DOWNTOWN LOS ANGELES

A WALKING GUIDE

REVISED

BY ROBERT D. HERMAN

WITH
MARIA GORSUCH
TRACEY REIM, ILLUSTRATIONS

Gem Guides Book Co.
315 Cloverleaf Dr., Suite F
Baldwin Park, CA 91706

Production Editor: Richard D. Burns and Janet Francisco
Book Design: Mark Dodge
Copy Editing: Rochelle & Jay Winderman
Maps: Christian Curtis and Robert Thomas

10 9 8 7 6 5

ISBN 1-889786-30-6
Library of Congress Card Number 2004104783

Manufactured in the United States of America

TABLE OF CONTENTS

Page

Downtown Los Angeles

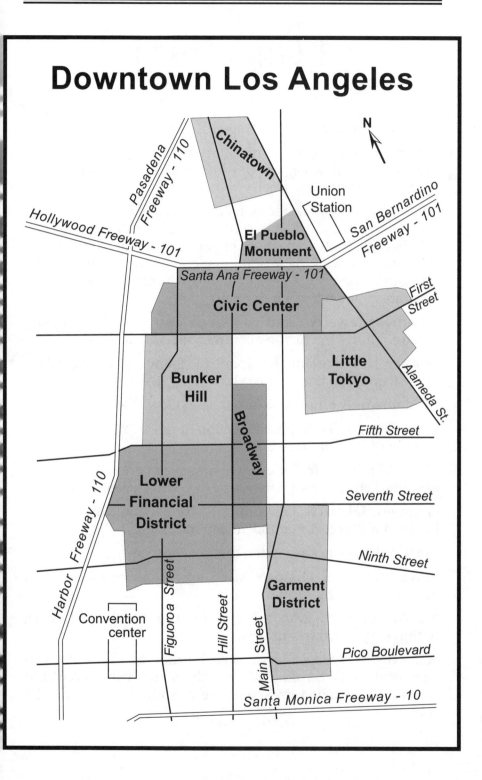

1. Getting Started

There is a Downtown Los Angeles!

It is a great place to visit! Safe! Fascinating, vibrant, and diverse! Most districts are destinations for the whole family. And the admission is free!

All you have to do is get there, and that's easy. Once you are there, you can choose from nine different neighborhoods (we call them districts). These are big areas, and you could spend an entire day walking around just one or two of them. Fine, you can come back another time to see others. We devote a separate chapter to each district.

Broadway-Jewelry District- Which also contains Pershing Square. This is the historic commercial core of the city.

Bunker Hill- Part of the financial district, with the tallest office towers on the west coast.

Chinatown- A bit of Asia in our own Downtown.

Civic Center- The largest collection of government buildings outside of Washington, D.C.

El Pueblo Historic Park- A circular plaza and Mexican village marketplace that dates back to L.A.'s earliest years.

Garment District- Downtown's connection to Southern California's largest manufacturing industry.

Little Tokyo- Another Asian district.

Lower Financial District- More office towers mixed with beautiful older buildings.

MacArthur Park- Mexican and Central American District within easy reach by subway.

Some districts are adjacent to each other; to visit both, you need only walk across a street. Others are farther apart but connected, reached by convenient shuttle buses or the subway.

GETTING THERE

Driving

If you drive to Downtown, you can park in inexpensive lots that are either close to your destination or within easy reach of the frequent shuttle buses (DASH buses: only $.25) or the Red Line Subway ($1.35).

Taking the Train – Metrolink

The Metrolink system offers the safest, most relaxing ride from the suburbs, and it takes you directly to Union Station. The trains are fresh, clean and fast. Park your car at one of the big parking lots next to your nearest Metrolink station, and hop on the train. The cars have wide doors for easy entry, seating in upper levels for scenic viewing, and whisper smooth rides. When you arrive at Union Station, you walk a few paces to the Red Line Subway or DASH buses that whisk you to the district you want to visit.

Getting around Downtown

Subway (Red Line)- L.A.'s subway is squeaky clean, very fast, and well guarded. The trains to and from Union Station are free to Metrolink riders.

Shuttle Buses (DASH buses)- Frequent buses ply several convenient routes connecting two or three districts. The buses are new, clean, and, when going to or from Union Station, free to Metrolink riders.

STEP-BY-STEP INTRODUCTION TO METROLINK

Why Drive When You Can Take the Train?

1) Find out when the Metrolink trains run from a station close to you. Your library, city hall, or chamber of commerce may have timetables in racks. Train schedules are also posted on your station platform near the ticket machines. Or call: (800) 371-LINK.

2) Buy a round-trip ticket from a machine on the platform of your train station. Get there a few minutes early in case there is a line of other folks trying to buy tickets. The machine takes credit cards or paper money. (Don't put in a big bill; the change is likely to be in heavy dollar coins.) If you are younger than nineteen or older than sixty-four, your ticket will be half price.

3) When the train arrives, board it promptly and take a seat either upstairs or down. The conductor will stroll by eventually and glance at your ticket. (In the good old days, conductors used to punch tickets. Times have changed.)

4) At the end of your ride, the train will deliver you to a platform at Union Station. Now you have some choices:

   a) You can visit Union Station itself. Then you can walk through the station to visit the old Plaza & Olvera Street–the neighborhood where the city of Los Angeles was born.

   b) You can walk farther north to Chinatown or south to the Civic Center or Little Tokyo.

   c) You can go directly down a ramp to the Red Line Subway platform for a short, fast ride to the Civic Center, Pershing Square, the Lower Financial District, or beyond.

   d) Other destinations can be reached by DASH buses.

5) To learn how to visit any one of the Downtown districts, turn to the appropriate chapter in this book and read the directions.

FREE TRANSPORTATION
AFTER YOU ARRIVE

When your train arrives at Los Angeles Union Station, your Metrolink ticket will get you a free ride on the Red Line Subway or a DASH bus. So keep your tickets handy until you have returned home.

Tip: This book tells you where to find public rest rooms in each of the districts. Nevertheless, before you leave Union Station, you might wish to use a rest room in the station. From your Metrolink train, enter Union Station through the pedestrian tunnel beneath the tracks, and bear left. The rest rooms are near the tunnel entrance.

Visiting Union Station

When you detrain from Metrolink, head for the pedestrian tunnel under the train platform. The tunnel is about half a block long. (See "Chapter 2 – Union Station and the Gateway Center" for information about Union Station and the neighborhood around it.)

Riding the Red Line Subway

After you have detrained from Metrolink, just follow the signs to the Red Line. You don't have to go into Union Station at all, unless you want to visit the station itself or go through it to nearby neighborhoods.

You will descend escalators to get to the subway platform. Simply step on board the first train that comes along. Union Station is at the northern end of the Red Line–the first station on the system–so you can't go wrong.

The Red Line can take you to:

• Civic Center (Hill Street, between First and Temple),

• Pershing Square (Hill and Fifth Streets),

• Seventh Street/Metro Center (Seventh and Figueroa Streets) where you can change to the Blue Line which goes south to Long Beach.

• MacArthur Park (Wilshire Boulevard and Alvarado Street), beyond to Western and Wilshire, or to Hollywood and North Hollywood.

Drawbacks of Using the Red Line

• There are no rest rooms at any of the Red Line stations except upstairs in Union Station. (Don't worry. This book tells you where to find them in each district.)

• There are no comfortable places to sit while waiting for subway trains. Each station does have one or two marble benches that look like ten-foot long caskets. Security guards will shoo you off stairs. Fortunately, the trains arrive every five minutes or so.

• Security guards check occasionally to see whether people have paid for their rides or have Metrolink tickets for continuing travel. Be sure to have a ticket–either a Metrolink ticket that shows you are going to or from Union Station, or a $1.35 ticket purchased from a Red Line machine.

• Sometimes you can hear the public address announcements on Red Line trains–but usually not. You should stay alert as you come into stations and try to spot the one you want. That's not easy, because the names of the stations are widely spaced and are almost invisible through the right side windows.

Taking the DASH Bus

DASH shuttle buses- They can take you to Chinatown, the Garment District, Civic Center, Bunker Hill, or the Lower Financial District. They are free to passengers arriving on Metrolink trains; $.25 otherwise. DASH buses run every day.

DASH buses to *Chinatown* stop at a small shelter on Alameda Street at the corner in front of Union Station. From the Metrolink train, walk into and straight through Union Station, and out the front door.

DASH buses to the *Garment District* depart from a bus platform at the Gateway Plaza. Instead of walking through the tunnel to Union Station, turn right and go in the opposite direction. The bus will take you to the Garment District by way of Civic Center and Spring Street.

DASH buses to parts of the *Civic Center, Music Center, Bunker Hill,* and the *Central Library* are found just across Alameda Street from Union Station–about where the street curves to the left by the Plaza. From the train, walk into Union Station, go straight through, exit the front door, and cross the street.

Temperature and Smog

The climate of Downtown is generally more moderate and cleaner than most other parts of Southern California. Only those towns closer to the ocean offer more comfortable temperatures and purer air.

Check this yourself. Each day, the *Los Angeles Times* Metro section reports temperatures and smog levels for a dozen locations in L.A. County including the Civic Center.

In contrast to the suburbs (the "inland valleys" as weather people call them), Downtown is spared the more severe pollution levels for which L.A.'s summers and autumns are infamous. This is especially true of ozone, the chemical that, in many locations, increases dramatically in the afternoon sun.

So, for a healthier outdoor excursion, go Downtown!

The Red Line Subway is faster than the DASH bus, but the bus gives you a view of the city as you travel through it. Four Downtown districts–El Pueblo/Olvera Street, Garment District, Chinatown, and Little Tokyo–can be reached only by DASH buses or by walking, not by the subway.

No need to hurry, Red Line trains and DASH buses run frequently.

Enjoy your tour of Downtown Los Angeles. L.A. is one of the easiest and most interesting cities in the world to visit.

HISTORICAL NOTE

Metrolink

If your branch of Metrolink serves San Bernardino, Rialto, Rancho Cucamonga, Upland, Montclair, Claremont, Pomona, Covina, Baldwin Park, El Monte, and Cal State LA, your trip is mostly on the reconstructed tracks of what was once the Pacific Electric Railway, or simply the P.E. The Blue Line to Long Beach also uses an old P.E. right of way–the last one to be closed in 1961 after a twenty-five year decline in patronage.

The P.E. was created around the turn-of-the-century by Henry Huntington. The railway spread itself across the length and breadth of Southern California, laying the groundwork for the famous urban sprawl we know today. The P.E. was, in fact, the largest electric rapid transit system in the world! Its trains connected Downtown L.A. to towns as far away as Redlands, Newport Beach, Redondo Beach, and San Fernando.

If your Metrolink train uses one of the branches serving the San Fernando Valley or Ventura County, you travel on the route of the Southern Pacific Lines, now leased by Metrolink. The Southern Pacific was created by the infamous "robber barons" of California: Leland Stanford, Charles Crocker, Mark Hopkins, and, the most notorious of all, Collis Huntington (Henry's uncle).

The history of the Southern Pacific is a saga of powerful and ruthless men and a gullible federal government which provided most of the financing. The Southern Pacific was first built to the San Francisco Bay area from the interior of the country in 1869 and then extended south to Los Angeles in 1876. Nine years later, the competing Santa Fe Railroad came to Los Angeles from the east. The ensuing rate war between the Southern Pacific and the Santa Fe resulted in the first great surge in population in Southern California–the "Boom of the Eighties."

Trains to Oceanside travel over the Santa Fe's tracks. Trains from Riverside use the tracks of the Union Pacific Railroad.

Metrolink, then, is a modern system of trains running on new rails set upon historic pathways. If you take the train to Downtown, you'll discover that getting there is half the fun!

2. Union Station and Gateway Center

Among America's great railroad terminals, Los Angeles *Union Station* (John and Donald Parkinson, consulting architects, 1939) stands in a class by itself.

Train stations in other American cities mimicked classical government buildings, royal palaces, or even Victorian fortresses. Their architecture proclaimed the overarching importance of railroads in American life–their power, wealth, and prominence as the nation's largest industrial enterprise.

In contrast, L.A.'s Union Station, with its lavish color, soft light, and beautiful flower garden waiting areas, represents Southern California rather than the railroads serving it. Spanish tiles, great rounded arches, richly patterned floors, and wood-toned interiors suggest a warm welcome for the arriving passenger and the promise of a new beginning–a new life.

DRIVING AND PARKING

From the north: Drive toward Downtown on the Pasadena Freeway (I-110 South) and take the transition ramp to the I-101Freeway going east. Take the Alameda exit, follow the loop around to the right. Turn right on Alameda, cross over the freeway and drive to the entrance to the parking lot in front of Union Station ($10.00 all day).

From the east: Take the I-101 Freeway. Exit at Alameda; turn right. Drive a long block to the driveway entrance of the parking lot in front of Union Station ($10.00 all day).

From the south and west: Drive north on the Harbor Freeway (I-110). Take the transition ramp to the I-101 Freeway going east. Take the Alameda exit, follow the loop around to the right. Turn right on Alameda, cross over the freeway and drive to the entrance to the parking lot in front of Union Station ($10.00 all day).

From the northwest (Hollywood and the San Fernando Valley): Take the Hollywood Freeway (I-101 East). Take the Alameda exit, follow the loop around to the right. Turn right on Alameda, cross over the freeway and drive to the entrance to the parking lot in front of Union Station ($10.00 all day).

Note: Parking is only $3.00 all day in front of the Terminal Annex north across Cesar Chavez Street from Union Station's lot.

WHAT TO SEE IN UNION STATION

Union Station mixes two architectural styles–Spanish Colonial Revival and Art Deco (See "Glossary"), each contributing color, ornamental detailing, and decorative tile. Earlier rail stations in L.A., on East First Street near the Los Angeles River and on East Fifth Street at Central Avenue, had been built in Victorian or Greek styles, reminding newcomers of the cities they had just left, but by the 1930s, city boosters were pushing the romantic fantasies of Southern California.

It's no accident that the floor plan for Union Station is a cross, like that of a cathedral. Near the west end of the main waiting room (the "nave") stands a wooden information booth. Just south of that is a "transept" that continues through the doors, becomes a covered arcade, and connects with the restaurant.

The Fred Harvey Restaurant was one of the famous chain of eateries along the *Santa Fe Railroad*. It is a wonderful place inside. You can see through the windows the sumptuous southwestern colors and details. It awaits an expensive upgrade before it can be used again as a restaurant.

The north transept was the ticket hall. In the days before local travel agents and computers, several ticket clerks from each of the three railroads (*Southern Pacific, Santa Fe,* and *Union Pacific*) manned the positions, and often the entire counter would be busy.

Notice the absence of an echo. The lining on all the walls, cork, absorbs the sound. You can even hear what the public address loudspeaker is saying.

Union Station is *California* all the way. It combines abiding themes in L.A.'s mythology: This is the land of beguiling climate, so the building has outdoor waiting rooms–a cathedral in a garden. This is the land of casual and friendly people, Spanish–like serenity, Western individualism, and new opportunity. Out here, one can find not just a new job, but a whole new persona, a new spirit!

Union Station was once home to great and beautiful long-distance trains with imposing names: *The Chief, El Capitan, The Super Chief, The City of Los Angeles*–all running to and from Chicago; *The Sunset Limited*–to and from New Orleans; and *The Coast Daylight*–to and from San Francisco. These were luxury trains, sleek, impressive, whose absence is now tearfully mourned. May they rest in peace!

However, Union Station itself is alive again–with Metrolink and Amtrak trains, MTA and DASH buses, and the Red Line Subway all serving the terminal.

Jack Benny on the radio from 1932-1955

If you are older than fifty, you may recall "the golden years of radio." Every Sunday evening, the Jack Benny comedy program would broadcast a variety show whose set pieces formed vivid images of L.A. for listeners across the United States. In one of his best remembered routines, Benny would find himself in Union Station. Mel Blanc intoned the voice of the public address announcer in the background: "Train leaving on Track Five, for Anaheim, Azusa, and Cuuck–ahmonga." This was always greeted by huge laughter and applause from the studio audience.

Today, the City of Rancho Cucamonga remembers Jack Benny with a charming sculpture of the bemused comedian holding his violin. Nearby, a street named "Rochester" recalls the character of Benny's valet.

PUBLIC ART

City of Angels- (Carlson, Cynthia, 1992) Mural, western entrance to Red Line. One of many artistic efforts to interpret the name, "Los Angeles". Eleven wings, one each for the eleven founding families of Los Angeles. The wings are labeled:

Ram'khastra=Angel of Rarefied Air;
Mika'll=Angel of Insomnia;
Janax=Angel of Monday;
Nogah=Cools the Earth in Summer;
Sofiel=Angel of Vegetables;
Zahun=Angel of Scandal;
Sui'el=Angel of Earthquakes;
Gabriel=Angel of Mercy;
Sut=Angel of Lies;
Dagiel=Angel of Fish;
Rohab=Angel of the Sea.

Traveler- (Schoonhoven, Terry, 1992) Mural, ceramic. East entrance to Red Line. L.A. on-the-move through space and time.

Union Chairs- (Sproat, Christopher, 1992) Sculpture, granite benches. Red Line platform. Stripped version in cold stone of the streamlined Art Deco chairs in the waiting rooms over head.

Nick Patsaouras Transit Plaza – East of Tracks

Atrain- (Bell, Bill, 1996) Moving light patterns and images. Top of escalator leading down to Red Line platform. Alternately abstract and realistic graphics seen in twelve vertical slits in the wall. Watch it long enough to see the trains, buses, cars, and human faces flash by.

Los Angeles, 1870, 1910, 1960, after 2000- (Doolin, Jim, 1995, 1996) Four striking murals, inside main lobby of *MTA Building*, first level, revealing the grand scale of the City of Los Angeles across a 130-year time span.

Epoch- (Nagatani, Patrick, 1996) Collage mural. *MTA Building*, third level, east side. Over five hundred postcards of trains, ships, and other transit images from 1900 to 1995 in a circular pattern suggesting a view from space of the edge of planet earth. Among images of heavenly bodies, Nagatani placed selections from the famous photographic studies of a man running. First published in 1887 by Eadweard Muybridge. The fact that the man in the series is nude scandalized someone from the MTA shortly after the collage appeared, and a sheet of opaque plastic was taped over the work for a couple of days, only to reappear after a public furor.

L.A. Dialogs- (Nielsen, Margaret, 1996) Mural. Third level; cafeteria entrance. Oversized postcards of famous Los Angeles images: Griffith Observatory, other landmarks, and giant oranges.

River Bench- (Sun, May, 1995) Chinese crockery, bottles, and other artifacts found in this neighborhood when Union Station and other buildings were constructed. They are shown imbedded in a "river bed" and the conical mound next to it.

Aquarium- (Weathersby, Oscar, marine biologist)

City of Dreams/River of History- (Wyatt, Richard, 1996) Mural, twenty-two feet by seventy-nine feet, over tunnel leading to the trains. Faces of the diverse populations that make up Los Angeles.

ReUnion- (Yasuda, Kim, Noel Korten, Torgen Johnson, Matthew VanderBorgh, 1995) Six pavilions marking places where buses stop. Steel grilles and guard rails designed by Michael Amescua.

CONVENIENCES & NECESSITIES

Public Rest Rooms

In Union Station near the pedestrian tunnel leading to the trains; next to ticket windows.

In Gateway Center, just south of main entrance, lower level.

RESTAURANTS

Price Guide for average lunch entrees:

$ = $3.00 - $8.00 $$$ = $13.00 - $17.00
$$ = $9.00 - $12.00 $$$$ = $18.00+

In Union Station

Union Bagel- near front of building. Fresh bagels, sandwiches, coffees. ($)

TRAXX Restaurant- near front of building. Elegant lunches and dinners inside the building or in the North Courtyard. Monday through Friday 11:00 a.m. to 10:00 p.m., Saturday 6:00 p.m. to 10:00 p.m. (213) 625-1999. ($$$)

In the MTA Building in the Gateway Center

Metro Cafe- third level. Big, new, cheerful cafeteria, open to the visiting public. Sit indoors or out. Stunning views through large windows of Union Station and Bunker Hill office towers beyond. Broad menu of tempting dishes at truly bargain prices–for example brandied mushroom chicken with two side dishes for $3.90. 6:30 a.m. to 3:00 p.m. ($)

HISTORY

In the decades before Union Station was built, three transcontinental railroads, the *Southern Pacific*, the *Atcheson, Topeka*, and *Santa Fe*, and the *Union Pacific* systems brought their trains into two separate stations several blocks east of Downtown. The Southern Pacific's "Arcade" station, shared with the Union Pacific, was on Fifth and Central Streets. Santa Fe's station was located at Santa Fe Avenue and Second Street, near the Los Angeles River.

In the 1920s, civic leaders wanted a single terminal to replace competing stations that were too far from the center of activity. They also wanted a grand entryway for tourists and newcomers, suggesting pleasures and opportunities here at hand. Several plans were considered before settling on the proposals of a design team led by John and Donald Parkinson (father and son) who a few years earlier had designed *City Hall*, and *Bullock's Wilshire*, an Art Deco masterpiece.

Ironically, Union Station contains a cruel skeleton in its closet. Long before it was built, Chinese people had settled around Alameda Street and on the streets bordering the El Pueblo Plaza and its eastern slope. Although Chinatown was one of the oldest neighborhoods in Los Angeles, the City required its demolition to make way for Union Station and sent its people to two new locations. One was three blocks north at Ord and Alameda Streets, there to make a "China City." The other was "New Chinatown," north of Alpine Street. A tantalizing fragment of the original community survives on Los Angeles Street–the Garnier Building, just south of the old firehouse in *El Pueblo Historic Park*. The Garnier Building is currently boarded up awaiting rediscovery and rescue.

John and Donald Parkinson

1994 marked the 100th anniversary of the oldest architectural firm in Los Angeles. Born in England, John Parkinson (1861-1935) came to Los Angeles by way of the 1893 Chicago World's Fair, the Columbian Exposition that would prove to be a powerful inspiration for many American designers. He set up his offices on Spring Street, between Second and Third Streets. In time, he would design fifty Downtown buildings that still survive today. Joined by his son, Donald B. Parkinson (1895-1945), the firm designed *City Hall* (1928), *Bullock's Wilshire* (1929), *Memorial Coliseum* (1921 and 1931), the original campus of *University of Southern California* (1918-1938), and *Union Station* (1939). A firm still carries the name today, *Parkinson Field Associates*, specializing in historic preservation.

Union Station was built at the end of the Great Depression and just before the Second World War. It quickly became a key element in the enormous task of transporting soldiers and factory workers in and out of Southern California. After the war, trains soon began losing business to automobiles and airplanes. By 1971, when Amtrak began running the nation's long distance rail passenger service, Union Station had lost much of its vitality. However, the building itself, though empty much of the time, was cared for, its gardens were properly tended, and the fabric of the structure remained in good condition.

With the arrival of Metrolink's commuter rail service to the suburbs and the start of the Red Line Subway, Union Station awoke from its torpor. People now mill through the waiting rooms even in the periods between trains. The restaurants and newsstand are well patronized. Things are looking up.

Union Station and its site of fifty acres is owned by Catellus Development Corporation, founded as the real estate arm of the *Santa Fe* and *Southern Pacific Railroad*s. In 1995, *Catellus* constructed a huge multi-use development just east of the tracks–*Gateway Center*. When fully developed, it will include hotels, offices, retail stores, and other services. First up was the new twenty-six-story headquarters building, priced at $100,000,000.00, for the *Metropolitan Transportation Authority* and the bus plaza. The *Metropolitan Water District* has moved into a newly-built complex.

There's talk of an even larger development in the distant future, the *Alameda District Plan*. It would refurbish the beautiful *Terminal Annex*, the old post office on Alameda and Cesar Chavez Avenue just north of Union Station. This plan would try to make historical and ethnic connections between *Union Station, Terminal Annex, Chinatown*, and *El Pueblo Monument*.

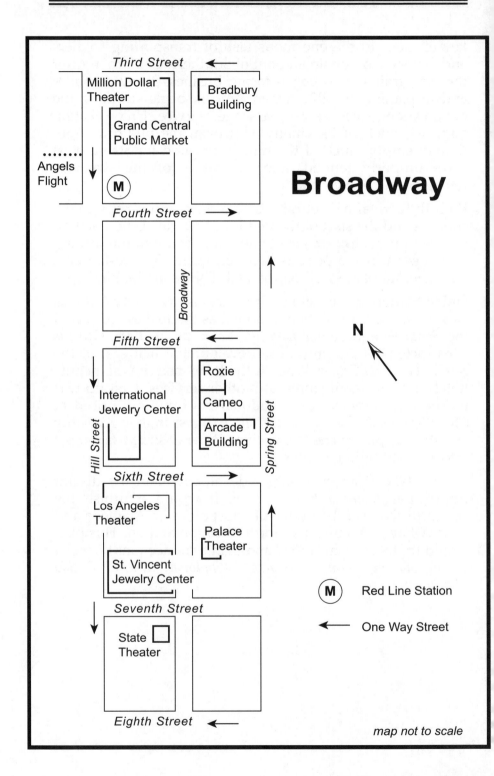

3. Broadway, Pershing Square, Jewelry District

THE HISTORIC CORE

If you visit nowhere else but Downtown, Broadway is the street to see!

From 1890 to the 1950s, Broadway was the main corridor of Downtown Los Angeles. It was the principal shopping and entertainment street, with department stores, jewelry stores, and, above all, movie palaces. Here was the largest concentration of great movie theaters in the world, the "Great White Way" of Los Angeles, and the stage for premiers with all the hoopla for which Hollywood became famous.

Some of the great movie theaters have, in recent years, been demolished, and others are on the endangered species list. *The United Artists* and *State Theater* are now churches. The *Tower Theater* and several others have been converted into stores while retaining their original facades. *The Orpheum* presents occasional stage plays, but *The Palace, The Los Angeles,* and the *Million Dollar Theater* are empty most of the time.

Broadway has become an urban bazaar–mainly aimed at Latinos. Between Fifth and Seventh Streets, the west side of Broadway merges with the Jewelry and the Garment Districts. The street is lined with handsome old buildings that give it texture and drama. Everywhere are sights and sounds of L.A.'s most urban thoroughfare.

Broadway is also a promenade–noisy, colorful, vital, and teeming with people. It is L.A.'s stage for ceremonies. When a local sports team celebrates a winning season, Broadway is the parade route. In fact, it has long been the true center of the city.

Broadway is a safe street!

In fact, Downtown, in total, is the safest district in Los Angeles! Why? Because there are lots of people on the streets. With so many others around, crime is rare. Of course, in any crowd, you should hold onto your purse, but you need not fear other kinds of crime.

LOCATION

• Broadway (really *South* Broadway, not to be confused with Chinatown's North Broadway) extends south from the Civic Center, and comes truly alive between Third and Ninth Streets.

• Pershing Square is a public park located one block west of Broadway between Fifth and Sixth Streets in the very center of Downtown.

GETTING THERE FROM UNION STATION

Red Line Subway: Free to Metrolink riders, $1.35 to others. From your Metrolink train, walk down into the tunnel beneath the tracks and follow signs to the Red Line Subway trains–you can walk either right or left. The subway takes just three minutes to get from Union Station to the *Pershing Square* station, the second stop. Walk out the exit labeled *Pershing Square* and ride the escalator up to Fifth and Hill Streets for Pershing Square, or take the other exit to Fourth and Hill Street for Angels Flight and the Grand Central Market.

DASH bus, Route D: On weekdays catch this shuttle (free to Metrolink riders, $.25 to others) at the *Nick Patsaouras Transit Plaza*. When you detrain, go down the ramp to the pedestrian tunnel and turn *right*–away from Union Station. Don't go into the station itself. DASH bus, route D travels down Spring Street which is parallel to, and just one block east of, Broadway. Hop off anywhere between Third and Ninth Streets and walk west to Broadway. On weekends, catch the DASH bus across Alameda Street from Union Station. Get off at Third and Hill Streets.

DRIVING AND PARKING

From the north: Drive toward Downtown on the Pasadena Freeway (I-110 South) and take the transition ramp to the I-101 Freeway going east). Take the exit marked Broadway, but drive across Broadway to Spring. Turn right on Spring and continue to just past Third Street. Park in the structure on your right, across the street from the Ronald Reagan State Building ($3.00 all day on weekends).

From the east: Take the I-101 Freeway. Exit at Spring and drive just past Third Street. Park in the structure on your right, across the street from the Ronald Reagan State Building ($3.00 all day on weekends).

From the south: Drive north on the Harbor Freeway (I-110) to Sixth Street exit. Drive seven blocks to Main Street and turn left. Drive three blocks to Third Street and turn left. Turn left again on Spring, but swing into the right lane immediately. Park in the structure across the street from the Ronald Reagan State Building ($3.00 all day on weekends).

From the west: Take the Santa Monica Freeway (I-10) to the Harbor Freeway North (I-110). Drive to Sixth Street exit. Drive seven blocks to Main Street and turn left. Drive three blocks to Third Street and turn left. Turn left again on Spring, but swing into the right lane immediately. Park in the structure across the street from the Ronald Reagan State Building ($3.00 all day on weekends).

From the north-west (Hollywood, and San Fernando Valley): Take the Hollywood Freeway (I-101 East). Take the exit marked Broadway, but drive across Broadway to Spring. Turn right on Spring and continue to just past Third Street. Park in the structure on your right, across the street from the Ronald Reagan State Building ($3.00 all day on weekends).

WHO'S THERE ?

This area is a great place for people watching. You'll see rich people and poor, Latinos, Caucasians, African-Americans, Asians, Native Americans, Middle Easterners, and

Midwesterners. But most of Broadway's people are Latinos, and you'll hear mostly Spanish. Women shoppers, families with children, young couples, teenagers, panhandlers, and retirees all converge from miles around by buses, trains, and cars, and even by walking.

Like many of Downtown's streets, this district comes to life late in the morning as shops begin to open and people pour in. By 5:30 p.m., the day is done, and the sidewalks rapidly empty.

What draws all these people to Broadway? Inexpensive merchandise and credito facil (easy credit). But many are attracted to the color and life of a street richly populated with other people. This is society! This is vitality! This is life!

Music

What about the pulsing rhythms and profoundly amplified sounds that give so much electricity and color to Broadway? The music comes in various forms: You might hear *mariachi*, with its strings and trumpets, popular in Los Angeles since the 1930s. Or maybe *salsa*, based on Caribbean rhythms. Or you might hear Latino versions of rock and roll. Listen for the *banda* sound, derived in part from German polka music, Germans having settled in portions of northern Mexico and south Texas in the late nineteenth century. You'll hear the strong, bass oom-pah-pahs under trumpets and vocals. Latino teenagers, especially those of Mexican origin, dance the *la quebradita* (little break) to this music.

Broadway is especially vibrant on weekends. Families shop for clothing, audio tapes, gifts, and food. Religious zealots hand out fliers and shout dire warnings. Stores selling electronic goods aim loudspeakers at the passing crowd and boom out Mexican dance music with such force that you can feel the bass notes in your stomach.

WHAT'S THERE FOR THE VISITOR?

Stores, shops, movie theaters, office complexes, restaurants, a large park (Pershing Square), a small park (Biddy Mason Park), Angels Flight, and art. And the old buildings on Broadway are extraordinary.

As you walk along the street, don't forget to look *up*. Most old buildings are richly ornamented, usually in *terra cotta* (glazed tile, see "Glossary"). In the 1950s and 1960s architects scorned the elaborate detailing of theater and office buildings, and slapped on the flat, dreary street-level facades we see so often today.

SHOPPING

Suburbanites may want to shop on Broadway for themselves, but, even if not, it's an adventure to look. A stroll down Broadway will take you past stores crammed with children's wear, watches, perfumes, video games, jewelry, telephones, bridal gowns, burgers, tacos, tamales (*Mexicanos y Salvadorenos*), pupusas, burritos, fruit juices, cutlery, magazines, electronic gadgets, cameras, shoes (*zapatas*), maternity apparel (*maternidad*), ceremonial dresses and suits for Latino traditions of baptism (*bautizo*), *First Communion*, and the celebration marking a fifteen-year-old girl's entrance into adulthood (*quince anos*)–clothes to carry you from cradle to grave.

Step into the *Arcade Building* (542 South Broadway), and just look at the stuff! If you've been hunting for a green plastic dancing frog band or a feather-trimmed plaid taffeta codpiece, this is your place. Or here's a perfect gift for that certain someone: a revolving, internally lit, multi-colored jeweled sphere, or maybe a Count Dracula with flashing green eyes rising out of a coffin. Need a telephone shaped like a helicopter, or a baseball hat bearing the name of a Mexican state, or a clock with rotating light bursts around a picture of the Last Supper, or a watch faced with the American flag? There are enough shoes (white ones wrapped in plastic) and bundled socks to outfit a high school. You can get three tee-shirts for $10.00. You can examine stereo equipment (including karaoke machines), bead curtains, animated singing and guitar–playing cacti, and tons of other battery-operated plastic toys, some for kids, some definitely not.

Broadway has one of only three full-service drug stores in Downtown L.A., Rite-Aid, (Broadway and Fifth Street). There are dozens of stores specializing in Levi's. You can find a Julio's Burgers, a Pollo Ole', Newberry-TG&Y (437 Broadway), and a Pic 'N' Save. Best of all, there's the colorful and wonderful *Grand Central Market*.

Grand Central Market- (Parkinson, John, 1897; 1905 addition, department store at street level replaced by food market in 1917). 315 Broadway. Also known as the *Central Market*, this is one of L.A.'s great, authentic destinations. For many Angelenos, this is the true heart of the city. A full block in depth, from Broadway to Hill, the fifty-stall *mercado* serves people of modest and low incomes. They travel here from miles around to pick up bargain meats, sugary breads (*pan dulce*), three-day-old bakery items, beans, peppers, grains, Latino food, soul food, Chinese food, and fruit juices. Don't expect packaged, canned, or bottled groceries. You can stand or sit down for Mexican or Chinese lunches, or cappuccino, or other refreshments. (see "Restaurant" section). *Central Market* hours are Monday through Saturday 9:00 a.m. to 6:00 p.m. and Sunday from 10:00 a.m. to 5:00 p.m.

The Central Market was owned by Ira Yellin, who upgraded this immediate block, including the former Million Dollar Theater Building, now the *Grand Central Square Apartments*, and the Bradbury Building. Preservation architect Brenda Levin has been restoring the building; she brought the return of the many neon signs that give much of the color to the place. She also recently removed an inappropriate modern facade and installed a more appealing entrance. This is the first earthquake and fire-proof building in Los Angeles; it uses structural steel in the Broadway side and reinforced concrete on the Hill Street side.

Farmacia Million Dollar- in the *Million Dollar Theater Building*, now called *Grand Central Square*, on Third and Broadway. A small drug store but also something more. Here are shelves of nostrums, elixirs, and potions for whatever ails or fascinates you, from *amor* (love) to *trabajo* (work). You can buy small packages of herbs, roots, and bark for your medicine cabinet. See your doctor first. Safer, perhaps, are charms, amulets, and talismans which are not taken internally.

There are other institutions too:

A & A Jewelers Tools and Supplies- 319 West Sixth, between Broadway and Hill Street. Study the fascinating instruments and materials used by craftsmen working in the buildings nearby. A great shop to buy tools for any kind of small work.

The Escuela de Costura- (school of needlework) advertises *"mucho trabajo"* ("much work", maybe in the sweatshops of the adjacent Garment District).

New York Hardware Trading Co.- 410 West Eighth, near Hill Street. A big, old-fashioned hardware store with everything you would want in such a place, Downtown's last example of its breed.

Notice all the shops devoted to wedding clothes! You can even get married in a shop near Broadway and Third Streets, *La Catedral de Los Angeles Wedding Chapel & Bridal Shop*. This all-in-one shop handles fifteen to twenty weddings a week.

Hours: Most Broadway stores are open from 9:30 a.m. until 7:00 p.m. Monday through Saturday, and 10:00 a.m. to 6:00 p.m. Sunday. *Grand Central Market* hours are Monday through Saturday 9:00 a.m. to 6:00 p.m., Sunday 10:00 a.m. until 5:00 p.m.

The Jewelry District

The Jewelry District- The boundaries are indefinite, but jewelry businesses are concentrated in several square blocks between Hill Street and Broadway and from Fifth Street down to Eighth Street. The streets are lined with jewelry stores, and inside several large former department stores, jewelry stalls have taken over the former display counters. All stalls are separately rented by competing merchants. If you stroll among them, you will draw their eager attention.

Gold chains, rings, bracelets, precious stones, and watches are staple items in most of the stalls, but some of the dealers specialize, say, in decorative brooches, or bejeweled key chains, or luscious pearl necklaces. There's enormous variety. You can find just about anything you want.

Check out the *Jewelry Theater Building* (formerly the *Pantages Theater* and *Warner's Downtown*)at Seventh and Hill Streets and *St. Vincent's Jewelry Center*, Seventh between Hill and Broadway. Even if you're not looking to buy, you can find interesting items not seen in the newer, fancier establishments. In the *Jewelry Theater*, don't miss the spectacle of jewelry stalls in an old-style movie palace, complete with chandeliers, proscenium, balcony, and boxes. It's surreal. Their jewelry? How about ID bracelets engraved with the Virgin of Guadalupe, or watches so ornate you can hardly tell the time?

The upscale jewelry stores may be more appealing; they are concentrated on Hill Street between Sixth and Seventh. Try, for example, the *Jeweler's Mall* at 625 Hill. The *California Jewelry Mart*, 607 South Hill Street has over two hundred show rooms, some of them exclusively wholesale, selling gold, pearls, gems, and watches. Open Monday through Saturday from 8:00 a.m. to 6:00 p.m.

The International Jewelry Center- 550 South Hill, is a modern glass, gray stone, and stainless steel building located across from Pershing Square. Many of its shops are wholesale only, but the first nine floors are open to the public. A New York-style deli, *City Deli*, is in the north end of the building on the sidewalk level.

In the buildings of the Jewelry District, you'll find appraisers and licensed buyers, casters, custom designers of jewelry, diamond and gem cutters, setters, engravers, estate and antique jewelry specialists, jewelry repairers, manufacturers, pearl importers, polishers and platers, bead and pearl stringers, watch dealers and repairers, wax carvers, and stores that sell tools and materials to all the above.

This district employs 55,000 to 60,000 people. There are two hundred wholesale diamond dealers and cutters alone. With such enormous forces, you really should consider shopping here for any important jewelry purchases. You can comparison-shop easily, merely by stepping to the next stall or building a few feet away instead of driving from one suburban mall to another.

There are many security guards in the Jewelry District, and they help make it one of the safest neighborhoods in Los Angeles.

Shopping in the Jewelry District

Here is advice from Ralph Shapiro, president of *The Diamond Club, West Coast*, one of only twenty-two wholesale diamond exchanges in the world. (The *Diamond Club's* offices are in the *International Jewelry Center*, 550 South Hill Street):

- Unless you are an expert on jewelry, you must depend on the integrity of the person presenting an item to you. You should ask for proof that the seller is a *Certified Gemologist*, or that the seller's word is guaranteed by a Certified Gemologist in the shop.
- When you are close to buying something, you should ask for a certificate describing that item issued by either the *Gemological Institute of America (G.I.A.)* or the *European Gemological Laboratories (E.G.L.)*.
- Then you should require the seller to stipulate in writing that the object is just as it is described. What is the color, clarity, cut, and carat weight of a stone (the "Four C's")? Who is the maker of a watch? What materials are used in a jewelry piece?

Mr. Shapiro says, if you do your homework in advance and take care to learn about the jewelry you intend shopping for, you can get a better deal from responsible retailers in the *Jewelry District* than in most other shops back home, if only because the selection is so enormous.

Remember! Get it in writing!

Note: The *Jewelry District* takes its time waking up each morning. Don't expect much action in the retail shops before 11:00 a.m.

BUILDINGS ON BROADWAY

Two Operating Movie Palaces

The term movie *palace* is exactly appropriate for these spectacular theaters. Facades and marquees were designed to provide diversion and excitement even before you reached the building. Once inside, elaborate decor, florid lighting, and mood music anticipated the movie. Many of these theaters were previously vaudeville houses, and they often produced musical and dance preliminaries to the movies, greatly adding to the fun.

Palace Theater- (Landsberg, G. Albert, 1911) 630 Broadway. Italian on the outside, French on the inside, with elaborate pastel decor. It once produced performances of the Orpheum vaudeville circuit before it became a movie palace. The theater is owned by developer Tom Gilmore who plans to refurbish the rooms above the theater for his own offices.

State Theater, formerly Loew's State- (Wees, Charles and William Day, 1921) 703 Broadway. When the State was built, Seventh and Broadway was the busiest Downtown intersection, and this was the most profitable theater for many years. It presented both movies and vaudeville and had its own orchestra and chorus line. Judy Garland appeared here in 1929 as one of the Singing Gumm Sisters. This twelve-story building is the largest brick-clad structure in Los Angeles. The elaborate interior mixes Spanish, medieval, classical, and Eastern ornamentation, including a seated Buddha in a niche over the stage. Now it is a church, the *Iglesia Universal.*

Orpheum Theater- (Landsberg, G. Albert, 1926) 842 Broadway. Built as a vaudeville theater, with extravagant French appointments, this theater has received help from an enthusiastic club of restorers. Its Wurlitzer is the last remaining original theater organ in Los Angeles.

Guided Tours of the Broadway Theaters

The *Los Angeles Conservancy* offers guided tours to a dozen Broadway theaters, with a look inside some. Every Saturday at 10:00 a.m. Free to members; otherwise $5.00. Call (213) 623-CITY for reservations.

The Conservancy also runs a popular series each summer called *Last Remaining Seats*–old-time movies in three of these theaters. Call (213) 623-CITY for information.

Former Movie Theaters

Million Dollar Theater- (Martin, Albert C. and William Lee Woollett, 1918) Third and Broadway. The theater is in the base of an office building originally occupied by the Edison Company and later by the Metropolitan Water District (The name of the M.W.D. was recently renewed high up on the west side). Albert Martin created an elaborate exterior facade, a Churrigueresque screen around the entrance and movie-inspired terra cotta sculptures on the exterior. From 1950 through the 1980s, the *Million Dollar Theater* was a popular spot for Mexican stage shows. Be sure to see the elaborate terra cotta ornamentation on the Third Street side, more exotic references to Hollywood fantasies (best viewed from across the street). The floors above it contain the *Grand Central Square Apartments.*

Los Angeles Theater- (Lee, S. Charles and S. Tilden Norton, 1931) 615 Broadway. Sadly closed in 1994, this was the last of the movie palaces to be built on Broadway, and the gaudiest of them all. Imitations of Versailles in the lobby, staircase, and rest rooms. As with the other movie palaces, the *Los Angeles* is architecturally and historically significant and cannot be divided into multiplexes.

Globe Theater- (Morgan, Walls & Morgan and Alfred F. Rosenheim, 1913) 744 Broadway. Go into this building, now a "swap meet," and stroll all the way back. You will see the ornate, gilded balconies and proscenium. For a look at two other theaters now used for retail spaces, visit the *Pantages/Warner Bros.* (below) or the *Westlake Theater* in MacArthur Park.

Tower- (Lee, S. Charles, 1927) corner of Eighth and Broadway. The first Downtown theater to play "talkies." Delightful Art Deco detailing on the exterior of this small (900-seat) building. Look at the movie references in the small details over windows. A fine example of what architects could accomplish in terra cotta designs.

United Artists Theater- (Walker & Eisen; C. Howard Crane, 1927) 933 Broadway. Elaborate Gothic designs on the facade, complete with gargoyles–one holding a camera. United Artists movie stars are depicted in the auditorium. The building now houses the church of Dr. Gene Scott. Many Angelenos recall the earlier home of Scott's congregation on Sixth and Hope, the building with "Jesus Saves" signs on the top.

Pantages/Warner Bros. Theater- (Priteca, Benjamin Marcus , 1919) Now called the *Jewelry Theater Building*. Seventh and Hill Streets. This was an office building and movie palace built by Alexander Pantages but later made part of the Warner Brothers chain. It was changed into a church in the 1950s, then sold to Wanis Koyomejian and his partners who removed the theater seats and opened the space to jewelry stalls. Go inside and look around at the baroque decor of the theater stage, drapes, and chandelier. You can see the *Warner Bros.* shields here and there.

The *Pantages* has a garish history: In 1929, Alexander Pantages was accused of raping a 17-year-old dancer in his office on the second floor, but he was acquitted after a long trial. A biographer of Pantages later wrote that the dancer had been bribed by Joseph Kennedy, father of J.F.K., Robert, and Edward. Joe Kennedy spent some years in Los Angeles in shady jazz-age businesses and affairs. He hoped, by ruining Pantages's personal reputation, to gain control of his theater empire.

More recently, Koyomejian and several other Jewelry District businessmen were the targets of a major federal investigation called "Operation Polar Cap." In 1991, they were convicted of money-laundering, taking tainted cash from the drug trade and using the jewelry business as a cover for sending money to foreign banks. The federal judge said the scale and sophistication of money-laundering was "without parallel" and handed down a sentence of 505 years to *each* man.

OTHER BUILDINGS AND PLACES

Pershing Square- This is a public park one block west of Broadway, between Fifth and Sixth Streets and Hill and Olive Streets. A $14,500,000.00 reconstruction project was dedicated February 6, 1994 in the hope that Pershing Square would become a bridge between two cultures–the historic Broadway and the Jewelry District on one side and the newer office towers on the other.

Mexico City architect, Ricardo Legoretta, designed the yellow buildings, pink columns, and purple water tower and sluice which pours water into a tidal basin (which rises and falls in a half-hour period). Benches, walls, and pillars enclose the park, but also isolate it from the streets. Legoretta subdivided the original over-scaled space into "rooms" by marking them off with cement curbs. He also bunched together the old statues like the Spanish American War Monument (1896), the oldest piece of public art in Los Angeles. Another represents World War I, a doughboy under the command of General John Joseph Pershing. The statue of a scowling Beethoven once stood across Fifth Street from *The Auditorium*, the venue for orchestra concerts before the *Music Center* was built. The structure was razed and replaced by the vacuous parking lot on Fifth and Olive. Pershing Square needs the enclosure that was once provided by the buildings encircling it. Oddly, there is no statue of General Pershing in this park.

Why such emphatic colors? Legoretta says he and other Mexicans have a powerful emotional affinity for strong colors. If you doubt his concept, stroll to the corner of Hill and Sixth Streets and look northwest. This is one of L.A.'s most spectacular views! The grand and colorful office towers on Bunker Hill are framed by Legoretta's constructions on the Square in the foreground.

Barbara McCarren created the art program. Old postcards of Los Angeles are embedded in a bench; two constellations of stars (of the heavens, not Hollywood) are on the plaza floor; a jagged earthquake fault surfaces in the tidal basin and runs toward Olive Street; and a long quotation on another bench from historian/activist Carey McWilliams may put a lump in your throat. The landscaping was designed by Hanna/Olin of Philadelphia. The trees, planted in 1993, will not grow much higher because the surface of the park is really the roof of a multilevel parking structure.

A deli sells sandwiches and salads for *alfresco* lunches. The park has a stage for public performances, and lots of benches and low walls to sit on. Park rangers, city police, and grounds keepers are in sight. The whole idea in redeveloping the park was to provide a warmly inviting, amiable place to mix the people of Downtown–all of them. Everyone should feel welcome.

Buildings on Spring Street
(one block east of Broadway)

Ronald Reagan State Building- (Welton Becket Associates, 1990) 300 South Spring Street. The funds to build this elegant structure came through the pipeline before the recession of the early 1990s hit. This 850,000 square foot building holds 2,000 state employees in 16 different departments. Blessings should be heaped upon the designers for committing 12,000 square feet to retail space on Third Street instead of making that side a blank wall on the sidewalk. The atrium contains several large, stunning works of art (See "Public Art" section later in this chapter.)

Herman W. Hellman Building, (now *Banco Popular)-* (1903) Fourth and Spring Streets. Elegant marble entrance on Fourth Street. The *Community Redevelopment Agency (C.R.A.)* occupies several floors.

Alexandria Hotel- (Parkinson, John, 1906) 210 West Fifth Street, corner of Spring Street. The Alexandria was the leading hotel in the city until the Biltmore was built in 1923. The Great Depression, coupled with Downtown's growth west of Pershing Square, was hard on the Alexandria. The hotel's original baroque marble lobby was remodeled beyond recognition in 1970, but the banquet room, now called the Palm Court, was beautifully restored after a period of service as a training gym for boxers. Ask someone to show it to you.

Buildings on Broadway

Los Angeles Times Parking Structure- Second Street between Broadway and Spring. Artist Tony Sheets carved images of street scenes, buildings, important episodes, and people from L.A.'s history on the east and west walls of the parking structure. It's worth a contemplative look. This site was the location of the first Jewish temple in Los Angeles (see "History" later in this chapter).

Bradbury Building- (Wyman, George, 1893) Third and Broadway, across from the *Million Dollar Theater*. Open weekdays and Saturdays. Built for Lewis Bradbury, a gold mining magnate whose huge mansion stood on Bunker Hill. Architect/author Charles Moore calls the interior of the Bradbury Building "one of the most thrilling spaces on the North American continent.... The thrill of discovery is there each time: it's always far more wonderful, more ineffable, more magic than memory allows."

When you walk through the arched entrance from noisy, crowded, Latino Broadway you are propelled back to elegant, ordered, nineteenth century Paris. The space is a five-story atrium, roofed by a wall-to-wall skylight, framed all around by French-made wrought-iron, and linked together vertically by two old-fashioned, open-cage elevators. The iron work was shipped from France to Los Angeles by way of the Chicago World's Fair of 1893, the Columbian Exposition. Entrances and windows of offices on each floor look onto the balconies that surround the interior.

The Bradbury Building evokes urban Europe's loveliest age, making it a major attraction for tourists. The building has starred in many a movie; the most famous, *Bladerunner* (1981), offered an apocalyptic view of the future of Los Angeles. The building was dirtied up to play the role of Sabastian's grimy residence. A blimp occasionally appeared floating over the skylight advertising escape trips to other planets. In real life, the building offers dignity, calm, reassurance, and a solid connection to history.

George Wyman, the designer of the Bradbury Building, was a lowly draftsman working for architect Sumner Hunt. Wyman got the job of planning the building when Bradbury was dissatisfied with Hunt's proposals. Wyman accepted the assignment only after consulting, by way of a Ouija board, his dead brother who told him that taking the job would make him famous. The departed brother was right. The result was a masterpiece, Wyman's only recognized accomplishment. But what a glorious achievement it is!

[One of the shops occupying the front of the Bradbury Building, *Ross Cutlery*, figured prominently in the O.J. Simpson murder pre-trial. While he was acting in a movie nearby, Simpson allegedly bought a dagger in Ross's.]

Biddy Mason Park- (de Brettville, Sheila Lebrant and others, 1991) 331 South Spring Street, or you can enter through the gates next to McDonald's on Broadway, across from *Grand Central Market*. This delightful little pocket park offers a calm, tree-shaded retreat from the hubbub of Broadway. You'll find metal sculptures and fountains, comfortable benches, and a history lesson artfully worked into a wall. Designed by UCLA-based artists, the wall honors Biddy Mason (1818-1891), an African-American woman who lived at this very location. Born a slave, she *walked* from the South to Los Angeles, obtained her freedom, became a midwife, founded an orphanage, and helped found the First A.M.E. Church. This park is a moving tribute to "Grandma Mason," one of the authentic angels of L.A.

Architects *John Parkinson and Edmund Bergstrom*, with whom he was associated for ten years, are honored by a plaque on 453 Spring Street. John Parkinson (1861-1935) founded the oldest architectural firm in Los Angeles on Spring Street between Second and Third. His Braley Building, on Fourth and Spring Streets, is the first "skyscraper" in town–twelve stories. Both men designed many of the other office buildings that, for half a century, defined L.A.'s financial district. Later, Parkinson and his son Donald B. led a team of other architects in designing three masterworks: *City Hall* (1928), *Bullock's Wilshire* (1929), and *Union Station* (1939). Fifty buildings designed by Parkinson still stand Downtown. Today the firm of Parkinson Field Associates specializes in historic preservation.

Outdoor magazine stand- A rare, old-fashioned institution in L.A. on St. Vincent's Place, a short alleyway on the south side of Sixth Street between Broadway and Hill.

Eastern Columbia Building- (Beelman, Claude, 1930) Broadway at Ninth. The most colorful Downtown Art Deco building; turquoise, green, and gold terra cotta. Two stores owned by the same man, Adolph Sieroty, *Eastern Outfitting Co.* (furniture) and *Columbia Outfitting* (clothing) occupied lower floors, and the rest is an office building topped by a clock tower with neon hands. Much photographed. Yes, the gold tile is made with genuine gold dust!

Broadway/Spring Arcade Building- (MacDonald, Kenneth , 1924) 542 South Broadway or 541 South Spring. Spectacular arched entrances on both Broadway and Spring lead into a large atrium court covered by a glass roof. Intended to be a replica of London's Burlington Arcade. The Community Redevelopment Agency (C.R.A.) wants to convert the office building above the atrium to residences and studios for artists.

Grand Central Square- (Levin and Associates, 1995) Third Street between Broadway and Hill. This includes the structure rising above the *Million Dollar Theater* which was once occupied by the Metropolitan Water District. Ira Yellin converted the building to a mixed-use facility which includes offices, apartments, retail shops, and parking. (see "History: section) This project will help bridge the gap between the business culture on Bunker Hill and the vibrant life of Broadway's people.

On Hill Street –
One Block West of Broadway)

Subway Terminal Building- (Schultz and Weaver, 1925) 415 Hill Street. The "Big Red Cars" of the Pacific Electric Railway once rolled westbound from this building through a one and one-tenths mile tunnel under Bunker Hill, heading for Hollywood, Glendale, and the San Fernando Valley. The Art Deco lobby is dominated by a copy of Odin's sculpture "The Thinker," adding a somber, incongruous note to the entrance of the building which has not served trains since the late 1950s. At the time of this writing, the building is closed, awaiting respect, funding, and renovation.

Look hard at the north exterior of the building. The New York-based artist, Jeff Greene, designed a delightful *trompe l'oeil* scene of painters working high up the wall. Are they painting the words on or off? The long rope and its shadow are uncanny.

Because the *Subway Terminal Building* is empty and boarded shut, this block is now nearly dead. The old *Clark Hotel*, on the east side of Hill Street between Fourth and Fifth, is being remodeled, and may brighten the street again after several dark decades.

Title Guarantee Building- (Parkinson, John and Donald Parkinson, 1931) Northwest corner of Fifth and Hill. This gem currently has no close neighbors to detract from its handsome Art Deco Gothic features; it stands alone and proud across Fifth Street from Pershing Square. Note the flying buttresses at the top.

International Center- (formerly *Bankers Building*) (Beelman, Claude, 1930) 629 South Hill. Beautiful green terra cotta Art Deco twelve-story building, brutally cut off at the knees by a tacky facade added to the lower floors.

Angels Flight- This is a "funicular" (a short cable railway) running up to the top deck of *California Plaza* from Hill Street between Third and Fourth Streets. On December 31, 1901, the counterbalanced cars, *Olivet* and *Sinai*, began carrying people from Third and Hill in the downtown commercial district up the steep hill to their homes. Built by engineer J.W. Eddy and modified a bit in the first few years, *Angels Flight* served the public (at a penny a ride until the 1910s when the fare was raised to a nickel). It was dismantled and put into storage in 1969 when all the buildings on the top of Bunker Hill were bulldozed away. In 1995 the shortest railroad in the world was refitted to the hill half a block south from where it lived for sixty-eight years. The original archway structures at the top and bottom ends of the track are made of concrete and have safely survived years of exposure and neglect. An accident in 2001 forced the closure of Angels Flight. Reopening -- to be announced.

PUBLIC ART

Biddy Mason- (de Bretteville, Sheila and others, 1990) 331 South Spring Street. This small park can also be entered from Broadway just south of McDonald's. Timeline wall created by U.C.L.A. artists for the "Power of Place" project honoring people who lived or worked in the places identified. This wall celebrates the life of an amazing woman who was born a slave and later became a guardian angel for the fledgling city. It also lifts what would otherwise be an anonymous alley from obscurity to a real "place" with a history and meaningful identity.

Biddy Mason's House of the Open Hand- (Saar, Bettye, 1990) 331 South Spring. Collage of photographs. Wall inside parking structure, next to elevators.

Bride & Groom- (Twitchell, Kent, 1972-76) Mural. North exterior wall of *Victor Clothing Co.* 242 South Broadway. Seventy foot tall Latino couple, beautifully painted in blue tones.

Ed Ruscha Monument- (Twitchell, Kent, 1978-87) Mural. North exterior wall of 1031 South Hill Street overlooking a parking lot between Eleventh Street and Olympic Boulevard. This is a photographically accurate portrait, 6-stories tall, of Twitchell's friend and fellow artist.

Fountains in Biddy Mason Park- (Eino, 1990) Between Third & Fourth Streets on Broadway. Look at these constructions with the high-rise office towers as a backdrop. Best of all, this is water, and you can touch it!

L.A. Grows- (Sheets, Tony, 1988) Broadway and Spring Streets at Second. Relief mural incised in west wall of parking structure of *Los Angeles Times*. An illustrated history of Southern California. See his *History of Printing* on the east end of the same structure.

Neons for Pershing Square Station- (Antonakos, Stephen, 1992) Sculpture, Hill Street between Fourth and Fifth. Twelve neon abstractions suspended over the tracks inside the Red Line *Pershing Square Station*.

Pershing Square Art Program- (McCarren, Barbara, 1994) "Earthquake fault," constellations of stars (in space, not Hollywood), old postcards embedded in a bench, quotation from Carey McWilliams, and three telescopes–two looking into the past.

The Pope of Broadway- (Torrez, Eloy, 1985). Mural. Movie actor Anthony Quinn dancing on south wall of *Victor Clothing Company*, Broadway & Third. Looks down on old Downtown's most exciting corner.

Inverted Clocktower- (Hawkinson, Tim, 1994) Mirror image of a "historic" clock tower. Southeast corner of Third and Hill Streets in *Grand Central Square*. The parking structure is made to appear to have been molded around a clock tower that, in fact, never existed on this corner. The clock dials are negatives. The Roman numerals are reversed, but–is this confusing? The hands move clockwise.

Calle de la Eternidad "Street of Eternity"- (Poethig, Johanna, 1992) Mural on wall of 351 South Broadway. Sponsored by the Social and Public Art Resource Center (S.P.A.R.C.). Dramatic use of Mexican themes applied to Broadway itself. "Street of Eternity" is an appropriate name for this part of Broadway.

Treaty of Cahuenga- (Ballin, Hugo, 1931) Mural in lobby of *Title Guarantee Building*, Fifth and Hill Streets.

Inside Ronald Reagan State Building, 300 South Spring Street

California- (Hooper, Melvinita, 1990) Mural. Dining area. Celebration of California's natural, historic, and demographic diversity.

California Cougars- (Murrill, Gwynn, 1990) Sculptures, bronze. Central atrium. Alert, powerful, ready to strike.

California Dreamscape- (Flores, Elsa and Carlos Almaraz, 1990) Mural, acrylic on canvas. Above the pool in central atrium. A freeway swoops in from an urbanized beach, past Los Angeles icons, and immediately connects with San Francisco. Kissing lips in the sky and a burning heart in San Francisco reveal the poignant fact that this public statement is also a private one–a tribute and love letter by Elsa Flores to her husband Carlos Almaraz who had died at the age of forty-eight only a year before this was painted.

California Grizzly- (Chomenko, Mary, 1990) Sculpture, bronze. Central atrium. Half-size model of an extinct species. Too engaging to be taken by most viewers as a commentary on our fragile natural environment.

Redwood Moonrise- (Gold, Betty, 1990) Sculpture/fountain, stainless steel, bronze. Central atrium. The mist created by the water slowly spilling off the upper surface and into the large pool helps balance the humidity inside the building.

Sedan 98- (Bengston, Billy Al, 1990) Mural and painted columns and cross bars. fifty-one feet long. From the main floor of the lobby, you see this scene from above. It is a view of a planet in the foreground with the more distant heavens beyond. The red framework gives the painting a three-dimensional quality-looking out from inside a spaceship.

CONVENIENCES & NECESSITIES

Public Rest Rooms

Biddy Mason Park- Broadway, a few doors south of the Bradbury Building. The rest rooms are just inside the back entrance of the *Ronald Reagan State Building's* parking structure.

Pershing Square- Entrance area to underground parking structure, under yellow cafeteria building on west side of the Square. Get key from attendant at news/candy stand.

Ronald Reagan State Building- 300 South Spring Street, 1st floor near elevators. Also 2nd floor near cafeteria.

Drinking Fountains

Grand Central Market- Upper level near Hill Street side.

Biddy Mason Park- Broadway, several doors south of the Bradbury Building. Fountain is near back entrance of the parking structure.

Pershing Square- South side of the yellow building near Fifth and Olive, across from the Biltmore Hotel.

ATMs

550 Hill Street- (International Jewelry Center).

First Street & Broadway Street- (Bank of America).

Places to Sit

Biddy Mason Park- Broadway across from Grand Central Market. Benches, tables and chairs.

Grand Central Market- Near Third and Hill Street. Sit at tables just inside the west (Hill Street) entrance.

Pershing Square- Between Fifth and Sixth, and Olive and Hill Streets. Many concrete benches throughout the park.

Parking

Broadway- Between Second and Third Streets.

Parking structure across from Ronald Reagan State Building- 300 block of Spring Street.

530 Spring Street- next to the *Theater Center*.

Hill Street- just south of *Grand Central Market*, between Third and Fourth.

Beneath Pershing Square- Expensive.

Full Service Drug Store

Thrifty- 501 South Broadway. Open 8:00 a.m. to 8:00 p.m.

RESTAURANTS

Price Guide for average lunch entrees:

$ = $3.00 - $8.00	$$$ = $13.00 - $17.00
$$ = $9.00 - $12.00	$$$$ = $18.00+

Cafeteria in the Ronald Reagan State Building- 300 South Spring Street. Second floor, overlooking the central atrium, or you can sit outside and see Little Tokyo to the east. Excellent food, bargain prices, and cheerful surroundings. Monday through Friday, lunches. ($)

Grand Central Market- 317 Broadway. Many shops and stalls. You can make a lunch by selecting, from different stalls, some *pan dolce*, fruit, dried fruits, sliced luncheon meats, coffee or espresso, deli items, seafood, and a hunk of chocolate for desert. Or you can try one of many fast-served meals: pizza, tacos, burritos, and roasted chicken (*El Pollo Loco* or several other stalls). The *China Cafe* seems out of place in this Latino environment, but it is very popular. All food counters are inexpensive. ($)

The *Grand Central Market* is often delightfully jumbled and crowded. If the Historic District has a center–a heart–this great, old marketplace is it!

Fiesta Grill- 327 Broadway, next to *Grand Central Market*. This place is trying to develop into a Mexican food court. It's main attraction is loud music, either from a juke box or a live Mariachi group. ($)

Pan Mexico- (delicious fresh, sugary, doughy rolls, *pan dulce*), 224 Fifth Street, just east of Broadway. Note: You can also get pan dulce at a counter in *Grand Central Market*, north aisle near the Broadway entrance. ($)

Smeraldi's Deli and Bakery- in the *Biltmore Hotel*, Olive & Fifth Streets. You could buy a salad or lunch box and carry it to Pershing Square. Try a delicious combination salad for a reasonable price. ($)

Cole's P.E. Buffet- 118 East Sixth Street on north side of *Pacific Electric Building* (1905), corner of Sixth and Los Angeles Streets. Claims to be the "Oldest Bar & Restaurant in Los Angeles." It is, indeed, a designated historic monument with a fine mahogany bar and Tiffany lamps. Note old photographs of the building, the main terminal of the old rapid transit system. Delicious hot sandwiches of fresh-sliced roast beef, pork, or turkey. Claims to be the originator of French-dipped sandwiches (but so does *Philippe* in Chinatown). Closed Sundays ($)

Clifton's- 648 South Broadway. Try if you are interested in recalling memories of a once-loved place. *Clifton's* does have a colorful history: This was Clifford Clinton's first cafeteria in his chain. In 1935 he decorated the room in a redwood forest theme with waterfalls and fountains.

During the Great Depression, Clinton experimented with low-cost meals for the poor and returning the price of a meal to any dissatisfied customer. Notice the elaborate terrazzo sidewalk in front. ($)

Pete's Café and Bar- 400 South Main Street. Popular New York bistro in the Old Bank District.

The Sultan- 311 West Sixth Street. Small, popular Middle Eastern eatery. You can sit on stools at a counter by the front windows. Good place to people watch. ($)

In the Alley of St. Vincent Jewelry Center – Seventh Street between Broadway and Hill:

St. Vincent Deli- Middle Eastern take-out, or sit at tables in the gritty alley. Atmosphere! Try an Armenian coffee for $1.25. ($)

Farid Middle East Cuisine- Greek salads, kabobs, yogurt appetizers, spiced-up rice, and vegetable dishes. Casual, small tables that can be pushed together for larger parties. ($$)

Garo's Deli- Take-out only. Fresh sandwiches. Tantalizing imported packaged foods from England, Armenia, Turkey, India, Afghanistan, Italy, Indonesia, and elsewhere. Lots of tea, pasta, fresh pita, canned and preserved vegetables, dried fruits, soup mixes, and cookies. Experiment with a new ingredient for tonight's dinner! ($$)

HISTORY

Ponder how much of our past we have thoughtlessly destroyed!

Consider the block of Broadway between Second and Third, just up the street from the Bradbury Building. A City Hall, one of a succession of buildings designed to house L.A.'s government, once stood at 226-240 Broadway. Close by was L.A.'s first synagogue. Designed by Ezra Kysor, Temple *B'nai B'rith* stood at 273 Broadway from 1872 to 1896. Kysor was also the architect of the *Pico House Hotel* (1870) and, just two blocks away, *St. Vibiana's Cathedral* (1876). The west side of Broadway, then called Fort Street, was the "choicest residence neighborhood in the growing city" according to the businessman-author Harris Newmark, who built his own home there. (After twenty-four years, the Jewish congregation moved to a new synagogue at Ninth and Hope Streets and later west to the Wilshire Boulevard Temple.)

In time, the old City Hall, the elegant residences, and the temple were razed, replaced by various commercial buildings, and finally by a parking structure built to serve the needs of the *Los Angeles Times*.

The transformation from residential neighborhood to parking structure is the dreary story of much of the Main-Spring-Broadway District, often called L.A.'s Historic Core. Since the 1950s, when the Santa Ana Freeway (I-101)/San Bernardino Freeway (I-10) plowed through the center of town, large, vacuous parking lots replaced blocks of stores and offices. Much of Downtown became a social vacuum. Although the freeways shortened driving times, their effect on Downtown itself was dramatic and disheartening.

The Downtown District was split apart. The visual connections between the Plaza, the Civic Center, and the Broadway District were lost. The north-south streets–Main, Spring, Broadway, and Hill–which once had clear identities, now had so many holes and gaps, they no longer made sense.

You can see faint suggestions of what we have lost and what the Broadway area looked like 100 years ago, by studying the Victorian houses and commercial buildings on North Main Street near *El Pueblo Plaza–Sepulveda House* and its neighbors, *Pico House, Merced Theater,* and the *Masonic Hall.*

Yet, there still remain some wonderful old buildings along South Broadway. The *Bradbury Building,* at the corner of Third and Broadway, was built in 1893. In 1917, the Metropolitan Water District building, with its *Million Dollar Theater,* and the *Grand Central Market* were built in the same block. This corner of Third and Broadway was once the commercial center in a half-mile long, seamless urban district.

Between 1900 and 1930, flagship department stores were built southward along Broadway and westward along Seventh Street. In 1906, *Bullock's Department Store* was built on the northwest corner of Broadway and Seventh where St. Vincent's College had stood earlier. In 1908, the *Hamburger and Sons Department Store* (later *May Co.*) was built on Broadway and Eighth. The *Broadway Department Store* had occupied much of the block on Broadway and Fourth Streets since 1897. *Barker Brothers* furniture store was a huge emporium on Broadway between Fourth and Fifth before it moved to an even more magnificent building at 818 West Seventh. The *Fifth Street Store* appeared on Broadway and

Fifth. And the spectacular Art Deco *Eastern Columbia* store at Ninth Street appeared in 1930. All these buildings are still standing!

Broadway was the commercial heart of Los Angeles. It also became the entertainment center of the City. Great movie palaces materialized in the 1910s and 1920s, marching in step with the booming motion picture industry. The production studios were in Hollywood, Culver, City, Studio City and elsewhere, but the glittering premieres were on Broadway. Along with the theaters came shops, hotels, restaurants, and night spots as each new attraction added crowds to the mixture.

Spring Street, one block east, began life as a residential neighborhood, lived in by Biddy Mason, among others. (see listing for "Biddy Mason Park"). Spring Street began to change in the 1890s to become L.A.'s Financial District, with banks, title insurance companies, office buildings, hotels for businessmen, and the *West Coast Stock Exchange*. Until the 1970s, Spring Street was the "Wall Street of the West."

In the days before freeways, people traveled Downtown by rail. The "Big Red Cars" of the *Pacific Electric* would disgorge passengers in two Downtown spots, the *Pacific Electric Building* at Sixth and Main, and the *Subway Terminal Building* on Fourth and Hill. Streetcars (trolleys) brought people in from far flung residential neighborhoods.

Traveling to Downtown was convenient and inexpensive when interurban trains and streetcars ran. However, in the 1920s, real estate developers in more distant parts of the city began to see the advantages of automobile access to their tracts. A new stage of urban evolution was at hand–and heavily promoted. Stores, hotels, office buildings, and theaters began to be relocated in new subdivisions. The expansion of the city, in turn, encouraged people to buy cars. And so it goes–each process driving the other. In 1927, *Bullock's* constructed a satellite store with a huge, newfangled space called a *parking lot*. *Bullock's Wilshire,* one and a half miles west of Downtown, became the model for many ensuing stores and offices as Wilshire Boulevard was extended to Santa Monica and the coast.

Jewelry District: Wholesale jewelry businesses and manufacturers have been well represented Downtown for most of this century. However, the conversions of old department stores and theaters to *retail* jewelry shops is more recent, dating from the 1970s when many Middle Easterners and Asians came to this country. These are the entrepreneurs and salespeople we see today. Wholesalers were originally concentrated near Broadway and Fifth; in 1920s, there were a dozen wholesale jewelry companies housed in 220 West Fifth Street building alone. In the last twenty years, the center of jewelry retailing has shifted a couple of blocks south to Hill Street between Sixth and Seventh.

World War II and the Zoot-Suit Riots: If Broadway was a place where diverse groups and cultures could mix, it could also be an arena for carousing and even conflict. During World War II, military servicemen on weekend passes crowded into Downtown streets, bent on drinking and hell raising. Many of these men came from small towns in the rural Midwest and South and were unfamiliar with "foreigners," especially those who publicly flaunted their distinctiveness. Mexican-American teenagers did just that by wearing symbols of adolescent rebellion, loose-fitting, zoot-suits, "serape shaped" jackets, pegged trousers, and broad hats.

For ten days in June, 1943, zoot-suiters and military men, young people in contrasting uniforms, engaged in protracted, noisy brawling along Broadway's Theater District. There were few serious injuries, no deaths, and little property damage, but Southern California's military commanders were embarrassed, and the long-term symbolic consequences, especially among Latinos, are still debated today.

The Wall Street of the West: Financial institutions decamped from Spring Street in the 1970s, moving several blocks west to the office towers on Bunker Hill. Since then, the Community Redevelopment Agency (C.R.A.) has made fitful attempts to preserve and recycle a few buildings on Spring Street. For example, The *Los Angeles Theater Center* (514 South Spring) was an effort to convert an old bank building into a set of small theaters. However, because the surrounding neighborhood was left to deteriorate, audiences were tentative and small, and the L.A.T.C.'s future is uncertain. It is now available as a rental.

Main Street: As a reminder of where the center of town used to be, *St. Vibiana's Cathedral* (1876) still stands on Second and Main. The Los Angeles Catholic Archdiocese abandoned St. Vibiana's after the Northridge Earthquake in favor of the new *Cathedral of Our Lady of the Angels* near the Music Center (on Grand Avenue and Temple Street). Developer Tom Gilmore now owns the property and expects to refurbish it for mixed uses. In the decades of interurban trains and streetcars, Main Street was a colorful mixture of small theaters, cut-rate stores, newsstands, pawnshops, and small cafes. Main Street was anchored by the *Pacific Electric Building* (1905) at Sixth Street (still standing).

Following the Second World War, Main Street evolved into a zone of minor vices, with burlesque houses, all-night movie theaters, greasy-spoon joints, x-rated book stores, and cheap hotels and bars. Such places also served as shelters for otherwise homeless people on Skid Row. Finally, with the cancellation of the last interurban trains in 1961, the neighborhood was neglected to death.

Scruffy buildings were demolished or shuttered. A few inexpensive hotels were converted to S.R.O. (single room occupancy) hotels, having spartan, but clean, rooms for low prices. The old burlesque houses and gaudy stores disappeared, and parking lots took over much of the neighborhood. Today, Main Street is nearly empty, a melancholy borderland separating Skid Row on the east from the commercial district on the west.

PROSPECTS

A major private investor in the Historic Core is Ira E. Yellin, who owns the *Bradbury Building*, the *Million Dollar Theater* building (now called *Grand Central Square Apartments*) and the *Grand Central Market*–all in the neighborhood of Third Street and Broadway. Preservation architect Brenda Levin has overseen the $7,000,000.00 refurbishing of the Bradbury Building. She also relit the many neon signs over food stalls inside the Central Market and removed an ugly modern facade from its Broadway side.

Yellin and an investment firm owned by Roy Disney recently built *Grand Central Square* on Third Street between Broadway and Hill. It is a mixed-use complex of old and new office, retail, and residential spaces. Like the reinstalled *Angels Flight* and the remodeled Pershing Square, Grand Central Square hopes to bridge the "Hill Street wall," a physical and psychological barrier now separating Bunker Hill's office workers from the color and excitement of Broadway.

In 1987, with the help of C.R.A. funds, Yellin and others organized a movement called *Miracle on Broadway*. The huge mural on 351 Broadway is a product of this effort. Sadly, at the time of this writing, *Miracle on Broadway* had been disbanded, a victim of the inability of the district's merchants to unite for their mutual advantage.

The State of California plans to become a major player in the district. In 1995, it bought (for $1,800,000.00) the old Luby Building (the original *Broadway Department Store*, vacant since 1966) on the southwest corner of Fourth and Broadway. The rehabilitated (for $62,000,000.00) *Luby Building* will hold about 1,700 workers who previously occupied forty different sites. The state wants to do the same for a couple of other old buildings nearby in an effort to consolidate more than 3,000 workers in this neighborhood. This would help stabilize the district, perhaps leading to other upgrades. The streetside retail spaces so carefully fitted into the new *Ronald Reagan State Building* remain mostly unrented. More state workers might generate the needed customers.

Downtown Strategic Plan (D.S.P.): In 1994, the City Council accepted a visionary design published, after five years of work, by the Community Redevelopment Agency.

The *D.S.P.* argues that Downtown's separate parts must be woven back into a whole. Walkways should connect formerly separated districts. Electric trolley "circulator" buses would sail up and down Broadway. The rebuilt *Angels Flight* would be joined by one or two other "flights." Second Street would be made into a major east-west thoroughfare. Pershing Square has been remodeled as a centerpiece of the anticipated re-centering process.

Neglected buildings should be refurbished and used again. The spectacular *Herald Examiner Building* (1111 Broadway) might be made into a *Museum of Fashion*. A few Broadway movie palaces would be spruced up for continued use as theaters. The *Broadway/Spring Arcade Building* would be converted into mixture of artists' lofts and residences with a Performing Arts Community College on the second and third floors.

An effort is also under way to reintroduce a residential population to the Broadway District. The apartments of *Grand Central Square* and *Angelus Plaza* are current examples, as are three former office buildings on 4th Street between Main and Spring Streets, an area now called the *Old Bank District*. Developer Tom Gilmore has successfully remodeled these beautiful buildings for residential purposes, and eager tenants have filled the buildings.

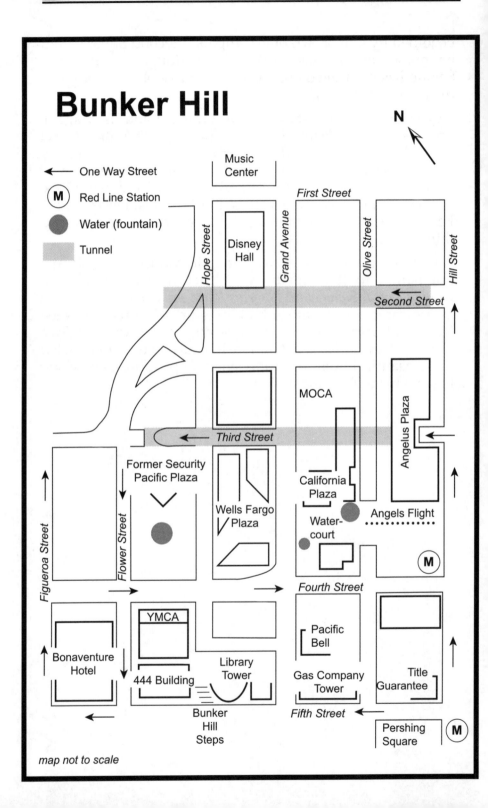

Bunker Hill

N

← One Way Street

(M) Red Line Station

● Water (fountain)

▬ Tunnel

Music Center

First Street

Hope Street

Disney Hall

Grand Avenue

Olive Street

Hill Street

Second Street →

MOCA

Angelus Plaza

Third Street ←

Former Security Pacific Plaza

Flower Street

Figueroa Street

Wells Fargo Plaza

California Plaza

Water-court

Angels Flight

Angeles Flight

(M)

Fourth Street →

YMCA

Bonaventure Hotel

444 Building

Library Tower

Pacific Bell

Gas Company Tower

Title Guarantee

Bunker Hill Steps

Fifth Street ←

Pershing Square

(M)

map not to scale

4. Bunker Hill

The gleaming skyscrapers of Downtown's skyline stand in two districts–Bunker Hill and the Lower Financial District. The two neighborhoods are separated by Fifth Street which runs along the southern edge of Bunker Hill.

The buildings on Bunker Hill, all constructed after 1980, are glistening and monumental–in sharp contrast with the older, more textured, historic district. Views of Bunker Hill from below are spectacular, as are views of the city from Bunker Hill.

Most of these buildings are also sumptuous inside. Their lobbies enclose dramatic atriums or solariums displaying works of art, special exhibits–and more views of the city.

It's easy to explore this district. You can stroll through plazas and lobbies, ponder creations by some of America's best known artists, and try a wide variety of restaurants. Two of the city's most spectacular fountains splash through computerized high jinks on Bunker Hill plazas.

Bunker Hill has a few apartment structures, but it consists mostly of office towers. It is more active and engaging on weekdays when business people are bustling about. Except for a few hotels, the *Museum of Contemporary Art*, the *Central Library*, the *Disney Concert Hall*, and the *Music Center*, Bunker Hill is nearly empty on weekends.

LOCATION

The Harbor Freeway (I-110) is the western border, Fifth Street is the southern edge, Hill Street is the eastern side, and Temple Street is the northern one. Grand Avenue is the north-south spine of Bunker Hill.

Fifth Street is the east-west dividing line separating Bunker Hill from the Lower Financial District. However, the *ARCO Plaza*, *Central Library*, and the *Biltmore Hotel* really belong to both neighborhoods. *Angels Flight* is shared with the Broadway District below and connects the two neighborhoods.

GETTING THERE FROM UNION STATION

Red Line Subway: Your Metrolink ticket gets you a free ride on the Red Line. Get off at the "Pershing Square" Station and either:

    1) Walk to the Pershing Square (Fifth Street) exit. From the surface, look west on Fifth Street past Pershing Square itself. The *Biltmore Hotel* sits on the opposite side of the Square with Bunker Hill's business towers beyond and to the right. Walk two and a half blocks on Fifth Street to Bunker Hill Steps and take the escalator up the hill.

    2) Or exit the Pershing Square Station by the Fourth Street exit, and then catch the *Angels Flight* rail cars going up to the *Watercourt* on the *California Plaza*.

DASH bus- From the front of Union Station, walk across Alameda Street, and look for the DASH sign on a pole. Catch a DASH bus (route B) which appears every five minutes on weekdays. Show the driver your Metrolink ticket, otherwise the bus costs only $.25. The bus travels west to the Music Center and heads south on Grand Avenue. You can be dropped off across the street from the *Museum of Contemporary Art, (M.O.C.A.)* or at the foot of the hill in front of the Bunker Hill Steps on Fifth Street. On weekends, get off at Hill and Third, and take Angels Flight to the top of Bunker Hill.

DRIVING & PARKING

Best Parking Deal in Town

If you own a Los Angeles Public Library library card (not a *County* library card) and you can begin your visit after 3:00 p.m. on weekdays or any time on weekends. Drive to the lot under the Maguire Gardens (524 South Flower Street. Flower is one-way, going south). Only $1.00 flat rate!

From the north: Take the Pasadena Freeway (I-110) south to the Sixth Street exit. Turn immediately left onto Figueroa and drive two blocks to Fourth Street. Turn right onto Fourth and right again onto Flower Street. Park either in the structure across Flower Street from the Bonaventure Hotel (under Bunker Hill) or, in the next block under the Maguire Gardens just south of Fifth Street.

From the east: Take the 101 Freeway west; exit on Grand Avenue. Follow the curve around and turn right onto Grand. Consider parking in the lot south of The Music Center or drive down to Fifth Street and turn right. Park under the Maguire Gardens just south of Fifth on Flower Street.

From the south: Drive north on the Harbor Freeway (I-110) to the Sixth Street exit. Turn immediately left onto Figueroa and drive two blocks to Fourth Street. Turn right on Fourth and right again onto Flower Street. Park either in the structure across Flower Street from the Bonaventure Hotel (under Bunker Hill) or, in the next block under the Maguire Gardens just south of Fifth Street.

From the west: Take the Santa Monica Freeway (I-10) to the Harbor Freeway North (I-110) to the Sixth Street exit. Turn immediately left onto Figueroa and drive two blocks to Fourth Street. Turn right on Fourth and right again onto Flower Street. Park either in the structure across Flower Street from the Bonaventure Hotel (under Bunker Hill) or, in the next block under the Maguire Gardens just south of Fifth Street.

From the north-west, Hollywood, and San Fernando Valley: Take the Hollywood Freeway east. Go through the transition to the Harbor Freeway South (I-110) south to the Sixth Street exit. Turn immediately left onto Figueroa and drive two blocks to Fourth Street. Turn right on Fourth and right again onto Flower Street. Park either in the structure across Flower Street from the Bonaventure Hotel (under Bunker Hill) or, in the next block under the Maguire Gardens just south of Fifth Street.

WHO'S THERE?

The high rise office towers are headquarters of law firms, banks, accounting firms, insurance companies, oil companies, and other corporations. During lunch and rush hours, you'll see executives, business professionals, secretaries, paralegals, receptionists, clerks, janitors, food delivery runners, security guards, tourists, and shoppers.

L.A. LAW- The top five law firms in the city are all located Downtown. *O'Melveny & Myers*, (400 South Hope); *Gibson Dunn & Crutcher* (333 S. Grand); *Paul Hastings Janofsky & Walker* (ARCO Plaza); *Latham & Watkins* (in the Library Tower); and *Sheppard, Mullin, Richter & Hampton* (333 South Hope Street). In fact, eighteen of the top twenty-five law firms in L.A. are located in downtown. Also, most law firms are adding attorneys as the economy of the region improves.

Source: *Los Angeles Business Journal.*

L. A. ACCOUNTING FIRMS- The top firms in the city are located Downtown: *Deloitte & Touche* (350 South Grand Avenue), *PricewaterhouseCoopers* (400 South Hope Street), *Ernst & Young* (Seventh Street and Figueroa Street), and *KPMG* (335 South Grand Avenue).

WHAT'S THERE FOR THE VISITOR?

Bunker Hill- Offers an amiable spaciousness with lofty views from the crown of the hill. Pedestrians can also enjoy colorful stores, new architecture, public art, playful fountains with antic imaginations, and restaurants–some fancy and expensive, others interesting and affordable.

SIGHTS

Angels Flight- Funicular (a short cable railway), running up to *California Plaza* from the corner of Fourth and Hill Streets. On December 31, 1901, the counterbalanced cars, *Olivet* and *Sinai*, began carrying people from Third and Hill Streets in the downtown commercial district up the steep hill to their Victorian homes and residential hotels. Built by engineer J.W. Eddy and modified a bit in the first few years, Angels Flight served the public at a penny a ride until the 1910s when the fare was raised to a nickel. It was dismantled and put into storage in 1969 when all the buildings on the top of Bunker Hill had been bulldozed away. In February 24, 1996 this "shortest railroad in the world" was refitted to the hill one-half block south from where it had operated for sixty-eight years and reopened to the public. The archway structures at the top and bottom ends of the track are of concrete and have safely survived years of exposure and neglect. *Olivet* and *Sinai* have been carefully refurbished, and would run today exactly as they did originally. (A tragic accident in 2001 forced the closure of Angels Flight. Reopening to be announced.)

Panoramic view of the city- From the 35th floor of the *Westin Bonaventure Hotel* you can get a 360 degree view of downtown and beyond. But there are equally intriguing vistas from several street level positions. Try the view from the rim of *California Plaza*'s Watercourt or from the second floor cafeteria of the Wells Fargo Court.

Bunker Hill Steps a.k.a. "Spanish Steps"- (Lawrence Halprin, 1990; *Source Figure*, Robert Graham, 1992) This is a "step-fountain," a stream flowing down from the top of the hill to a small pool on Fifth Street. It doubles as a pedestrian way (either by escalator or by regular steps) linking two business districts–Bunker Hill and the Lower Financial District. The Bunker Hill Steps is also a destination itself. Its informal landings and small courtyards are great spots for lunch and to catch the sun, enjoy the terrific view, or grab a moment of repose. This is a fascinating urban place; it is part of the urban street action but lifted above it. You are up in air, but, at the same time, you also feel comfortably enclosed by the structures around the various perches. At the top of the stairs, Robert Graham's sculpture of an exquisite nude, *Source Figure*, looks down on the stream in front of her. She is giving water to the thirsty city.

There are three other fountains on Bunker Hill- The **California Plaza**, 350 South Grand Avenue, has two of them–the Watercourt and a smaller circular fountain between the *California Plaza Towers*. The *Music Center* fountain, 135 North Grand, located between the Dorothy Chandler Pavilion and the Mark Taper Forum, is the older brother of the other two. All are lively, computer-controlled show-offs, and great fun to watch.

BUILDINGS

Westin Bonaventure Hotel- (Portman, John, 1976) Taking up the entire block between Fourth and Fifth Streets and Flower & Figueroa Streets, the Bonaventure is the largest hotel in L.A., with 1,474 rooms. Five glass cylinder-shaped towers rise from a mammoth concrete bunker. Step inside to experience an impressive, six-story lobby/atrium. The space is airy and relaxed; you hear the pleasing sounds of fountains; there are inviting places to sit either near ponds or suspended in space.

However, inside this collection of cylinders, the visual references are all circular and dizzying. The whole space is concrete gray except for spots of color on the four elevator columns. Suggestion: Memorize the color spot near the door by which you entered so that you know how to leave the building when the time comes. Better still, carry a compass!

Take one of the Red elevators to the thirty-fifth floor. If you don't like heights, stand near the door, away from the glass sides because the elevator shoots through the roof of the atrium and up the *outside* of the building. At the thirty-fifth floor, enter the restaurant and stroll around it for a 360 degree view of L.A.

The outside of the Bonaventure is best appreciated from the Harbor Freeway, half a block away, but it offers mostly blank concrete walls and huge garage cavities to its own sidewalk. You are meant to drive, not walk, into this building. Who cares? Walk through one of the glass doors anyway.

Library Tower (formerly *First Interstate World Center)-* (Cobb, Henry of I.M. Pei, Freed/Harold Fredenburg, 1990) 633 West Fifth Street. This is the tallest building on the west coast, seventy-three stories, one thousand seventeen feet. Three thousand people work here, carried up and down by forty-four elevators. A painting of three renaissance angels on the lobby walls facing the windows is best studied inside the entrance. The mural is one of many artistic commentaries on the city's Spanish name, *The Angels.* When the curtains were parted at the public dedication of the mural in 1993, someone exclaimed, "They're all white!"–embarrassing, for the most diverse city in the country.

Maguire Thomas Partners has been the most prominent developer in downtown Los Angeles in recent years. This firm, with the help of public subsidies from the Community Redevelopment Agency (C.R.A.), built three projects on Bunker Hill and along the Fifth Street neighborhood: *Wells Fargo Center, Library Tower,* and the *Gas Company Tower.* Maguire Thomas is also the principal force behind such "placemakers" as the *Bunker Hill Steps, Maguire Gardens* at the Central Library and the remodeled *Pershing Square.*

Wells Fargo Center, formerly *Crocker Center-* (Skidmore, Owings & Merrill, 1983) 333 South Grand Avenue. In 1986, when many banks were troubled by the failures of overly optimistic loans, Wells Fargo Bank swallowed–that's the word for it–the *Crocker Bank.* Logos on the buildings were changed to *Wells Fargo.*

Wells Fargo History Museum- Open every banking day. Heavy on promotion, but its star attraction is a genuine stagecoach you can look at, but not touch. You can then sit in a full-size, mock stagecoach to ponder the pleasures and pains experienced by our pioneer ancestors. You'll not detect any reference to the extermination of other banks in this museum.

Wells Fargo Court Restaurants- In the middle of the Wells Fargo Center. A delightful, visually exciting structure enclosing several fine restaurants. (See "Restaurants" below.) Several fine works of art, fountains–and aromas!

California Plaza- (Erickson, Arthur, 1985, 1992) 350 South Grand Avenue. A complex of office towers, residential blocks, hotel, and entertainment spaces. Its high-rises are among the most striking office towers on Bunker Hill because of the rounded corners on the two opposite sides of each building. The forty-two-story and fifty-two-story buildings rise from a platform that bridges Olive Street. The funicular railroad Angels Flight, lifts people from the Red Line station at Fourth and Hill Streets up to this platform overlooking the Watercourt at California Plaza.

Museum of Contemporary Art (M.O.C.A.)- (Isozaki, Arata, 1986) 250 South Grand Avenue. Isozaki, a Japanese architect well-known for his museums in Asia, created this delightful, two-colored, post-modern building–really a work of sculpture itself–to hold works of art created after 1940. Deep red sandstone from India covers all exterior walls except the green painted ones. The exhibition spaces are mostly under street level, so the building we see on the plaza is smaller, more human in scale than other structures on Bunker Hill. Twenty-four hour information (213) 626-6222. Open Tuesday through Sunday 11:00 a.m. to 5:00 p.m., Thursday 11:00 a.m to 8:00 p.m., closed Monday and some holidays.

M.O.C.A. Store- Tuesday through Sunday 11:00 a.m. to 6:00 p.m., Thursday 11:00 to 8:00 p.m. (213) 621-1710. The museum's large gift shop is an outstanding place to find books, paintings, toys, gifts, and other fine mementos.

Watercourt- (Robinson, Alan, 1992) Fountain. One of the great delights of Bunker Hill is its collection of several water fountains. The sights and sounds of water splashing, shooting, gushing, popping, and hiccuping are counterpoints to the noise of car and bus traffic. This huge fountain-waterfall can be quickly turned off, drained, and converted to a stage for noon-time or evening concerts or other performances.

Tables and chairs are set at the water's edge, and granite benches are arranged on a viewing platform above.

Closer to the front of the plaza on Grand Avenue you'll find the fountain's smaller sibling, a perky circular fountain with a madcap personality. It skips merrily through a program made all the more comical by sound effects. Don't miss it!

But be careful! This smaller fountain subsides completely now and then, hoping you'll be tempted to dash across its shallow basin. Make sure your health insurance policy is paid up before trying it.

Omni Los Angeles Hotel (formerly Hotel Inter-Continental) - (Myers, Arthur and Flatow, Moore, Bryan, Shaffer, McCabe, 1993) 251 South Olive Street. Newest luxury hotel Downtown.

Floor Space

To get an idea of how much space is included in office towers, the taller of the two *California Plaza* buildings has 1,270,000 square feet of "rentable area." The shorter one has 1,000,000 square feet.

The largest Downtown building is the *333 South Hope Building* (formerly *Security Pacific Plaza*) with 1,400,000 square feet.

The tallest building is *Library Tower* with 1,300,000 rentable square footage.

Source: *Los Angeles Business Journal.*

Angelus Plaza- (Dworsky, Daniel L., 1980, 1981) Hill Street at Third. Senior housing apartments in three massive blocks on the east side of Bunker Hill. The 1,057 one-bedroom units were built by the United Church of Christ and the C.R.A., with funds also from H.U.D. No complaint about that, but the structures constitute a barricade between the white-collar Bunker Hill and the blue-collar Broadway District. The city hopes to reunite the two neighborhoods by Angels Flight at Fourth Street and another funicular at Second Street.

Los Angeles Music Center- (Welton Becket & Associates, 1969) 135 North Grand, between First and Temple Streets, and between Grand and Hope Streets. Charles Moore, architect and author of *City Observed: Los Angeles*, calls this "official Late Modern Architecture" marked by "windy grandiosity." It must be said that the *insides* of these buildings are splendid!

The plaza of the Music Center is a platform for looking down the *Paseo de los Pobladores*, anchored at the east end by City Hall. You can also catch views of the *Los Angeles Times* building just south of City Hall–an important visual link, because the *Times* and Dorothy Buffum Chandler, the wife of editor and publisher, Norman Chandler, were the pushers, money raisers, and arm-twisters who brought forth the Music Center and erected it here on land belonging to Los Angeles County.

Dorothy Chandler Pavilion- This is the largest of the three performance halls, with 3,197 seats, the home of the Los Angeles Philharmonic unless and until the *Walt Disney Concert Hall* is built across the street. It is also used regularly by large touring orchestras, opera and ballet companies, and the Los Angeles Master Chorale. For an auditorium this size, the *Dorothy Chandler Pavilion* has excellent acoustics and sight lines.

Mark Taper Forum- Sitting inside a moat, surrounded by a rectangular frame, this is a theater-in-the round, with a stage that projects into the 737-seat auditorium.

Ahmanson Theater- Ideal for large musical-theater and dance productions. Remodeled in 1995, this theater holds 2,071.

Fountain- The plaza between the Dorothy Chandler Pavilion and the Mark Taper Forum contains a bronze sculpture by Jacques Lipchitz, *Peace on Earth*, (1969) surrounded by a computer-controlled fountain. The water shoots up from the flat "basin" which is a continuation of the plane of the plaza floor. It taunts theater patrons to dash in and out of the fountain during one of its quiescent moments. (Kindly notice our warning about the circular fountain at the *California Plaza*, above. They are in the same family of tricksters.)

Walt Disney Concert Hall- (Gehry, Frank), Grand Avenue between First and Second Street–across the street from the Dorothy Chandler Pavilion. This astonishing structure, has become one of L.A.'s most distinctive landmarks–and a spectacular venue for the Los Angeles Philharmonic. The Disney family made a $100,000,000 gift to get things started, but others contributed to the full cost of $274,000,000. The main hall holds 2,300 people who surround an open platform stage. A smaller theater, two outdoor amphitheaters, and gardens provide additional spaces for public gatherings and concerts.

Will the Walt Disney Concert Hall rival Sydney's famous Opera House? Time will tell. The exterior walls of both buildings are unusual–and large. The Walt Disney Concert Hall is clad in huge carved and folded stainless steel panels, rather like those Gehry used for his acclaimed Guggenheim Museum in Bilbao, Spain.

Colburn School of Performing Arts- (Pfeiffer, Norman, 1998) Next to the Museum of Contemporary Art on Grand Avenue. Teaches music, drama, and dance in a demanding program to 1,300 children, starting as young as possible.

Gas Company Tower- (Skidmore, Owings & Merrill, Richard Keating, 1991) Fifth Street between Olive Street and Grand Avenue, across from *Biltmore Hotel*. A contrasting slice of glass is fitted into the top of the tower, meant to suggest the shape of a gas flame. But the most intriguing feature of this building is found inside, in the main elevator lobby. You look through the glass walls at Frank Stella's enormous mural, the largest abstract painting in the world. You will also be able to walk on water, something you may have been hoping to do but somehow never found the time to try before now.

What are These Office Towers Made of Anyway?

A modern high-rise building is supported entirely by the steel skeleton inside the structure. Huge I-beams are bolted and welded together and anchored to a massive steel-reinforced cement foundation poured many stories below street level. What we see on the outside is a *curtain wall* composed of thin slabs of stone, brick, metal, glass, or even plastic. These materials are attached or "hung" on the steel framework to form the skin of the building; they do not help support it.

This technique makes possible the variety of textures and colors seen on tall structures today. Architects are no longer limited to the natural colors of brick, concrete, or stone.

One Bunker Hill, formerly *Edison Company Building-* (Allison & Allison, 1930) Northwest corner of Fifth Street and Grand Avenue. Aristocratic Art Deco office building. Above the entrance are carved stone panels by Merrill Gage representing hydroelectric power. Go inside and admire what a major utility could build when it wanted to, a luscious gold and marble lobby. Mural by Hugo Ballin (1930), *Apotheosis of Power* celebrates electric energy.

Los Angeles Department of Water and Power- (Martin, A.C., 1964) 135 North Hope Street. This was the first commercial building erected on Bunker Hill after the Victorian houses were destroyed and the landscape shaved clean. Surrounded by a moat, the D.W.P. marks the western end of the Civic Center whose axis extends across the plaza of the Music Center and down the hill until it bumps into City Hall. Visit the "Historical Gallery" in the main lobby, a collection of photographs and artifacts from the days (1913) when William Mulholland built the aqueduct that brought water from the Owens Valley, 233 miles away, to thirsty L.A. This is a promotional exhibit, and you'll find no mention of the struggle between Los Angeles and the once-productive farming region. And there is nothing in the exhibit about the 1928 collapse of Mulholland's St. Francis Dam in the Santa Clara Valley in which almost 400 people died.

333 South Hope Building (formerly *Security Pacific Plaza*)- (Martin, Albert C., 1974) Hope Street at Third. A fifty-five-story office tower set at an angle on its site, which looks like a park but is really the top of a multi-level parking garage. With 1,400,000 square feet. *Security Pacific Plaza* is Downtown's largest office building. Alexander Calder's red painted *Four Arches* sculpture is a striking punctuation mark. In the south corner of the lobby, nearest the Calder sculpture, you can find an evocative little model showing the Victorian houses that occupied this site in 1895. The *Security Pacific Bank* was absorbed by the *Bank of America* in 1993, so the building now has other tenants, mostly, at the time of this writing, law firms.

Office Tower Rents and Occupancy Rates

The square foot rents in Downtown office towers dropped in the 1990s and have become bargains—lower than the downtown rents of several other big city markets in the U.S. and lower than satellite office complexes on the perimeter of Los Angeles.

This has helped maintain reasonably strong occupancy rates (approximately twenty percent) in spite of the loss of several large tenants due to mergers and acquisitions.

Stuart M. Ketchum Downtown Y.M.C.A.- (Martin, Albert C., 1986) 401 South Hope Street. Smack in the middle of office towers, this wedge-shaped post-modern building offers exercise and recreation for stressed—out office workers. Walk by the "Y" at noon on a weekday and gaze up into the two-story workout gym. An array of sweating, puffing yuppies will glare right back—one of the funniest sights in the city. The Downtown Y.M.C.A. also conducts recreation and fitness programs for kids, seniors, and homeless people living within the district. Monday through Friday from 5:30 a.m. to 10:00 p.m., Saturday 8:00 a.m. to 5:00 p.m., Sunday 9:00 a.m. to 4:00 p.m. (213) 624-2348.

MOTION PICTURE THEATERS

Laemmle's Grande- 345 South Figueroa Street. This is the only multiplex theater Downtown and has four screens. Park in *World Trade Center*, Fourth Street between Figueroa and Flower. (213) 617-0268.

PUBLIC ART

Four Arches- (Calder, Alexander, 1974) Sculpture, painted steel sixty-three feet high. *Security Pacific Plaza*, 333 South Hope Street. Calder is famous for his mobiles; this is a "stabile". Visible from many Downtown viewpoints.

Le Dandy- (Dubuffet, Jean, 1973-82) Sculpture, painted fiberglass ten feet high. West entrance of Wells Fargo Court, 333 South Grand Avenue.

Sequi- (Graves, Nancy, 1985) Sculpture, bronze with polychrome finish, Grand Avenue side of *Wells Fargo Plaza*, 333 South Grand Avenue. Colorful big bird pecking for seeds?, coins?, credit cards?

Crocker Fountain Figures, Numbers 1, 2, & 3- (Graham, Robert, 1984) Sculptures, bronze. In *Fountain Court* atrium in *Wells Fargo Court*, formerly Crocker Bank Plaza, 333 South Grand Avenue. Athletic nudes caught in mid-event.

Source Figure- (Graham, Robert, 1992) Sculpture, bronze. Exquisite nude at the top of the Bunker Hill Steps' step-fountain. Her hands are cupped and held open to the stream in front of her. She is presenting precious water to the thirsty city below.

Uptown Rocker- (Hamrol, Lloyd, 1986) Sculpture, painted steel. Fourth Street below Grand Avenue bridge. Jammed alongside Fourth Street, this huge, colorful image of cars on a rocker runner could be the icon for the Planning Department of the City of Los Angeles.

North, East, South, West- (Heizer, Michael, 1967-81) Sculptures, brushed stainless steel, eight feet high. Ground level of 444 Building, corner of Fifth and Flower Streets.

Unity- (Komar, Vitaly and Alexander Melamid, 1993) Mural. Lobby of *Library Tower*. 633 West Fifth Street Three Renaissance angels, a brunette and two blondes, represent figures painted in the chapel called *Porciuncula* ("little place") attended by St. Francis of Assissi. The word was part of the original Spanish name given to the *Rio de Los Angeles de Porciuncula*.

Peace on Earth- (Lipchitz, Jacques, 1969) Sculpture, bronze. Plaza of Music Center, 135 North Grand Avenue.

Prenatal Memories- (di Suvero, Mark, 1976-80) Sculpture, corten steel. In front of *Omni Los Angeles Hotel* on *California Plaza*. Of course! What else could this sculpture be named?

La Caresse d'un Oiseau- (Miro, Joan, 1967) Sculpture, painted bronze. South side of Wells Fargo Court. Engaging humanoid in bright red, blue, and yellow.

Night Sail- (Nevelson, Louise, 1985) Sculpture, painted aluminum and steel. Wells Fargo Plaza near Grand Avenue. Across the street, M.O.C.A. holds some of Nevelson's other works.

Long Beach- (Stella, Frank, 1982) Sculpture/painting, painted aluminum. Twenty-two feet wide. Ground level of 444 Building, corner of Fifth and Flower Streets.

Dusk- (Stella, Frank, a part of his *Moby Dick Series*, 1991) Mural, on south wall of *Pacific Bell/AT&T Building* on Grand Avenue, above corner of Fifth and Olive Streets. This, says Stella, is the world's largest abstract mural (40,000 square feet), a backdrop to the *Gas Company Tower*. Go inside lobby of the *Gas Company Tower*; you'll feel you are inside the painting.

Shoshone- (di Suvero, Mark, 1982) Sculpture, painted steel I-beams on third level of 444 Building overlooking Flower Street, across from *Bonaventure Hotel*.

Handstand- (Hibald, Milton, 1986) Sculpture, bronze. East end of high foot-bridge over Flower Street connecting the *Y.M.C.A.* to the Bonaventure Hotel.

Ulysses- (Liberman, Alexander, 1988) Sculpture, painted steel. Southeast corner, Hope and Fourth Streets. Assertive punctuation mark, well-scaled to this corner.

CONVENIENCES & NECESSITIES

Public Rest Rooms

California Plaza- 350 South Grand Avenue, near the sporty little fountain.

Wells Fargo Building- 333 South Grand Avenue, next to Wells Fargo History Museum.

Westin Bonaventure Hotel- Fifth and Flower Streets, street level, lobby near yellow elevators and near red elevators. Also on Fourth floor, "Market on Fourth" food court.

Library Tower- Second floor. Enter from *El Fornaio* level of Bunker Hill Steps.

Central Library- Fifth and Flower Streets.

444 Building- Northeast corner of Fifth and Flower Streets; escalator up to Carl's Jr.; from order counter, walk left through double doors, left again, then right.

Places to Sit

Wells Fargo Plaza- 333 South Grand Avenue, outside benches. Also *Wells Fargo History Museum* (inside).

California Plaza- 350 South Grand. Tables and chairs around Watercourt, also stone benches on deck above the fountain level.

Bunker Hill Steps- across Fifth Street from Central Library. Benches and chairs on the landings.

RESTAURANTS

Price Guide to average lunch entrees:

$ = $3.00 - $8.00 $$$ = $13.00 - $17.00
$$ = $9.00 - $12.00 $$$$ = $18.00+

At the Music Center

Otto's Grill and Beer Bar- 135 North Grand Avenue. Restaurant and cocktail lounge. Fresh fish, steaks, microbrews. Monday 11:30 a.m. to 2:00 p.m., Tuesday through Sunday 11:30 a.m. to 12:00 a.m. (213) 972-7322. ($$)

Impresario Ristorante e Bar- Top (fifth) floor of *Dorothy Chandler Pavilion* in the *Music Center*, 165 North Grand Avenue. (213) 972-7318. This space was formerly occupied by the *Pavilion Restaurant* which had lost its earlier polish and distinction. But new management, and consultant, Piero Selvaggio, have created this super-elegant, California-Italian dining experience in a grandiose restaurant with the "grand feel of theater." (*Downtown News*, 1-15-96). Lunches from 11:30 a.m. to 2:00 p.m. only on the Chandler's opera matinee days; dinners Tuesday through Sunday 5:30 p.m. to 8:00 p.m. (213) 972-7333. ($$$$)

Cafe on the Plaza- In front of Mark Taper Forum. Sandwiches, salads, pizza. Monday 8:00 a.m. to 3:00 p.m.; Tuesday through Friday 8:00 a.m. to 8:00 p.m.; Saturday, Sunday 11:00 a.m. to 8:00 p.m. ($)

[There's not much choice at the Music Center. Try going across Hope Street to the excellent *Cafe Current* in *Department of Water & Power Building*. Modern food court with several ethnic stations. ($)]

On Fifth Street

Starbucks- 601 West Fifth Street, corner of Grand Avenue. Specialty coffee, tea, and pastries. There are tables on the busy sidewalk across from the Central Library.

McCormick and Schmick's- in *Library Tower*. Famous for its huge selection of fresh seafood. Menu changes according to what's in season. $12.95 lobster every Friday. Sporty atmosphere. Also has an extensive wine list, a bar, and a "$1.95 Menu," happy hour Monday through Friday 3:00 to 7:00 p.m. Open Monday through Thursday 11:00 a.m. to 10:00 p.m., Friday. 11:30 a.m. to 11:00 p.m. Saturday & Sunday 5:00 p.m. to 11:00 p.m. (213) 629-1929. ($$)

Cafe Pinot- in Maguire Gardens of Central Library, Fifth and Flower Streets. When the *Central Library* was reconstructed in 1993, this glass-sided restaurant building was placed in the Maguire Gardens apparently to insure there would be lively activity there. Success! On weekdays, the place is filled with office workers from the surrounding district. "Casual indoor and patio dining featuring rotisserie chicken." This popular restaurant is an offspring of the esteemed *Patina/Pinot* on Melrose Avenue. Weekdays breakfast and lunch, Monday through Saturday 5:00 p.m. to 9:30 p.m. (213) 239-6500. ($$-$$$)

In 444 Building, Fifth and Flower Streets

Turkey Basket- Third level. Indoor or outdoor seating. Turkey as fast food. How about Turkey Teriyaki, or Lemon Turkey, or Turkey Chili Bowl, or, of course, Turkey Burgers? Monday through Saturday 7:00 a.m. to 3:00 p.m. (213) 892-9500. ($)

Carl's Jr.- Second level. The most interesting, airy Carl's you are likely to find. Great views from indoor or outdoor seating, looking across Fifth Street at the Central Library and the Maguire Gardens. Burgers, sandwiches, salad bar. Monday through Friday 7:00 a.m. to 7:00 p.m. Saturday lunch. ($)

In Westin Bonaventure Hotel – Fifth & Flower Streets

Sidewalk Cafe- ground floor of *Westin Bonaventure Hotel*. A classy coffee shop. Salads, sandwiches, seafood, and meats served American-style with occasional Asian and Mexican accents. Salad bar. Frequented by business people, hotel residents and tourists. Open Sunday through Thursday 6:00 a.m. to 11:00 p.m., Friday and Saturday 6:00 a.m. to 12:00 p.m. ($$)

Top of Five- in Westin Bonaventure Hotel, thirty-fifth floor. High up, with a terrific view of the city. Rotating bar (*Bona Vista Lounge*) on the level below restaurant. Serves French-

American food at tables arranged so all have fine views. Salads, mesquite broiler, prime rib, and seafood. Monday through Friday, lunch; Sunday through Thursday, dinner 5:30 p.m. to 10:00 p.m.; Friday and Saturday 5:30 to 10:30 p.m. (213) 624-1000. ($$$)

Mandarin West- In Westin Bonaventure Hotel, Figueroa Street side, 6th floor. Mandarin and Szechwan food. Also pork, beef, and lamb dishes. Sleek modern decor. (213) 488-1111. Luncheon specials $5.00-$6.00, otherwise ($$).

Bonaventure Brewing Co.- On the plaza deck by the swimming pool. Lunches, happy hours, and dinners. Closed Sundays. ($$-$$$)

"Market on Fourth," a food court on fourth level. Wide selection of ethnic fast food shops arrayed along the balcony ringing the central atrium:

Cap'n Lee's Seafood- Fried and grilled seafood. ($)
The Health Winner- Salads, sandwiches, baked potatoes. ($)
Jyokamachi- Japanese. Steak, sushi. ($)
Korean BBQ Plus- Korean BBQ combination platters. ($)
Uncle Mustache Falafel- Middle Eastern fast food. ($)

In Y.M.C.A., Fourth & Hope Streets

California Crisp- Salads, sandwiches, turkey and vegi-burgers. Catering. Open to 8:00 p.m. (213) 622-6749. ($)

Wells Fargo "The Court" Restaurants – in Wells Fargo Center, 350 South Hope Street

All restaurants have seating under skylight roofs as well as inside their own enclosures. The *Wells Fargo Court* is mostly aimed at weekday lunch crowds.

Court Cafeteria- Second level. Monday through Friday breakfast and lunch. Excellent selection of soups, salads, burgers, burritos, and other hot dishes. Additional balcony seating with terrific view. ($)

Taipan- Second level. Standard Chinese/Mandarin restaurant menu. Quiet, sleek interior seating. Lunch specials include appetizer, soup, and entree. Monday through Friday 11:00 a.m. to 9:30 p.m., Saturday 11:30 a.m. to 9:00 p.m., Sunday closed. (213) 626-6688. ($)

California Pizza Kitchen- First level. Pizza with toppings you've never tried before. Also pasta, soups, and salads. Additional outdoor seating. Monday through Friday 11:00 a.m. to 10:00 p.m., Saturday noon to 10:00 p.m., Sunday noon to 9:30 p.m. (213) 626-2616. ($)

Fountain Court- First level atrium. Gracious, open, garden-like atmosphere. Enchanting bronze sculptures by Robert Graham and lovely fountains. Salads, sandwiches, pasta, and rich desserts; espresso and cappuccino. Overlaps with the menu of *Stepps*, of which it is an off-shoot. Monday through Friday lunch. ($$)

Nick and Steff's Steakhouse- First level–where *Stepps* used to be. One of the many famous Joachim Splichal restaurants in town. Named for his twin sons, this is a BIG place (320 seats), well located to appeal to concert go-ers and Staples Center crowds. Indoor and outdoor tables. A glass-walled meat locker shows off the prime cuts to hungry customers. (213) 680-0330. Monday through Thursday 11:30 a.m. to 2:30 p.m. and 5:30 p.m. to 9:30 p.m. Friday and Saturday from 5:00 p.m. to 10:30 p.m. Sunday from 5:00 p.m. to 9:30 p.m. ($$$)

McDonald's- First level. Make a list of the ways this fancy franchise differs from the standard ones. Also has balcony seating. ($)

Pasqua- First level. Snacks, sandwiches, coffee. ($)

In California Plaza, Fountain Level and Spiral Court – 300 South Grand Avenue.

Dan's Deli- Sandwiches, small salad bar, drinks, and a huge selections of chips and candy bars. Grab a bite to eat and sit out by the fountain. ($)

Panda Express- Chinese fast food. Monday through Friday 10:00 a.m. to 4:00 p.m. ($)

Patinette- Under entrance to *M.O.C.A.*'s front entrance, down the stairs; open air, but below street level. Joachim Splichal's contribution to Bunker Hill (see *Patina* at the Central Library's Maguire Gardens). Salads, sandwiches, soup, wine & beer by the glass. Tuesday through Sunday 10:00 a.m. to 5:00 p.m., Thursday 11:00 a.m. to 8:00 p.m. ($-$$)

Tesoro Trattoria- By Spiral Court just south of *M.O.C.A.* Tuscan, al fresco pizza, pasta, and secondi. A good before–concert option. Reservations suggested. (213) 680-0000. ($$-$$$)

Angels Flight- In the *Omni Los Angeles Hotel.* Named for the old funicular recently returned to service. Exclusive club atmosphere with prices to match. A special pre-theater menu as well. Seafood, fowl, and steak prepared with international influences. Monday through Friday lunch, Saturday dinner only. (213) 356-4100. ($$$)

Grand Cafe- In the *Omni Los Angeles Hotel.* Large American breakfasts with European frills; California cuisine for lunch: hearty sandwiches, beautiful salads. Daily specials. Artsy interior, perhaps influenced by the Museum of Contemporary Art next door. Monday through Friday 6:30 a.m. to 10:30 p.m., Saturday and Sunday 7:00 a.m. to 10:00 p.m. (213) 356-4155. ($$)

Wall Street Deli- Lower level on Grand Avenue. Popular, cheerful. Full of office workers. Cafeteria/food court: deli sandwiches, bagels, salad bar, and soup. Try the all you can eat potato/salad bar, less than $5.00. Monday through Friday 6:30 a.m. to 4:00 p.m. ($)

Koo-Koo-Roo- 255 South Grand, across the street from M.O.C.A.. Indoor/outdoor eating. Skinless flame broiled chicken, turkey, ten vegetable soup. ($)

In Marriott Hotel –
Third and Figueroa Streets

All restaurants entered from the street-level lobby.

Moody's Bar and Grille- Hearty American food. Hunting club atmosphere, polished brass and dark wood. Sports bar at the center. Steak, seafood. (213) 617-6023. Lunch (**$$**) and dinner. (**$$$**).

Three Thirty Three- American. Subdued lighting, elegant feel of an intimate dining room. Dinners only. (213) 617-6045. (**$$$$**)

The Back Porch- Earns its name by its location next to the pool. Salads, pastas, sandwiches, and seafood and meat dishes, prepared American-style with dashes of Asian and Cajun flavors. Breakfast and lunch. (**$$$**)

HISTORY

In the first two decades following the Gold Rush, the population of Los Angeles increased in small fits and starts. The old Plaza neighborhood was still a wild, dusty, unkempt area in the judgments of newcomers, and they looked generally south and away from El Pueblo Plaza for places to build their homes. The flat lands along Broadway and Spring Streets were allocated for commercial and civic purposes, and just beyond, farms were being acquired and transformed into neighborhoods of modest houses.

In 1867, businessman Prudent Beaudry paid $517.00 at a sheriff's auction to buy some acres on the hill just west of Broadway. He piped water up to it in 1875, and developed the land into a residential community. The year 1875 was the 100th anniversary of the Battle of Bunker Hill, so Beaudry named his subdivision accordingly. It became a tony neighborhood of houses and mansions overlooking the changing scene below. Big Names like the Crockers (1886) and Bradburys (1887) built homes there, and some of their houses even managed to survive until the 1960s.

Bunker Hill was then higher and more convoluted than it is today, a steep climb for horses and humans, and it blocked convenient access from the commercial streets on the east side. Anyone thinking of acquiring properties farther west of Downtown was confronted by the barrier which extended from El Pueblo Plaza down to Fifth Street. So, in 1885 developers created *The Second Street Cable Railroad* to carry people up and over the hill. Eventually other cable systems extended as far west as Alvarado Avenue. By 1893, those routes were converted to electric street railways.

Meanwhile, profound changes were afoot. From 1885 to 1888, the real estate market in Southern California, pumped up by the railroads, exploded. Bunker Hill began a commercial transformation. Several hotels and rooming houses were constructed, encroaching on the Hill's single family residences. In 1888, the bubble burst, signaling the arrival of a protracted decline in this and other old neighborhoods. Then in 1892, a new arrival to Los Angeles, an unsuccessful gold miner named Edward Doheny, discovered oil in the low-lying area just west of Bunker Hill, near the corner of Second and Glendale–right under the upturned noses of the rich. In 1908, the elegant Crocker Mansion, on Olive and Third, was demolished. Doheny himself, with his oil-based wealth, bought a mansion in *Chester Place*, two miles south, on what became the new up–scale corridor of West Adams running west from Figueroa. By World War I, other members of the elite had moved down and away from Bunker Hill, leaving it to shift for itself.

L.A. Noir

Raymond Chandler, in writing his detective novels and short stories, described L.A.'s experience with the Great Depression in gritty detail, using images now called *noir* (as in movies adapted from his writings–*film noir*). In 1942, Chandler wrote the most famous description of the Bunker Hill in *The High Window*:

Bunker Hill is old town, shabby town, crook town. Once, very long ago, it was the choice residential district, and there are still standing a few of the jigsaw Gothic mansions with wide porches and walls covered with round-end shingles and full corner bay windows with spindle turrets. They are all rooming houses now, their parquetry floors are scratched and worn through the once glossy finish and the wide sweeping staircases are dark with time and with cheap varnish laid on over generations of dirt. In the tall rooms haggard landladies bicker with shifty tenants. On the wide cool front porches, reaching their cracked shoes into the sun, and staring at nothing, sit the old men with faces like lost battles.

(Vintage Books Edition, p. 41.)

Angels Flight- In 1901 it was a block-long railway that climbed Bunker Hill at Third Street and connected it to Hill Street and the Broadway business. This funicular and the new network of streetcars took away Bunker Hill's isolation. Soon mansions and cottages were joined by more apartment hotels. Although many of the Victorian houses survived well into the years of Great Depression, most had been converted into multi-unit apartment houses, overcrowded, and eventually neglected by their owners.

Urban Renewal: After World War II, the federal government embarked on an aggressive "urban renewal" campaign in many of America's large cities, including Los Angeles. Aimed at clearing slums and, more to the point, preparing large plots of centrally located land for private developers to acquire and build on, the federal bulldozers scraped old buildings off such areas. By the early 1960s, Bunker Hill was shaved smooth. Curving alleys and intricate street arrangements were replaced by an empty, stretched-out street pattern which frightened away pedestrians. There was nothing to see anyway except weeds, dirt, and endless parking lots.

Then in 1964, the *Department of Water and Power*, the *Music Center* (1964-69), and Union Bank Plaza (1968) became the first structures to be built on the cleared land of Bunker Hill. A few condominiums and apartment complexes were built between the *Music Center* and the Harbor Freeway, but for years, most of the hill lay fallow–and alienating. The new apartment residents were marooned between howling freeways and a vast area of cleared, faceless land.

The pace of construction did not accelerate until *Security Pacific Plaza* (the largest Downtown building) was built in 1974, followed by the Bonaventure Hotel in 1976. The colorful mass of the *Crocker Center* (now the Wells Fargo Plaza) was completed in 1983. Although many other large structures have been erected on the hilltop, you can still find north of Third Street and east of Grand a few open lots, now parking lots on L.A. County property, still available for new buildings.

The most recent construction on Bunker Hill is the *Walt Disney Concert Hall*, a surrealistic fantasy in billowing sails made of stainless steel, and now the home of the L.A. Philharmonic. However, because its style is so completely disconnected from anything else within miles, it is hard to predict exactly how it will be regarded in the future.

The Downside of Bunker Hill: Since World War II, the city has given enormous subsidies and other inducements to the businesses who developed the structures on Bunker Hill. The mechanism for these incentives and grants is the Community Redevelopment Agency (C.R.A.). (See "Glossary")

Citizens have debated two issues: First, might the redevelopment money have more usefully gone to refurbishing the beautiful old buildings in the historic core–the Spring Street/Broadway District. That area now stands neglected, run-down, and the buildings are about thirty percent empty. Private developers successfully encouraged former L.A. Mayor Tom Bradley to direct the C.R.A. to spend heavily on Bunker Hill's new office towers.

Second, the citizens of the City, knowingly or not, saw their taxes used to chop Downtown into fragments, separated from each other–and from history. For example, Angels Flight was removed in 1968 and a row of apartment towers along Hill Street was put in its place, which turned Hill Street into a barricade, isolating Bunker Hill from the Latinized historic core. Churches, apartment houses, shops, and auditoriums have disappeared to make way for skyscrapers and parking lots. The C.R.A. has generated some residential construction, but not much.

If this was yesterday's policy, what about today's?

PROSPECTS

The C.R.A. has, at last, taken a sharp turn. It finally awakened to the damage caused by carving Downtown into single-function segments and now realizes that the whole of Downtown is vital to the economy and society of the entire region.

Led by architects Elizabeth Moule & Stefanos Polyzoides, a team of inspired designers, landscape architects, academics, and City agencies spent five years developing a Downtown Strategic Plan (D.S.P.). Published in 1994, it proclaimed that Downtown must be made healthy again!

The Main Elements of the Downtown Strategic Plan:

• Downtown's separate parts would be woven back into a whole. "Linkages must be formed to create greater access and more powerful economic interaction."

• Walkways would connect formerly separated districts. Priorities once given to car traffic would be shifted to pedestrians. Electric trolley "circulator" buses would connect Chinatown to the Convention Center via Broadway; another line would go up and down Grand Avenue; and another would go east and west on First Street.

• Most Downtown districts would be reconfigured to become "mixed-purpose" rather than single-purpose areas. In particular, the plan wants to add 18,000 new mixed-income apartments and condos Downtown (in contrast to only 2,500 units built in recent years). The new housing would be slotted into existing districts having a variety of things going on. Life must be made more interesting for Downtown dwellers; they must have things to do. Supermarkets, schools, and police substations would be brought in along with churches, and meeting halls. Downtown neighborhoods should be alive twenty-four hours a day.

• Many of the fine old buildings would be strengthened and spiffed up. For example, the spectacular *Herald Examiner Building* (on Broadway and Eleventh) which is close to the Garment District, might be made into a Museum of Fashion. Broadway movie palaces would be fixed up and used as theaters again. The *Broadway/Spring Arcade Building* would be converted into mixture of artists' lofts and residences with a Performing Arts Community College on the second and third floors. The Robinson's store on Seventh Street would be brought back to life.

• The D.S.P. wants to end Bunker Hill's isolation. The hill would be reconnected to the streets below by two "flights" (like Angels Flight), a trolley bus system, and a Metro Blue Line station at Flower and Third Streets. The unused land east of the Walt Disney Concert Hall of Music would be filled with residential structures along with stores and services for the people living there. Second Street, which now tunnels under the hill, would be rebuilt on the surface and become a sociable space.

Status of the Downtown Strategic Plan?: Although Angels Flight and the Bunker Hill Steps are already up and running, and the City Council has formally accepted the Downtown Strategic Plan, changes to Bunker Hill are moving at a snail's pace. Perhaps the arrival of the Walt Disney Concert Hall, the Colburn School of Performing Arts, and the Cathedral of Our Lady of the Angels will energize the process.

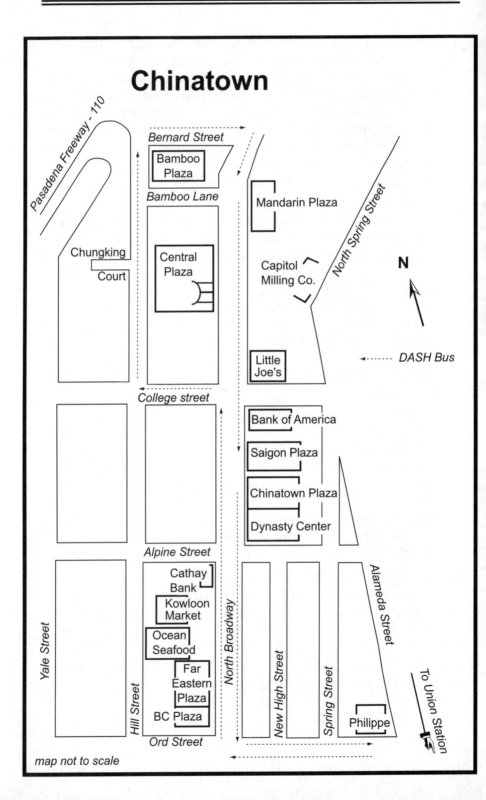

5. CHINATOWN

Los Angeles is lucky to have two Asian districts within easy reach of Union Station: Chinatown and Little Tokyo. You don't have to fly across the Pacific. You can visit an Asian culture right here!

Chinatown is several districts in one–tourist destination, commercial and market center, workplace, and residential neighborhood. It is the traditional hometown for many of L.A.'s Chinese people, even those who have moved out to the suburbs. Many shops on the streets and plazas sell traditional Chinese foods, medicines, household goods, magazines, newspapers, and the district is full of restaurants, large and small. For any tourist, Chinatown offers sights and sounds–and smells–that you won't find at home.

LOCATION

Chinatown's shops and restaurants are spread along North Broadway, starting three blocks north of Union Station or just two blocks from Olvera Street (in El Pueblo de Los Angeles Monument). The residential community lies west of the shops, between Hill Street and the Pasadena Freeway. Cesar Chavez Avenue (formerly Sunset Boulevard) defines the southern edge of Chinatown.

Landmark- North Broadway is aligned directly at City Hall which stands about half-mile south of Chinatown. If you look south, it will be straight ahead. Another landmark is Cathay Manor, a sixteen-story apartment building for retirees; it rises above Broadway at the southern end of Chinatown.

GETTING THERE FROM UNION STATION

DASH bus, Route B: On weekdays, you can catch this shuttle bus on Alameda Street directly in front of Union

Station. Look for the DASH sign on a pole near the bus shelter. (Every five minutes on weekdays, fifteen minutes on Saturdays. Free for Metrolink passengers; $.25 otherwise.) Get off at the second stop and begin your walk, or let the bus take you three blocks to the top end of Broadway for a preview of the territory. Then get off and stroll back.

Walking: You can easily walk to Chinatown, just three blocks from Union Station (Chinatown has no Red Line Subway station). From your train, go out the front door of Union Station and hike straight north on Alameda Street for about two and a half blocks to Ord Street and turn left. You will pass *Philippe, The Original French Dipped Sandwiches,* a much loved institution and a possibility for a non-Chinese meal.

DRIVING AND PARKING

From the north: Drive toward Downtown on the Pasadena Freeway (I-110) and exit from the *left lane* (watch for it) when you see the "Chinatown" sign. You will be riding south on Hill Street. If you are planning to visit the north end of Chinatown, drive into the three-level parking structure in Bamboo Plaza–the first chance you have to turn left.

From the east: Take the I-101 Freeway. Exit at Alameda; turn right and drive north on Alameda. Turn left into Chinatown at Ord, or Alpine, or College Street.

From the south and west: Drive north on the Pasadena Freeway (I-110). Exit when you see the "Chinatown" sign. The exit is a sharp U-turn onto Hill Street heading south. If you are planning to visit the north end of Chinatown, drive into the three-level parking structure in Bamboo Plaza–the first chance you have to turn left.

From the north-west (Hollywood and the San Fernando Valley): Take the Hollywood Freeway (I-101 East) to the Broadway off-ramp and turn left. Drive north on Broadway for two or three blocks. Parking lots are on both sides of Broadway.

If you want to drive around a bit, you will see many large and small parking lots. A stay of several hours will cost between $3.00 and $6.50, depending on the time of day.

WHO'S THERE?

You'll find shopkeepers, waiters, and clerks who are descendants of Chinese workers who first settled here 130 years ago. Others are newcomers freshly arrived from China, Hong Kong, Indochina, and the Philippines. Listen to the talk in stores, malls, and restaurants. You'll hear Cantonese, Mandarin, Vietnamese, Korean, and various other dialects from the nations of Asia.

Chinatown is intriguing but, for some, disconcerting. Outsiders are tolerated, but not courted. You'll not understand most store signs or see English labels on many products; prices are written in Asian characters, and restaurant menus give only enigmatic English translations. Waiters or clerks may offer only cryptic explanations. Most visitors find this only adds to the fun.

WHAT'S THERE FOR THE VISITOR?

Food markets- Browse the stores where the locals, old timers, and many new immigrants buy their native food, tea, spices, and other commodities.

Inhale! You don't have such rich combinations of aromas and flavors in your local supermarket. Starting with quantities of ginseng, a medicinal root, often thinly sliced and prepared as a tea, the air is enriched and complicated by open bins of ginger and other roots, big plastic bags of dried mushrooms, dried shrimps, dried oysters, dried octopus, dried sea snails, and dried white jelly fungus. Try it! You'll be fascinated.

The food shops have stacks of oversized tins of sugar cookies, huge sacks of rice, bags of fried pork skins, and bins of "white nut". You'll see aquarium tanks bubbling with many varieties of live fish and shellfish next to bewildering arrays of more dried food, including dried fish and sharks' fins.

Ginseng, Asian & American –

The labels on bins and packages of ginseng often identify the places they were grown: China, Korea, Canada, and Wisconsin! The root is a high risk/high reward crop for farmers. Extremely difficult to cultivate, it produces good earnings for growers of successful harvests. It must be grown under artificial shade and in raised beds to prevent root rot. In the stores, you will occasionally see the logo of the Ginseng Board of Wisconsin, the main U.S. source of the root, showing an American eagle superimposed on a red shield. It is a curious icon in an otherwise solidly Asian environment. An even larger supplier of ginseng to America's Chinese are farms in British Columbia, Canada.

Supermarkets- They sell every variety of imported food, tea in several different forms and flavors, ginseng, dried food, candy–and also woks and other cooking implements, crockery and plastic serving dishes, and small electric appliances. Don't hurry. You're visiting another culture! Nothing says as much about a people as its food.

Wing Hop Fung Gensing and China Products- 727 Broadway Street.

Kowloon Market- 750 North Broadway, in Chunsan Plaza.

Tak Shing Hong- 835 North Broadway.

99 Ranch Market- A conventional U.S. supermarket, but with an emphasis on Chinese goods. 988 North Hill (in Bamboo Plaza).

Han San- Bamboo Plaza, 988 North Hill.

TS Emporium- Corner of Spring and College Streets.

Check around to find the bargains, and stock up. Ginger is $1.39/pound; dried fungus is $2.19/four-ounce box; white nut is $4.49/pound.

Fish is not the only live food. Chinatown boasts several poultry shops–rows and stacks of cages holding chickens, ducks, and even rabbits.

Superior Poultry "Pollo Vivo"- Latinos also come here. 750 North Broadway.

Canton Poultry- 717 North Broadway.

Bakeries- They tempt visitors in every part of Chinatown. Cakes for family celebrations are the eye grabbers, but traditional treats–cookies, sugar rolls, and other delicacies easily conquer your resistance.

Phoenix Bakery- 969 North Broadway. The oldest and largest bakery in Chinatown.

Wonder Food- in Central Plaza, 900 North Broadway.

Maria's- Bamboo Plaza, 988 North Hill.

Queen's Bakery- 809 North Broadway.

KBC Bakery & Deli- 661 North Broadway.

Linh's Bakery- 685 D Ord Street.

Book stores- They offer magazines, posters, videos, and newspapers from various Asian countries. Not much in English, but intriguing!

China Book Store. 734-B North Broadway.

Sun Wah Book Store. 714 North. Broadway. Also sells shoes. Why not?

Antique stores- They are concentrated in a block called Chinatown West or "Chunking Court," 900 North Hill Street just across the street from the *Central Plaza* and *Bamboo Plaza*:

F. See On- 507-509 Chunking Court. This is the store made famous in Lisa See's book, *On Gold Mountain*, where members of her extended family still run the business. Perfectly gorgeous collection of Chinese antiques for sale.

Fong's- 943 Chunking Court (ring doorbell for service). A store in another branch of Lisa See's family.

The Jade Tree- 957 Chung King Road.

Beijing Cloisonné- 949 Chung King Road.

Li Hing of Hong Kong- 932 Chung King Road.

Enclosed shopping malls- They are located in several parts of Chinatown, with stores selling clothing, toys, jewelry, electronic gadgets, and, even very public karaoke contraptions cranked up to full volume and echoing down the aisles:

Bamboo Plaza- 988 North Hill. (Has multilevel parking structure.)

Saigon Plaza- (also Vietnamese). 828 North Broadway.

Chinatown Plaza- (largely Vietnamese). 818 North Broadway. (Parking entrance on Broadway.)

Dynasty Center- 800-812 North Broadway. (Parking entrance 821 North Spring Street)

Far East Plaza- 727 North Broadway.

Medicinal herb shops- They are among the most fascinating places to visit. Herbalists use hand-held scales to measure out prescriptions of dried bark, leaves, roots, bone and antler chips, and other ingredients. They may pulverize some of the items with mortars and pestles and then fold the whole collections into pink paper packets.

The herbalist, often with the guidance of a Chinese doctor, aims to correct internal imbalances in a patient and to enhance *ch'i*, vital energy. The body's system may need to speed up or slow down, heat up or cool down. You take this packet home, boil the herbs in water long enough to reduce the liquid to, say, one-fourth its original volume. The resulting brew is strained and consumed as a thick, bitter tea or "soup medicine." If you ask an herbalist about this process, you may be told only "Good for stomach," or "Good for skin," or "Long life".

Hong Ning Co.- 827 North Broadway.

Wing Fung Tai.- 811 North Broadway.

Tea shops- How can you visit Chinatown without buying some tea? Lots of stores carry a wide variety in all price ranges. One specializes only in tea and tea preparation items.

Ten Ren Tea Company- In the Far East Plaza, 726 North Hill. More than sixty varieties of tea displayed in a large, elegant, sedate shop.

"Free" wishes- There is a brightly painted and lavishly decorated wishing well at the back of the New Chinatown Central Plaza on Broadway. Throw a carefully-aimed coin at the part of the well labeled with your wish: "health," "wealth," "long life," or "happiness".

SIGHTS

New Chinatown Gateway- The most recognizable emblem of L.A.'s Chinatown is the gateway to the *New Chinatown Central Plaza* on the 900 block of North Broadway. Its formal name is *The Pailou of Maternal Virtue*. The buildings in the plaza are highly ornamented in traditional pagoda styles to attract tourists.

The majority of Chinatown's other buildings are the ordinary, functional storefront structures like those found along any other commercial street in the city. But those in the Central Plaza are declaratively Oriental, with animal icons and pagoda-style tile roofs. Animal forms are represented in stone or pottery sculptures. Foo dogs guard entrances against evil spirits. Fish, at the corners of roofs, are symbols of prosperity. Dragons represent power and fertility.

Colors are also potent symbols to the Chinese, and their logic makes sense even in Western culture: "Chinese red" (cinnabar) appears everywhere, symbolizing happiness and vitality. Blue suggests heaven and tranquillity. Green means life. Yellow means wealth. White means purity, but also mourning.

PUBLIC ART

Mural- (1995) Twenty-five by thirty feet. Designed by Christina Miguel Mullen and twenty-six Latino and Asian young members of the East/West Community Partnership. Southeast corner of Cesar Chavez Avenue and North Broadway Street. Depicts immigration experiences of the people in Chinatown.

Sun Yat-sen **Sculpture-** Central Plaza, 900 North Broadway. Sun was the leader of the Nationalist Party and the de facto ruler of the Republic of China until his death in 1925. He is called the father of modern China.

An Oddity

Today's Chinatown is a relative newcomer to this site. This "New Chinatown" was developed in the 1930s when the Chinese were forced to leave their older neighborhood to make way for the construction of Union Station (see "History" later in this chapter).

Capitol Milling Co.- A few older buildings survive from the days before the Chinese moved here. For example, on the north side of Chinatown, you can see a factory structure with a huge image of a flying eagle on the wall. The building looks like a misplaced movie set–the *Capitol Milling Co.* (1241 North Spring Street). In fact this is the oldest extant commercial building in Los Angeles! Although a sign on the wall says "Est. 1883," the building itself has existed since 1831 when Abel Stearns, a Massachusetts sea captain, built the mill 100 years before Chinese people moved into the neighborhood. Stearns became the largest landowner in Southern California. The bricks of the building were brought from Philadelphia and the first millstones from France. Power came from water–the *Zanja Madre* (see "Glossary"). The business was purchased by Jacob Loew and Herman Levi in 1883; hence, the date on the wall. The Riboli family, who have long owned the San Antonio Winery nearby, have recently purchased this building and will convert it to office, retail, and loft spaces.

Walking tours of Chinatown- Call Chinese Historical Society of Southern California (213) 621-3171. 969 North Broadway.

CONVENIENCES AND NECESSITIES

Public Rest Rooms

Bamboo Plaza- 988 North Hill, 2nd level.
Philippe's- (Inside toward rear), Ord and Alameda Streets.

Public Telephones

Along Broadway- On fronts of stores on every block.
Central Plaza- 900 block between Broadway and Hill Streets, phones in clusters inside plaza and at west gate.
860 North Hill
Corner of Ord and Spring-
Philippe's- Ord and Alameda Streets. Booths with seats.

ATMs

Bank of America- North Broadway and College Street.
Corner of Alpine and Hill

Places to Sit

Chinatown Plaza- 900 block between Broadway and Hill.
Chinatown West- 900 block Hill Street, west side.
Bamboo Plaza- 988 North Hill Street.

RESTAURANTS

In many of the tea houses and restaurants, mostly clustered at the north and south ends of North Broadway, the main offering for breakfast or lunch is *dim sum.* These places convert to regular Chinese meals for evening dining. Smaller restaurants often serve dim sum as well as regular lunches and dinners.

Dim sum are various forms of steamed or fried dumplings or other small dishes filled with bits of meat, bean, shrimp, or greens. In the larger restaurants (*Empress Pavilion, ABC Seafood,* or *Ocean Seafood*), carts carrying small plates or metal containers holding four or five dim sum will be wheeled by your table, and you can signal if you want a serving. You make your selection, as in a cafeteria, but here the food comes to you. With each delivery, the server will mark a card at your place, and this becomes your bill. Veterans of this game can tell the fillings by shape and appearance of the dumpling. If you ask, the waiters may or may not be of much help. Not to worry! Everything is delicious and usually inexpensive.

Many places have extensive seafood menus. Try the ultra-fresh fish and shellfish selections taken immediately out of the tank.

Chinatown's restaurants cater to several different crowds. Some places are informal, for locals; some are for mixed Asian and Spanish-speaking crowds; others are for more formal dining; and still others appeal to outsiders heading for main street establishments.

The following is not a exhaustive list of restaurants, so feel free to explore on your own. We encourage you to go into unfamiliar places as well as the European-American hideouts–and order something other than fried rice or Kung Pao chicken.

Price Guide to average lunch entrees:

$ = $3.00 - $8.00 $$$ = $13.00 - $17.00
$$ = $9.00 - $12.00 $$$$ = $18.00+

From Ord Street to Alpine Street, North 700 Block –

Listed from south to north

Thanh Vi- 422 West Ord Street. Vietnamese and Chinese food. Populated mostly by older people and families. Features noodle soups, rice stick dishes, vermicelli, steamed and fried rice dishes, and French bread served with duck, beef or egg. Informal. Open 8:00 a.m. to 7:00 p.m. ($)

ABC Seafood- 205 Ord Street. True to its name, this excellent restaurant has an extensive seafood selection. Abalone, sea cucumber, lobster, shrimp, crab, and various fresh fish. Dim sum is another option, as well as squab, duck, chicken, beef and pork dishes, prepared Cantonese style. Daily specials. On the formal side. Open daily 8:00 a.m. to 7:00 p.m. ($$$)

Regent Seafood- 739-747 Main Street, corner of Ord Street. Big dining place; popular. Open for lunches and dinners to 10:00 p.m., Friday & Saturday to 11:00 p.m. Parking in rear. (213) 680-3333. ($$)

Mon Kee's Seafood- 679 North Spring Street. Crab, lobster, shrimp, sea cucumber, scallops, squid, oysters, conch, clams, abalone, and ocean and fresh water fish. Well-known outside district, this place has a truly tempting menu of stir-fried, steamed, hot-pot, and deep-fried seafood dishes, many of them prepared with fresh vegetables. Poultry, beef, pork, rice, and vegetable dishes, too. Open Sunday through Thursday 11:30 a.m. to 9:45 p.m., Friday & Saturday from 11:30 a.m. to 10:15 p.m. ($$)

Dragon Inn- Ord & Spring. Mandarin and Szechwan cuisine. Features BBQ, lots of seafood, poultry, beef and pork, as well as fried rice and noodle dishes. Large, airy, comfortable dining room. Frequented by older people and families. ($$)

New Lucky Restaurant- 706 North Broadway. Informal, family style. Large round tables packed with local people. Offers soups, Lo Mein, barbecue meats, rice porridges, seafood, beef, pork, and poultry dishes, and even some vegetarian entrees. ($)

Lucky Deli- next to New Lucky Restaurant. Meat or bean buns, cakes and pastries, BBQ meat, noodles, poultry and seafood. You can have whole or half BBQ ducks and pig ribs. Take home some dim sum. ($)

Ocean Seafood- 750 North Broadway, 2nd floor. Much like the Empress Pavilion at the northern end of Chinatown. Huge dining areas, carts of dim sum, bustling staff. Great views to the north from big second floor windows. Daily 8:00 a.m. to 10:00 p.m. (213) 687-3088. ($$) (Parking in their lot, $.75 with validation. Often crowded.)

Far East Plaza, 727 North Broadway

Mandarin Deli Restaurant- A small, quiet place offering mandarin-style noodles, cold meat entrees, and side dishes. Noodles are prepared spicy or mild, in soups or "dry," with shredded meat, vegetables, or hot chili sauce. Cold entrees include aromatic beef and pork, beef tendon, tripe, and pig's feet. Combination plates if you want to try more than one of the cold dishes. Open 11:00 a.m.-9:00 p.m. ($)

Kim Chuy- A Chiu Chow restaurant with a trilingual menu: Chinese, Vietnamese, and English. Crowded with young people and families. Offers noodles, porridge, fried rice and fried noodle dishes. There are egg noodles and rice noodles, prepared with beef, pork, duck, or fish. Vietnamese influence in the fourteen-item beverage list, which includes iced coffee with condensed milk, hot soy milk, and plum drink. ($)

Pho' 79- One of several Vietnamese restaurants in Chinatown. Specializes in soups, but also has rice noodles, vermicelli, and rice rolls. Menu contains the standard lengthy Vietnamese beverage list, including guanabana juice. Cool interior, relaxed atmosphere. ($)

From Alpine Street to College Street – North 800 block

Sam Woo Chinese BBQ- 805 Broadway. Family-style restaurant, informal, packed with people. "BBQ" is only a small part of their menu. They have everything from Lo Mein to Kung Pao Chicken to Pig Trotters in Marinade Sauce. The barbecue smells wonderful–pork, spare ribs, and a Three Delicacy Combination platter. Vegetable dishes as well for those who are skittish about ducks hanging in windows. If you can't wait, go to the Sam Woo Express shop in the Far East Plaza, 727 North Broadway. ($)

Eden Restaurant- In the back of Chinatown Plaza, 818 Broadway. Vietnamese/French/Chinese cuisine, with dishes ranging from Cornish hen with red rice to steak with flank and tendon. Poultry, seafood, meat, and rice are prepared in each of the three styles. Long list of beverages, including soy milk and French coffee. ($)

Yang Chow Restaurant- 819 Broadway. Mandarin and Szechwan. Clean, quiet, and popular ($)

Hong Kong Harbor Chinese Restaurant- 845 Broadway. New, big place. Long list of week day lunch specials served with soup and steamed rice ($3.55) and seafoods ($4.25). Open daily 8:00 a.m. to 1:00 a.m. ($)

Hop Woo BBQ Restaurant- 853 Broadway. Popular, little place, across from Bank of America. 8:00 a.m. to 1:00 a.m. ($)

From College Street to Bernard Street – North 900 block

Golden Dragon- 960 North Broadway. Specializes in seafood, Cantonese style. Family style dinners for two or more orders. The specials are combinations of chicken, pork, and rice dishes with soup and appetizers. Patronized by local business people and families. Image of a large golden dragon on the wall of the plush, low-lit dining room. ($$)

Mandarin Plaza – 910 North Broadway

Mandarin Shanghai Restaurant- Seafood in Mandarin and Hong Kong style, pork, beef, and poultry prepared in sauces both spicy and mild. Also features the earthen pot dishes of Mandarin cuisine. Quieter than dim sum places; post-modern decor. Draws a mixed crowd of Asians, Anglos, and Latinos. Sunday through Thursday 11:30 a.m. to 9:30., Friday and Saturday from 11:30 a.m. to 10:30 p.m. ($$)

Fu Ling Restaurant- Features earthen pots, meats, seafood, poultry, noodles, vegetables prepared Mandarin style. Low-lit, comfortable atmosphere, appropriate for quiet business lunches or a relaxing evening for two. ($$)

Two Los Angeles "fixtures" from the Occident:

Little Joe's- (Italian) 900 North Broadway corner of College. This neighborhood, once called "Little Italy," contained about 5,000 Italian families. *Little Joe's* grew from a family grocery store to become a well-known lunch and dinner destination. Little Joe's closed in 1998.

(Another Italian institution, the *San Antonio Winery*, is half a mile northeast of here at 737 Lamar Street. It is the last of about twenty Los Angeles wineries whose grapes once grew in the immediate neighborhood.)

Philippe, The Original French-Dipped Sandwiches- 1001 Alameda (corner of Ord Street). Claims to be the originator of French dipping, but you can get your sandwich undipped if you wish. Sawdust on the floor; informal and inexpensive. You step up to one of nine lines at the counter to order your meal. Slower than McDonalds, but this is real food. Coffee is only $.10 a mug! Popular with every category of customer–business people, working people, concert-go-ers, patrons of Los Angeles Dodger games, tourists, and just folks. ($)

Bamboo Plaza –
988 North Hill

Empress Pavilion- Second floor. A truly impressive place–both in size (can seat 500 people!) and culinary prowess. Dining room is always bustling with waiters serving dim sum or Cantonese, Mandarin, and Szechwan dishes to an appreciative crowd. The menu of full meals includes an extensive seafood selection as well as poultry, meat and vegetables. Daily specials. Dress nicely, please. Open Monday through Friday 9:00 a.m. to 10:00 p.m., Saturday & Sunday 8:00 a.m. to 10:00 p.m. (213) 617-9898. ($$$)

Hop Louie- 950 Mei Ling Way (in Central Plaza). You can recognize this place by the five-story pagoda which has been featured in Hollywood movies. The dining room is in grand hotel style with chandeliers and plush carpets. Pictures of stars on the wall. Cantonese and Mandarin cuisine, including familiar dishes such as sweet & sour pork, chicken with cashew nuts, and fried rice. Sunday-Thursday 11:00 a.m. to 10:00 p.m., Friday & Saturday 11:00 a.m. to 11:00 p.m. ($$)

HISTORY

The first Chinese immigrants in California were gold miners, laborers, canal diggers, and farm workers. In the 1870s, the main group of Chinese to arrive in Los Angeles from northern California were mostly laborers who had been building the Southern Pacific Railroad. These workers, along with merchants and small manufacturing businesses, settled into the area where Union Station is today and extending west to a short block called *Calle de los Negros*. This street is now Los Angeles Street, on the east side of old Fire Station # 1 and the Plaza in El Pueblo Historic Park.

The *Los Angeles Times* in 1929 described Chinatown as a place where "a few shops, cafes, laundries and residential quarters remain of an exotic district that is ever growing smaller. Half a block from the plaza is a Chinese temple with quaint rites." The brick *Garnier Block* (1890), part of which still stands south of the Plaza on Los Angeles Street, was built to house Chinese businesses and meeting spaces. The only building remaining from the original Chinatown, the Garnier Block will soon reopen as the Chinese American Museum.

About one-third of the Chinese population in Los Angeles lived in this first Chinatown. They performed the heavy labor no one else would do, and they were willing to accept lower wages than others. When the gold mines slowed (after 1863) and railroad jobs declined (in the late 1870s), Chinese workers entering Los Angeles confronted a depressed labor market in which they found themselves competing with other recent arrivals for scarce jobs. Economic stresses combined with visible racial and cultural distinctions, and distrust, resentment, and open hostility soon developed.

Ethnic animosities reached a violent pitch in 1871 when an Anglo mob pounced on Chinese people on *Calle de Los Negros*, killed twenty of them, and looted and burned homes and shops. This "Chinese Massacre" brought new and unwanted attention from the whole country to this lawless Western town.

Undaunted by Anglo hostility, more and more Chinese people arrived in Southern California in the 1870s, mostly to work as truck gardeners, commercial fishermen, or construction workers.

Chinese Exclusion Act of 1882: A long series of restrictive federal laws, beginning 1882, forcefully contained and isolated those Chinese people who had already come to this country. The California legislature passed the *Alien Land Act of 1913* which prohibited the ownership of real property for more than three years by immigrants ineligible to become citizens. This applied directly to Asians rather than immigrant whites or people of African descent. Wives of Chinese merchants and American-born Chinese men could come to the United States, until the *Immigration Act of 1924* which stopped Chinese women from immigrating for several years. (These laws also constrained Japanese immigration in the same period. See "Chapter 9 – Little Tokyo").

For much of its history, Chinatown was feared and disdained by most midwestern and southern whites who had flocked to Los Angeles during the city's various booms, bringing their rural insularity and intolerance with them. In fact, Chinatown contained a mixture of both respectable and disreputable activities and people. Churches and retail stores were neighbors to brothels and gambling parlors. For most residents of the district, life was difficult but clearly more promising than in China.

In 1934, L.A.'s civic leaders fixed the site for the new Union Station–the very neighborhood where Chinese people were living and working. The residents were forced to move up Alameda Street–first to "China City" on Ord Street, and a bit later to today's "New Chinatown," the Central Plaza on Broadway and Hill north of College Street. Except for the now empty Garnier Building on Los Angeles Street, the last Chinese businesses in the original Chinatown near the old Plaza were demolished in 1951. (The popular movie, *Chinatown*, in *film noir* style (see "Glossary"), recalls the anti-Chinese climate of the Depression years. The last utterance of the movie, "It's Chinatown, Jake," reveals the dismissive attitude of much of the city before and after the Second World War.)

> When workers excavated the area under and around Union Station, including the tunnels for The Red Line Subway, they found long-buried relics of old Chinatown. You can see some of them embedded in the sculpture *River Bench* near the eastern entrance to the Red Line in the Gateway Center–the eastern portal of Union Station.

Though stigmatized and harassed over a period of many generations, Chinese-Americans managed to survive by hard work, persistence, saving their small earnings, and organizing community associations and "benevolent societies". Eventually the relocated Chinatown grew healthy and prosperous, aided by infusions of Asian immigrants. America's doors began to open to Asian countries in 1943, during the Second World War, in the first of a series of laws enacted over the next twenty years.

With no loans from Anglo banks, Peter Soo Hoo and other Chinese leaders formed the Los Angeles Chinatown Corporation, which still controls most of the district's commercial property. L.A.'s is the first Chinatown in the U.S. where Chinese people own the land.

A Riveting Book

On Gold Mountain: The One-Hundred Year Odyssey of a Chinese-American Family by Lisa See, St. Martin's Press, 1995. Ms. See personalizes the history of L.A.'s Chinatown in this study of her own family. Her great-grandfather was the founder of F. See On Company (and indirectly F. Suie One Company), imported-antique dealers in Los Angeles and Pasadena. The book is a fascinating *Roots*–style account that was on the L.A. Times best-seller list. The term "Gold Mountain" was the name Chinese workers used to refer to America in the days of gold mining and railroad construction.

Until the *Immigration and Naturalization Act of 1965* (which abolished country of origin quotas), most Chinatown residents were Cantonese. Now the immigrant stream includes Mandarin-speakers from Taiwan and refugees from Vietnam and other parts of Indochina. Signs in different languages on stores and restaurants reveal the current diversity of the population.

PROSPECTS

Chinatown's economy, at this writing, is diminished from what it was in its heyday. Most of L.A.'s Chinese people now live and shop in other parts of the region, particularly the San Gabriel Valley-Monterey Park, Alhambra, Hacienda Heights, and Walnut. Former residents of Chinatown have been attracted to quieter neighborhoods, lower rents for commercial spaces, and suburban life styles. Restaurant business in Chinatown is down about thirty percent from previous years; retail sales have fallen even more steeply.

Chinatown is also changing demographically. It has higher proportions of the aged and children than other parts of Los Angeles, but fewer middle-aged people. This is both a cause and an effect of economic sluggishness.

The economic changes are visible along North Broadway and the side streets. A few important markets and restaurants have closed. The Central Plaza honoring Sun Yat-sen (900 block between Broadway and Hill) is often listless–except for little groups of elderly men, members of benevolent associations, playing Mah-Jong, or just talking.

The Los Angeles Community Redevelopment Agency (C.R.A.) has put money into Chinatown (some new housing for the poor and elderly, a police service center, a few new sidewalks) but has done little to connect the district to the rest of Los Angeles or help it attract tourists. Business proprietors themselves have not promoted Chinatown to the general public or to the Metrolink passengers now pouring into Union Station and looking for interesting places to visit. Chinatown is hardly visible to people exploring the El Pueblo District just two blocks away. It is out of sight and out of mind.

Angels Walk: However, this isolation is about to change. Landscape architects are planning new visual connections and pedestrian walkways to bring Chinatown in closer touch with El Pueblo Plaza and Union Station. These changes are part of a larger project called *Angels Walk* that would link several of Downtown's now-separated districts. Chinatown's borders, which are now ambiguous and confused, would be ringed by a new series of gateways representing signs of the zodiac. This promises a more distinguishing identity and more visibility for the district.

Meanwhile, Chinatown offers visitors a colorful, exotic, fascinating experience. Spend some time there!

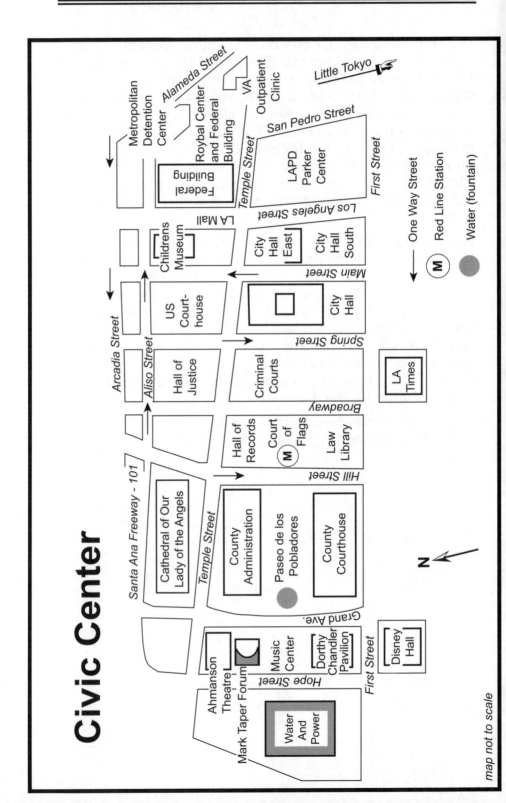

Civic Center

Metropolitan Detention Center

Alameda Street

Roybal Center and Federal Building

VA Outpatient Clinic

Little Tokyo

Federal Building

Temple Street

San Pedro Street

LAPD Parker Center

First Street

One Way Street

M Red Line Station

Water (fountain)

LA Mall

Los Angeles Street

Childrens Museum

City Hall East

City Hall South

Main Street

US Court-house

City Hall

Arcadia Street

Aliso Street

Hall of Justice

Criminal Courts

Spring Street

LA Times

Broadway

Hall of Records

Court of Flags

M

Law Library

Hill Street

Santa Ana Freeway - 101

Cathedral of Our Lady of the Angels

Temple Street

County Administration

Paseo de los Pobladores

County Courthouse

N

Grand Ave.

Ahmanson Theatre

Mark Taper Forum

Music Center

Dorthy Chandler Pavilion

First Street

Disney Hall

Hope Street

Water And Power

map not to scale

6. Civic Center

As your Metrolink train approaches Union Station, two sets of Downtown buildings appear off to the right. In the foreground, representing the "public sector," stand the institutional buildings of Civic Center. In the background are the "private sector" high-rise office towers of Bunker Hill and the Lower Financial District.

Civic Center boasts the largest collection of government buildings in the country except for Washington, D.C. The most likely destinations for visitors are: *City Hall*, the *Federal Courthouse*, and the *Ronald Reagan State Building* (which is not in Civic Center but three blocks south). The new Roybal Building has no public spaces for visitors except courtrooms, but its surrounding plaza contains impressive art works. Another much-visited building here, although it is not part of the government, is the distinguished headquarters of the *Los Angeles Times* standing across First Street from Civic Center.

Most of the other government buildings in Civic Center are products of the spare, functional architecture of the 1960s. Two huge examples are the Los Angeles County buildings across Grand Avenue from the *Music Center*–the *Hall of Administration* and the *County Courthouse*. They form two sides of a rectangle that encloses a park, *Paseo de los Pobladores (Walk of the Settlers)*. The park continues downhill to its neighbor, the *Court of Flags*.

Where is the Center of Downtown L.A.?

Los Angeles City Hall is one of two major exceptions to dreary sameness of the huge mass of government buildings. The Cathedral of Our Lady of the Angels is the other exception.

Dedicated September, 2002, the enormous Cathedral, with its plaza and outlying buildings, has become a popular destination for visitors from all religious traditions. Of course, its primary purpose is to serve as the seat of the most populous Catholic Diocese in the United States.

LOCATION

City Hall stands majestically about three blocks southwest of Union Station. Most other government buildings fill a swath a full mile long–from Alameda Street to Figueroa–and two blocks wide, between the I-101 Freeway and First Street. Five levels of government are found here–federal, state, county, city, and utility districts.

GETTING THERE FROM UNION STATION

Walking: Hike across Alameda Street from Union Station, go up to the Plaza, and walk south on Los Angeles Street about two blocks.

Red Line Subway: Civic Center is the first station on the Red Line after leaving Union Station, but it is close only to the County buildings west of City Hall (County Courthouse and Hall of Administration, Hall of Records, Criminal Courts Building, Law Library). The buildings east of City Hall (U.S. Courthouse, several federal buildings, Parker Center) are just as easily and quickly reached by walking. The Red Line is free to Metrolink riders; $1.35 otherwise.

DASH bus, Route B: (Weekdays only) If you are going to the western part of Civic Center (the County Court House or County Administration), you can ride free from Metrolink trains or $.25 otherwise. Catch the shuttle bus across Alameda Street from Union Station. The bus will travel up the hill and west for several blocks on Temple Street. Hop off at Spring Street for City Hall, or at Hill Street for the County buildings, or wait until it turns left onto Grand Avenue for the Music Center.

DASH bus, Route D: Catch this shuttle at the Gateway Transit Plaza (at the east end of the pedestrian tunnel under the tracks-opposite Union Station). It will take you to the Federal buildings, the front (Spring Street) entrance of City Hall, or down to Third and Spring Streets to the Reagan State Office Building.

DRIVING AND PARKING

From the north: Drive toward Downtown on the Pasadena Freeway (I-110) and take the transition ramp to the 101 East. Almost immediately, take the exit marked Broadway. Turn right onto Broadway. Drive past Temple Street to the parking lot under "Court of the Flags". For places east of City Hall, stay on the 101 Freeway until the Los Angeles Street exit, and park under the Los Angeles Mall.

From the east: Take the I-101 Freeway. Exit at Alameda Street but stay on Arcadia Street (parallel to the freeway) until you reach Los Angeles Street. Turn left for parking under the Los Angeles Mall, or continue to Broadway and turn left for parking under "Court of the Flags".

From the south and west: Drive north on the Harbor Freeway (I-110). Take the transition ramp to the 101 East. Almost immediately, take the exit marked Broadway. Turn right on Broadway. Drive past Temple Street to parking under "Court of the Flags." For places east of City Hall, stay on freeway until the Los Angeles Street exit, and park under the Los Angeles Mall.

From the northwest (Hollywood and the San Fernando Valley): Take the Hollywood Freeway (I-101 East) and continue to the exit marked Broadway. Turn right onto Broadway. Drive past Temple Street to parking under "Court of the Flags." For places east of City Hall, stay on the 101 Freeway until the Los Angeles Street exit, and park under the Los Angeles Mall.

WHO'S THERE?

About 35,000 people work in Civic Center in all levels of government. They include an amazing mixture of elected officials, commissioners, secretaries, lawyers, accountants, maintenance workers, staff workers, judges, jury members, police, and citizens/clients from all classes, cultures, and neighborhoods. Governments are big employers, and they are especially effective in hiring minorities, so you'll see many representatives of L.A.'s diverse populations.

WHAT'S THERE FOR THE VISITOR?

> **Tip:** There is not much to see or do in Civic Center on weekends—except for the Cathedral of Our Lady of the Angels.

City Hall- (Austin, John C., John Parkinson, Donald Parkinson, Albert C. Martin, Sr., interior by Austin Whittlesey, 1928) 200 North Spring Street. A Renaissance tower topped by a Greek temple supporting a Babylonian ziggurat, all resting on a classical base. You wouldn't expect a building so described to amount to much, but this strange architectural mixture works so well that City Hall has been the centerpiece of Los Angeles since 1928. The original cost of the building, $5,000,000.00, was enough to build a twenty-eight-story structure that reigned as the city's only high-rise tower until 1957 when the building code was changed.

Architect Charles Moore describes City Hall's interior Romanesque and Byzantine rotunda as "straight from Hollywood." Be sure to enter from the front porch on the Spring Street side for the full effect. The rotunda is a 135-foot circle centering on a replica of a ship set into an elaborate marble floor. This is a Spanish caravel that once sailed into California's ports. The walls are cut from French limestone.

Los Angeles Coat of Arms

A shield cut into quarters: 1) Stars and stripes representing the United States 2) Bear and star of the Republic of California 3) Lion and castle of Spain 4) Eagle, serpent, and cactus of Mexico.

City Hall underwent a seismic retrofitting of astonishing magnitude. A chunk of each of the building's 430 steel supporting columns was carved away at the foundation, held in place temporarily by hydraulic jacks, while a "base isolator" (a multi-layer sandwich of rubber and steel sheets) is jammed into the gap at the bottom of the column. This forms a flexible base for each column to rest on. Additional work, such as replacing the hollow block walls with reinforced concrete shear walls cost more than $154,000,000.00.

When the fifteen-member City Council or one of its committees meets, you can visit the impressive Council Chamber. You should also try to reserve some time for City Hall's observation deck which offers a stunning view of Downtown.

Lofty Quotations Carved on the Exterior of City Hall:

"The Highest Of All Sciences And Services–The Government"

(James Russell Lowell) north side

"A People Cannot Have The Consciousness of Being Self Governed Unless They Attend Themselves To The Things Over and Against Their Own Doors."

(Benjamin Ide Wheeler) east side

"He that violates his oath profanes the divinity of faith itself."

(Cicero) south

"Let us have faith that right makes might."

(Lincoln) west entrance

"Righteousness exalteth a people."

(Solomon) west entrance

Children's Museum- 310 North Main Street, just south of the I-101 Freeway. After decades of heavy use, this building was run down and too small to serve its intended purpose. Plans were to split and relocate the museum into two separate places – one at the north end of the San Fernando Valley, near Hanson Dam and the other, perhaps, in Little Tokyo. As this edition is published, the first is under construction, but the second will require more official pondering – and more money. Hope for the best!

The Cathedral of Our Lady of the Angels- (Moneo, Jose Rafael, 2001) On Temple Street between Hill Street and Grand Avenue. Taking up a two-block area, between the County Hall of Administration and the Santa Ana Freeway, this consists of three main structures, the large Cathedral church, an activities building, and the archbishop's residence. Spanish architect Moneo is one of the world's most distinguished members of his profession, and he has created a spectacular monument to stand among otherwise unimpressive government buildings. Note the beautiful statue over the main entrance, *Our Lady of the Angels* by Robert Graham. The windows are of slabs of alabaster rather than stained glass. For the *Communion of Saints* tapestries, artist John Nava painted the figures, then scanned the images, and sent the digital information to Bruges, Belgium where computer-driven machinery wove the tapestries.

Two historic markers are attached to a wall on the Main Street side of the *L.A. Mall*: The *Bella Union Hotel* was located here in the 1850s. Served by the *Butterfield Mail Stagecoaches* (twenty-one days from St. Louis), the Bella Union advertised itself as the best hotel south of San Francisco, but that wasn't saying much. Horace Bell wrote in 1881, "the rooms were not over six by nine feet in size.... The bar was well patronized."
The other plaque indicates the site of the first newspaper to serve the city, *Los Angeles Star (La Estrella)*, founded in 1851 and printed in English and Spanish. Its business lasted, off and on, until 1879.

A plaque you *won't* find on the L.A. Mall is one that would celebrate the Indian village of *Yang-na* that was located close to this spot. These were the Native Americans who greeted the Portola Party in 1769.

Los Angeles Times Building, a.k.a. *Times Mirror Square-* (Kaufmann, Gordon B., 1931-35; west wing, William L. Pereira, 1970-73) Southwest corner of First and Spring Streets. Often newspaper offices locate themselves close to government centers, hoping to borrow prestige and authority. The older building here is Moderne Art Deco, a style Kaufmann used also to put finishing touches on America's large dams, *Hoover, Grand Coulee,* and *Parker.* The presses are no longer located in this building, and even the editorial offices have outgrown it and are feeling squeezed. Visit the museum inside the entrance for a quick promotional history of the *Los Angeles Times.* Tours of the editorial department can be arranged for groups.

Harrison Gray Otis, the founder and editor, and his son-in-law, Harry Chandler, were two of the region's most powerful and ruthless businessmen. They were responsible for much of the maneuvering that produced such Los Angeles attributes as urban sprawl, hostility to organized labor, thirst for water from distant rivers, and a willingness to draw on public funds to subsidize private businesses–especially their own.

This noble building is the fourth home of the *Times* which was founded in 1881. The year 1910 witnessed one of the most shocking episodes in L.A.'s often violent history, the bombing of the third *Times* building on the northeast corner of Broadway and First Street.

Federal Building and Post Office, (now *U.S. Courthouse)-* (Simon, Louis A. and Gilbert Stanley Underwood, 1938) 312 North Spring Street, across Temple Street from City Hall. Handsome display of what government money could accomplish with Art Deco (WPA Moderne) style during the Great Depression. The building is handsome, dignified, and honest.

Hall of Justice Building- (Allied Architects, 1925) Northeast corner of Temple and Broadway. Beaux Arts exterior. Ornate entrance lobby. The top floors have barred windows; this was once the Main Jail. This building was damaged in the Northridge earthquake, and is now closed and vacant. The county administration is studying its potential for rehabilitation.

Federal Office Building and Post Office- 300 North Los Angeles Street, between the I-101 Freeway and Temple Street. Two blocks directly east of the older Federal Building (above). Designed in the post-war modernistic style common to several other Civic Center buildings.

Music Center- (see "Chapter 4 – Bunker Hill")

Metropolitan Detention Center- 535 North Alameda Street. This building, best seen from in front of Union Station, is a federal jail. Note the narrow windows and the fortress construction. There are about 925 prisoners here each day, guarded by 300 staff personnel. It costs taxpayers $23,000.00 per year to house someone in a federal jail. Mike Davis, author *City of Quartz*, thought this building could be an icon of L.A.'s social and political history and put it on the front cover of his book.

PUBLIC ART

The New World- (Otterness, Tom, 1982-91) Sculptures, fountain, and frieze on a curved arcade. Bronze and cast stone. Plaza behind Federal Building, 300 North Los Angeles Street. Startling image of a pudgy female holding a globe above the surface of the fountain's basin. Other characters, male and female, some in chains, are lifting, smashing, carrying huge objects or animals. Especially fascinating in the context of the site–federal courthouse on one side, federal jail on another, federal office building on the third side. You won't be surprised to learn that these images have managed to displease a judge who thinks they are obscene, so a barricade was constructed around the fountain–after four years. Apparently the railing keeps the sculpture from doing great harm to the public.

Broadway

Bunker Hill Steps

Chinatown Gate

City Hall

Olvera Street

Garment District

Little Tokyo

Lower Financial District
Grand Hope Park

Triforium- (Young, Joseph L., 1972-75) Sculpture, reinforced concrete, glass, steel, colored lights, loud-speakers. *Los Angeles Mall*, 300 North Main Street. A light-sound machine or oversized (sixty feet high) jukebox.

Our Lady of the Angels- (Graham, Robert, 2000) Corner of Temple Street and Grand Avenue, standing above the main entrance to the new Cathedral of Our Lady of the Angels. Beautiful, 8 foot tall sculpture of a welcoming, compassionate woman. She might well become the long-sought icon for the City of L.A.

Molecule Man- (Borofsky, Jonathan, 1991) Sculpture, brushed steel. Edwin R. Roybal Federal Building and U.S. Courthouse, 255 East Temple Street. Four men grappling with each other; each guy is a metallic slab, a huge cut-out, with Swiss cheese holes.

I Dreamed I Could Fly- (Borofsky, Jonathan, 1992) Sculpture, six fiberglass men suspended in air above Red Line Subway track in Civic Center station.

Untitled mural in glazed tile on *City Hall East*- (Sheets, Millard, 1971) 200 North Main Street. This building is connected to City Hall by a bridge over Main Street.

L.A. Freeway Kids- (Boltuch, Glenna, 1984) South wall of I-101 Freeway just below the Children's Museum. This is one of the most charming murals in town, and it is positioned to lighten the burdens of drivers stuck in traffic.

Abraham Lincoln- (Gage, Merrill, 1960) First Street at Grand Avenue. Bronze bust. Awkwardly positioned and hard for passers-by to study on this busy intersection.

Official Seal of Los Angeles County

Designed by Millard Sheets, 1957. See an example in the lobby entrance of *Los Angeles County Administration Building*, outside the Board of Supervisors Hearing Room. The goddess Pomona stands in the center surrounded by symbols of L.A.'s history and wealth: engineering instruments, Cabrillo's Spanish galleon, a tuna fish, a Christian cross, the Hollywood Bowl, an oil derrick, and a cow. Pomona is the Roman goddess of fruit trees.

CONVENIENCES AND NECESSITIES

Public Rest Rooms

County Courthouse- First Street, between Hill and Grand Avenue. Rest rooms are in centers of the long hallways on each floor.

City Hall- Between Temple and First Streets, Main and Spring Streets, second floor.

Department of Water & Power Building- Hope Street between First and Temple Streets, across from Music Center. lower level, near cafeteria.

Public Telephones

Near the rest rooms in **Civic Center buildings**.

Places to Sit

Benches and chairs in the **L.A. Mall**.

Benches on the **Paseo de los Pobladores**, between the **County Courthouse** and the **County Administration Buildings**.

ATMs

Near Pasqua Lunch on the *Paseo de los Pobladores* between the County Courthouse and the County Administration Building.

RESTAURANTS

Price Guide to average lunch entrees:

$ = $3.00 - $8.00 $$$ = $13.00 - $17.00
$$ = $9.00 - $12.00 $$$$ = $18.00+

Olive Tree- Southeast corner of First and Main Streets across from City Hall. Fast food. Small, bright, cheerful place. Pizzas, pasta, subs. ($)

Patisserie- In the south courtyard of *Los Angeles Mall*, corner of Temple and Los Angeles Streets ($)

Pasqua Lunch- Outside, Paseo De Los Pobladores, the green mall between the County Courthouse and the County Hall of Administration, between Hill and Grand. ($)

Los Angeles County Courthouse Cafeteria- 9th floor. Enter from Hill Street or Grand Avenue. ($)

Redwood Second Street Saloon- 316 West Second, between Broadway and Hill Street. Old-fashioned, beery atmosphere; authentic hang-out for *L.A. Times* staffers, government workers, and cops. Burgers, sandwiches, steaks. Big helpings. Monday through Friday 11:00 a.m. to 8:00 p.m. ($$)

Epicentre Restaurant- 200 South Hill Street, in the Kawada Hotel. Healthy meal-sized salads, northern Italian pastas, seafood, chicken and steak served grilled, broiled, or sautéed. There's also a "Curry on the Richter Scale" spiced to order, in "magnitudes" of 1 to 10. Trendy, lively atmosphere. Open Monday through Thursday 11:00 a.m. to 9:00 p.m., Friday 11:00 a.m. to 11:00 p.m., Saturday. 5:00 p.m. to 11:00 p.m., Sunday. 5:00 p.m. to 9:00 p.m. ($$)

Cafe in plaza of the Cathedral of Our Lady of the Angels- Temple and Hill Streets. ($)

Cafe Current- Food court. Across Hope Street from the Music Center in *Department of Water & Power Building*, lower level. 111 North Hope Street. Six separate food stations with excellent food choices. Eat inside or out on cheerful plaza. Note the clever names for food stations in this headquarters of a public utility. ($)

At the Music Center

Otto's Grill and Beer Bar- 135 North Grand Avenue Restaurant and cocktail lounge. Fresh fish, steaks, micro-brews. Monday 11:30 a.m. to 7:00 p.m., Tuesday through Sunday 11:30 a.m. to midnight. (213) 972-7322. ($$)

Impresario Ristorante e Bar- Top (fifth) floor of *Dorothy Chandler Pavilion* in the *Music Center*, 165 North Grand Avenue. This space was formerly occupied by the Pavilion Restaurant which had lost its earlier polish and distinction. But new management, with creative consultant, Piero Selvaggio, have created this super-elegant dining experience in a grandiose restaurant with the "grand feel of theater". (*Downtown News*, 1-15-96). Lunches are from 11:00 a.m. to 2:00 p.m. only on the Chandler's matinee days. Dinners are from Tuesday through Sunday between 5:00 p.m. to 10:00 p.m. (213) 972-7333. (**$$$$**)

Cafe on the Plaza- In front of *Mark Taper Forum*. Sandwiches, salads, pizza. Monday 8:00 a.m. to 3:00 p.m.; Tuesday to Friday 8:00 a.m. to 8:00 p.m.; Saturday & Sunday 11:00 a.m. to 8:00 p.m. (**$**)

HISTORY

Although the city of Los Angeles was founded in 1781, it didn't begin to govern itself until 1812. A City Council (*Ayuntamiento*) and a mayor (*alcade*) existed long before the city was formally incorporated under California law in 1850, but this government could not enforce law and order. Los Angeles was unruly and dangerous, and nearly everyone carried a gun. Public disorder reached a climax with the lynching of twenty Chinese people by a drunken mob just south of the Plaza in 1871 (See "Chapter 5 – Chinatown"). Eventually, increasing numbers of relatively sober and law-abiding citizens demanded a more orderly town.

A charter was written in 1878 establishing the main outlines of the present government. The size of the City Council was set at fifteen members, as it is today–even though the population was 11,200 then and 3,500,000 now. Called a "strong council" system, L.A.'s model also has non-partisanship as a political principle, a strong civil service, and citizen commissions. The "weak" Mayor is elected separately from the Council and can veto its actions. His power is exercised mainly through appointments of department heads and the preparation of the City's annual budget. The Council can override a veto by generating a larger vote than required to pass the measure on the first round, usually a two-thirds majority.

At first, L.A.'s government was housed in whatever buildings became available near the center of the Pueblo. The topography of the land boxed in the small pueblo, with hills just southwest of the Plaza. Still, even after those constraints were removed, the governmental district has remained concentrated in the very neighborhood in which it began.

The first *City and County Hall* (1853) was an adobe house located across Spring Street from the front steps of today's City Hall. In 1884, the city council moved to 213 West Second Street, and then in 1888 to a sandstone building on Broadway, between Second and Third Streets. The present City Hall, between First and Temple Streets, was dedicated on April 26, 1928.

The County government, meanwhile put itself in other quarters. The first approximation of a courthouse consisted of a space in the *Bella Union Hotel* on the east side of Main Street, where the 101 Freeway is carved today. From 1861 to 1891, the County occupied the *Clock Tower Courthouse* which resembled Boston's Faneuil Hall. Erected by Jonathan Temple to serve as a marketplace and theater, it stood on the west side of Main Street between Temple and First Streets–where City Hall is today.

In 1891 the County built a splendid Victorian courthouse, known to all as the *Red Sandstone Courthouse*. It stood proudly on *Poundcake Hill*, at the southeast corner of Temple and Broadway, where the first Los Angeles High School had been before it, and where the Criminal Courts building is today. The beautiful *Red Sandstone Courthouse* dominated the neighborhood until City Hall was built. After, the 1933 earthquake badly damaged the Courthouse–it was demolished in 1936.

One of the most dramatic events to shape the geography and politics of Civic Center occurred to a private enterprise, the *Los Angeles Times*. Its publisher, Harrison Gray Otis, had been spearheading a militant anti-union movement in Los Angeles, demanding "open shop" laws for Southern California, a political order that would disallow labor movements, strikes, pickets, and other collective actions benefiting workers. Unions from around the country poured money and energy into fighting the *Times*. As tensions mounted, both sides became increasingly strident and reckless. Finally, on October 1, 1910, a dynamite explosion demolished the *Los Angeles Times* building (on the northeast corner of Broadway and First Street), killing twenty workers. Labor agitators eventually confessed, but under ambiguous circumstances. The episode's immediate effect was to terminate a period of growth of the Socialist Party in Los Angeles. Its lasting effect was to reinforce in Southern California a continuation of hostility to labor unions.

When *City Hall* was built in 1928, the other, smaller government buildings were still haphazardly strewn around it. Planners had long tried to rationalize and organize the area, but little could be accomplished during the ensuing Great Depression except the construction of the Federal Building and Post Office (1938) and, a few blocks away, Union Station (1939). After the Second World War, Civic Center truly began to take its present form–that of a line-up of buildings going east and west from City Hall.

PROSPECTS

The Community Redevelopment Agency's Downtown Strategic Plan (D.S.P.) wants to concentrate more residential buildings close to Civic Center on Bunker Hill. The D.S.P. would also develop Second Street on the top surface of the hill (it is now only a tunnel through it), making it the central promenade of the neighborhood. They hope to turn Civic Center into a more diverse and friendly area linked to surrounding neighborhoods by tree-lined sidewalks.

A number of State of California departments are fragmented and scattered around Civic Center. In 1995, the state bought the old Broadway department store building on Fourth and Broadway in order to refurbish and recycle it as an office building. It is a block from the *Ronald Reagan State Building* on Third and Spring Streets, so the project makes sense and would clearly help the Historic Core.

A project, *First Street North*, that would have connected the eastern end of Civic Center with Little Tokyo, is on hold at this writing. The Mayor would rather first spend available funds on refurbishing the old buildings on Broadway, Downtown's Historic Core. However, the economy is better now and there may be funds to finance both tasks.

Plans are afoot to split the heavily used Children's Museum into two parts–one to be located near the Hansen Dam and the other possibly next to Little Tokyo between Temple and First Streets. There's much demand for at least two branches of the Children's Museum–and even more.

Dedicated in 2002, the most dramatic new architectural showpiece in the Civic Center is surely the *Cathedral of Our Lady of the Angels*. Designed by the Spanish architect, Jose Rafael Moneo, the cathedral building stands at the southwest portion of the huge, enclosed compound built immediately next to the I-101 Freeway. The whole complex is a fitting monument to the religious traditions and enormous size of the Catholic populations in this region. Its location is consistent with the history of the neighborhood; *La Placita*, L.A.'s original church, stands only three blocks away.

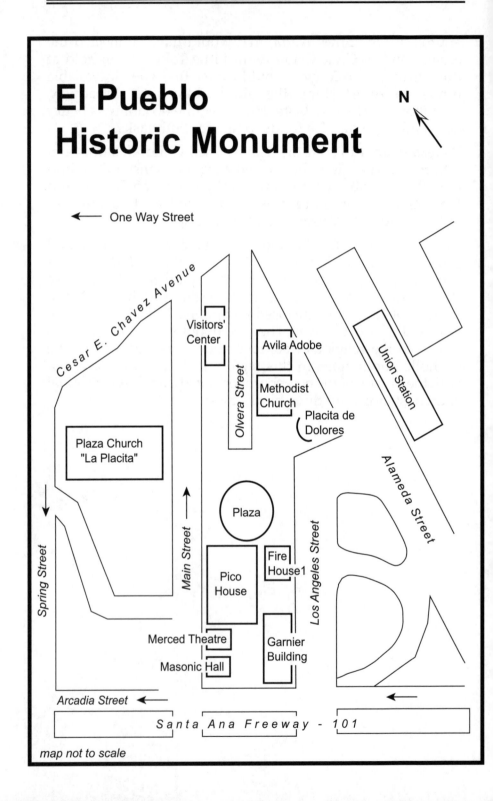

El Pueblo
Historic Monument

N

← One Way Street

Cesar E. Chavez Avenue

Visitors' Center

Avila Adobe

Union Station

Olvera Street

Methodist Church

Placita de Dolores

Plaza Church "La Placita"

Alameda Street

Spring Street

Main Street →

Plaza

Los Angeles Street

Fire House1

Pico House

Merced Theatre

Garnier Building

Masonic Hall

Arcadia Street ←

Santa Ana Freeway - 101

map not to scale

7. El Pueblo Historic Monument & Olvera Street

The plaza in the center of the *El Pueblo Historic Monument* is celebrated as the birthplace of Los Angeles, but the actual first settlement (1781) was close to the Los Angeles River, just east of where Union Station stands now. The plaza we see today is where the settlers moved after floods in 1818 washed away the first village (*pueblo*). The oldest church in Los Angeles, affectionately called *La Placita*, had just been built west of the plaza and across Main Street.

Olvera Street, extending one block north from the plaza, has often been called an early theme park. It is a lively replica of a Mexican village market street. Created in the 1930s–much later than the old buildings surrounding the plaza–Olvera Street has been popular with tourists ever since.

LOCATION

The El Pueblo District lies two blocks directly north of City Hall on Main Street. The I-101 Freeway is the southern border of the district, and Cesar Chavez Avenue is the northern border. It is across Alameda Street from Union Station.

GETTING THERE FROM UNION STATION

Walk: The plaza lies directly across Alameda Street from Union Station. Go straight out the front door of Union Station. On a slight incline across Alameda Street you will see the old circular Plaza ringed with huge trees and the handsome brick buildings of the Historic Monument.

DRIVING AND PARKING

From the north: Drive toward Downtown on the Pasadena Freeway (I-110) and take the transition ramp to the 101 East. Almost immediately, take the exit marked Broadway but continue two blocks to Main. Turn left onto Main Street. Parking lots are on the left side of Main Street.

From the east: Take the I-101 Freeway. Exit at Alameda Street. Turn right and drive north on Alameda to Cesar Chavez Avenue. Turn left onto Cesar Chavez Avenue and left again on Spring Street. Parking lots are on the left side of Spring Street heading south.

From the south and west: Drive north on the Harbor Freeway (I-110). Take the transition ramp to the 101 East. Almost immediately, take the exit marked Broadway but continue two blocks to Main Street. Turn left onto Main Street. Parking lots are on left side of Main Street.

From the northwest: (Hollywood and the San Fernando Valley): Take the Hollywood Freeway (I-101 East) to the exit marked Broadway but continue two blocks to Main Street. Turn left onto Main Street. Parking lots are on left side of Main Street.

WHO'S THERE?

Although this district once contained the houses of Los Angeles' first settlers, virtually no one lives close to the plaza today. This area is now a commercial and religious center, and a destination for visitors. As the term "Historic Monument" implies, it is a memorial, a reminder of the city's earliest days. Mostly, you'll find shopkeepers, waiters and waitresses, Mexican dancers, street musicians, and visitors and tourists by the busload. This is a great place for people watching!

WHAT'S THERE FOR THE VISITOR?

History

Bronze plaques and statues around the plaza tell the story of the founders of the pueblo in 1781. They include the Spanish King Carlos III, Governor Felipe de Neve, Father Junipero Serra, and the forty-four people recruited to be the first settlers, *los pobladores*. The plaza is not just a sculpture garden.

The Name, Los Angeles

The words were first given to the nearby river by a group of soldiers in 1769 commanded by Gaspar de Portola; they called it *El Rio de Nuestra Senora La Reina de Los Angeles de Porciuncula*, (The River of Our Lady, the Queen of the Angels of Porciuncula). "Porciuncula" refers to a little plot of land next to the church in Assisi, Italy where St. Francis of Assisi had lived and worshiped. He established the order of Spanish padres who founded the missions in the Americas.

Looking west across Main Street from the plaza, you'll see a small church, *La Iglesia de Nuestra Senora La Reina De Los Angeles De Porciuncula* (the Church of Our Lady, the Queen of the Angels of Porciuncula). Established by priests from the *Mission San Gabriel*, just eight miles east of this spot, the church stands on its first site, but the building has been altered frequently since 1818. The church took its name from the pueblo, which took *its* name from the river.

History alone makes the blocks of *El Pueblo Park* a draw for visitors of all ages and backgrounds. However, the main attraction for most people is Olvera Street, a facsimile of a Mexican village marketplace with vivid colors, sounds, and a buoyant atmosphere.

OLVERA STREET

In this short block, you'll find over eighty stalls and shops selling everything from clothing, leather goods, flowers, musical instruments, dishes, books, junk food, healthy food, junk toys, worthy toys, flags, hats, posters–the kind of small treasures you would expect to find in Tijuana, Mexico.

You can buy serapes, sombreros, dresses for women and girls, tooled leather belts and handbags, candles, rubber insects, rubber snakes, plastic puppets, mermaid dolls, castanets, guitars ($35.00), "quality sunglasses" ($3.95), and candy–candied sweet potato, candied cactus, candied water melon, candied pumpkin, coconut hay stacks, milk fudge, and pralines...There's enough sugar to make your cabeza buzz for a week.

You should certainly have your handwriting analyzed and your portrait drawn in charcoal. You might like a poster of Buffalo Bill, Emiliano Zapata, Pancho Villa, or Frida Kahlo. (You can find such posters and more costly examples of serious folk art in *Casa de Sousa*, #45 Olvera Street.)

It's all great fun. You can drop onto a park bench and watch the throng meander by. Olvera Street is a continuous street fair, a Mexican carnival.

You can step into L.A.'s oldest residence, the *Avila Adobe* (1818) for a free look into the past.

Visitors' Center- Check out this charming museum and shop on the first floor of the *Sepulveda House* (entrance is half-way down Olvera Street on the west side). The Visitors' Center also has a gift shop and book store. You can watch a free movie about L.A.'s early history while you give your feet an eighteen minute rest. Open Monday through Saturday 10:00 a.m. to 3:00 p.m. The movie is shown 11:00 a.m. & 2:00 p.m. Olvera Street is open every day until 7:00 p.m. in the winter; 10:00 p.m. in the summer.

HISTORIC SIGHTS AND SITES

Listed in chronological order:

Zanja Madre- (SAHN-hah MAH-dray), 1781-83. This is the "mother ditch" which brought water into the area and made a settlement possible. A wooden water wheel near Elysian Park lifted water from the Los Angeles River and sent it along a channel roughly parallel to Alameda Street. (The path taken by the zanja as it crossed Olvera Street is outlined in the main sidewalk just north of the Avila Adobe.)

> **Note:** A modern, stylized version of *Zanja Madre* was created by the artist, Andrew Leicester, for a small park next to one of the new office towers in the Lower Financial District, 801 South Figueroa, one and one-half miles southwest of Olvera Street. Los Angeles has not completely forgotten its origins!

The reason the early pueblo was established here is that this spot is high enough above the flood plane of the Los Angeles River to be safe but low enough so that a flow of water could be lifted to it from the same river.

La Iglesia de Nuestra Senora La Reina De Los Angeles De Porciuncula-(Church of Our Lady, the Queen of the Angels of Porciuncula)- (1818 to 1922) Affectionately called *La Placita*. Directly west and across Main Street from the circular plaza. The building, modified and repeatedly remodeled, is the first church to serve Los Angeles. Notice the mosaic placed above the front door in 1981 during the Los Angeles Bicentennial.

Fortunately, La Placita was built well away from the flood plane of the Porciuncula (later the Los Angeles) River which washed out the first group of houses in 1815. (After the flood, the Plaza was first relocated north-west of the church but, in 1818, it was shifted to the present spot.)

Don't be misled by the modest size of this church. It boasts the largest Catholic congregation in Southern California.

La Placita, and a newer church built back-to-back with it, are destinations for crowds of worshippers every Sunday. This is also the location of the annual "Blessing of the Animals" ritual on the Saturday before Easter.

In the 1980s, the church's role in the community was political and moral, not just religious. From 1981 until 1990, Father Luis Olivares was *La Placita's* pastor. He gained popularity, fame–and enemies–for sheltering and defending Latino immigrants, especially refugees from El Salvador and Guatemala who had fled repressive military regimes. Defying his superiors and the Immigration and Naturalization Service, Olivares declared *La Placita* to be a sanctuary for people threatened by the 1986 immigration law prohibiting hiring undocumented workers. Father Olivares, a diabetic, contracted AIDS from inadequately sterilized needles while on one of his many trips to Central America; he died March, 1993.

In front of La Placita Church see the C.L.A. Surveyor Post. When surveyor Henry Hancock officially mapped the village in 1858, he marked its boundaries with four posts. The one labeled "C.L.A. (City of Los Angeles) Post Number 1" is reproduced in bronze on its original spot.

Avila Adobe- (1818) Located halfway down Olvera Street on the east side. Built by Don Francisco Avila, this is the oldest surviving house in Los Angeles. Open for self-guided tours. In the 1930s, a group of civic leaders organized by Christine Sterling, saved the house from ruin and restored it. Preservation of the Avila Adobe formed the catalyst for creating the entire Olvera Street Marketplace. Open daily, except Sundays and Mondays. Free.

Pelanconi House- (1855-57) Now contains La Golondrina Restaurant. Built originally as a residence.

Masonic Hall- (1858) Located south of Pico House on Main Street. Open Tuesday through Friday 10:00 a.m. to 3:00 p.m.

Pico House- (Ezra Kysor, 1870) Pio Pico was the last Mexican governor of California. Twenty years after Anglo-Americans took over the state, Don Pio built this extravagant, beautiful hotel. The Italianate structure encloses an elegant interior courtyard which you can barely glimpse through the front windows. Portions of the building were restored in 1981 and 1992, but the only complete element left in the interior is the grand staircase. (The architect, Ezra Keysor, also designed St. Vibiana's Cathedral on the corner of Main and Second Street just three blocks south and the first synagogue near Second and Broadway.)

Merced Theater- (Ezra Keysor, 1870) 420 North Main Street, just south of Pico House. Delightful Victorian building with four cast iron columns framing the front windows and door. Named for the wife of the builder, William Abbot, the theater was on the second floor, and the Abbots lived on the third. The first floor had a bar and billiard saloon serving patrons of the Pico House next door. After sixteen years as a theater, the building switched to other purposes including the Salvation Army and Barker Brothers department store. In the 1960s, a tunnel was cut from the back of this building to the Garnier block on the other side of an alley (Sanchez Street).

Los Angeles should make more of a fuss over this charming little theater. The city thinks of itself as the entertainment capitol of the world. From this small acorn grew the mighty movie palaces on Broadway.

Firehouse #1- (1884) Located on Los Angeles Street, at the top of the hill across from Union Station, one of the first buildings you see as you approach the plaza. It is now a museum displaying hundred-year-old fire fighting equipment. Open daily except Sunday and Monday.

Sepulveda House- (1887) Eastlake Victorian commercial and residential house on Main Street. Now houses a museum and bookstore. The museum shows an informative film on the history of Los Angeles. Open Tuesday through Saturday 10:00 a.m. to 3:00 p.m., Sunday 10:00 a.m. to 4:30 p.m. Movie shown 11:00 a.m. & 2:00 p.m. Free.

Garnier Building- (1890) Los Angeles Street, south of Firehouse #1. This brick Victorian block was built when the commercial street of Chinatown was located here, on both sides of the street. The Chinese were pushed out of the area when Union Station was built in the 1930s. Note the cast iron posts framing the windows. Another matching brick structure extended south from the Garnier Building, but it was demolished in 1952 when the Santa Ana Freeway/Hollywood Freeway (I-101) plowed through here.

Plaza de Los Angeles- Over its long lifetime, this circle of land has served many purposes–marketplace, entertainment, venue for political demonstrations, and cultural center for Mexican and, later, Central American people. The visible elements today are the brick border wall encircling a central kiosko (1962), the huge Moreton Bay fig trees (*Ficus macro-phyllia*) planted in the 1870s, and three statues–Spanish King Carlos III of Spain, Felipe de Neve, Governor of the province of California when Los Angeles was founded, and Father Junipero Serra, standing just across Los Angeles Street from the Plaza Firehouse.

Placita De Dolores- (1978) at the Alameda Street entrance to the Historic Monument. A replica of the Bell of Dolores commemorates Mexican independence from Spain. Tile mural by Eduardo Carrillo.

The Indians of Southern California- Plaque and garden plot, in front of Placita De Dolores. This little garden contains native plants of Southern California whose uses to the Native Americans are identified by signs. The garden honors the native people who were encountered and nearly obliterated by the Spanish soldiers and missionaries. Anthropologists identify them by their language group–Uto-Aztecan.

Guided Walking Tour

You can take a guided walking tour of the Park (approximately one hour) conducted by volunteers of *Las Angelitas del Pueblo*. Tuesday through Saturday, 10:00 a.m. to 1:00 p.m. Tours leave on the hour. Meet at the office next to *Firehouse #1* on the south side of the Plaza. Free.

PUBLIC ART

Blessing of the Animals- (Politi,Leo, 1974-78) Mural on wall of Eugene Biscailuz Building on north side of the Plaza at the north end of Los Angeles Street. This delightful painting depicts an annual ceremony (on the Saturday before Easter) in which priests from *La Placita* bless pets of all descriptions brought here by children and adults from around Southern California.

America Tropical- (Siqueiros, David Alfaro, 1932) Currently hidden by a shed. High on the south wall of the Italian Hall, the northernmost building on Olvera Street. The shed protects a mural by one of the three great revolutionary Mexican muralists (the others are Diego Rivera, and Jose Clemente Orozco). Siqueiros painted an image of a crucified peon under an American eagle in front of a writhing jungle. Siqueiros had just escaped political violence in Mexico, and this was his symbol of exploitative capitalism. It so shocked the building's owners, who expected a picturesque tropical scene, that they fired him and painted over his work. Workers today are picking away at the whitewash to reveal, in time, the original work underneath. Ironically, the tile backdrop of the Plaza De Dolores (1978) (corner of Alameda and Los Angeles Streets) is a tribute to David Siqueirous. How attitudes change!

L.A. Freeway Kids- (Avilla, Glenna Boltuch, 1984) 225 foot mural on south wall of Hollywood Freeway (I-101) between Los Angeles and Main Streets. Children running and playing just under the L.A. Children's Museum. In the Civic Center, but seen only from El Pueblo side.

CONVENIENCES AND NECESSITIES

Public Rest Rooms

Under the circular stage (*kiosko*) in the center of the **Plaza**.

Near the northeast end of **Olvera Street**, close to Cesar Chavez Avenue, entrances from Olvera Street and Alameda Street.

La Placita Church- on the west side of Main Street; outside entrance from the courtyard.

Upstairs in **La Luz del Dia Restaurant** at southern end of Olvera Street, on the Plaza.

Public Telephones

Outside the gift shop in the courtyard north of *La Placita Church*, Main Street

At the southern entrance of **Olvera Street**, next to the Methodist Church.

ATMs

Bank of America, Main Street side, across from La Placita Church.

Places to Sit

Benches along **Olvera Street**.

Benches on the **Plaza courtyard** and in built into both sides of the circular wall.

Benches in courtyard of *La Placita Church*

RESTAURANTS

These two restaurants can seat you indoors or out, so you can enjoy the ambience of Olvera Street. Both places are visited by strolling musicians.

Price Guide to average lunch entrees:

$ = $3.00 - $8.00 $$$ = $13.00 - $17.00
$$ = $9.00 - $12.00 $$$$ = $18.00+

La Luz del Dia- (South end of Olvera Street, fronting on the Plaza). A cafeteria with a very limited menu. If you climb the open stairway along side the kitchen, you can watch an ancient activity, rarely seen in public in L.A. There are several women making tortillas by hand, clapping wads of corn dough, then tossing them onto a big iron stove. ($)

Casa La Golondrina- (Half-way down Olvera Street, west side). Wide range of Mexican dishes and drinks. This is in lower floor of the *Pelanconi House* (1855-1857). One of the oldest houses around. The restaurant was a haunt of movie stars, screenwriters, and Los Angeles' literati in the 1930s. (213) 628-4349. ($$)

HISTORY

Before 1769: *Yang-na*, a village of Uto-Aztecan speaking natives was located near the site of the present City Hall. They were peaceful hunters and gatherers. The staple of their diet was acorns, harvested from the many varieties of oaks in the region. With nutritious food and a mild climate, Southern California accommodated a larger population of native people than any other region in North America.

Then came momentous events–the turning points in the history of Los Angeles:

August 2, 1769: An expedition of Spanish soldiers camped on the bank of a river near *Yang-na*. King Carlos III had sent the men, commanded by Gaspar de Portola, north from Lower California to Monterey Bay (previously seen only by sea) to stake a claim to Alta California before the Russians got there. Indeed, the Russians were moving down the coast, and the British were also making plans for the area. Almost 300 years after Columbus, Carlos III had no desire to terminate the western expansion of the Spanish Empire.

On August 1, 1769: the Portola Party had observed the jubilee day of Saint Mary of the Angels of Porciuncula in the "little portion" of land next to the church in Assisi, Italy in which St. Francis had lived. So they named the river *El Rio de Nuestra Senora La Reina de Los Angeles de Porciuncula*–The River of Our Lady, the Queen of the Angels of Porciuncula. The river was called *Porciuncula* for years after that. Eventually the "Los Angeles" name was adopted for the river and the pueblo. The original spelling was kept, if not its Spanish pronunciation (lohs AHN-hay-lays).

1771: Father Junipero Serra (see statue across Los Angeles Street from the Plaza) established *Mission San Gabriel* eight miles east of here.

1777: Carlos III instructed Felipe de Neve, the Spanish governor of California (see statue on west side of Plaza) to recruit settlers to come up from Mexico to colonize this area in order validate the Spanish claim to the region.

September 4, 1781: After an arduous journey from the Mexican provinces of Sinaloa and Sonora, the "Pobladores" (settlers or founders) were officially granted property for houses and farming in a new pueblo. The year 1781 is the official founding date of the city of Los Angeles.

The settlers were forty-four men, women, and children; twenty-seven were of African descent, the others of mixed Indian and Spanish heritage (*mestizos*). Only two were Spanish.

A bicentennial plaque placed on the Plaza grounds in 1981 lists the names and races of each of the original settlers. "The Pobladores ranged in age from one to sixty-seven, and reflected the cultural heritage and racial diversity that link the city's past to the present."

Unfortunately, the Pobladores decided to build their little adobe houses on the flood plain of the river. They were washed out in 1815 and moved up to the present Plaza in 1818. The oldest surviving house in Los Angeles is the Avila Adobe (1818) on Olvera Street.

1784: Three retired soldiers were officially permitted to graze longhorn cattle, beginning the *rancho* period of California history six decades long. Several dozen other families quickly obtained ranchos, in effect dividing Southern California into huge feudal baronies and concentrating land ownership in a few hands. Cattle ranches dominated the economy for almost eighty years. The era came to an end when the ranches were hit by a terrible drought in 1862-1864 and a drop in the demand for beef when the Northern California gold mines played out.

1818: The pueblo church was built, *La Iglesia de Nuestra Senora La Reina de Los Angeles de Porciuncula,* now often called La Placita. The Avila Adobe, the oldest existing house in L.A., was built in the same year.

1821: Mexico won independence from Spain after an eleven year struggle. Spain had ruled for almost 300 years, but now the Mexican flag flew over Los Angeles. The population of El Pueblo was 1,000.

1833: The Mexican government secularized the mission lands. Political uncertainty anticipated the Mexican-American War, but ranchero life enjoyed a "golden age."

1846: Governor Pio Pico complained, "We find ourselves suddenly threatened by hordes of Yankee immigrants ...whose progress we cannot arrest." War broke out between the Mexican Californios and the (Anglo) Americans.

1848: California, along with several other western states, was seized by the United States in the Treaty of Guadalupe Hidalgo, signed on July 4th, ending the two-year war with Mexico.

1850: Los Angeles population = 1,610. California became the thirty-first state of the U.S.

Los Angeles Coat of Arms

This emblem represents our mixed ancestry. A shield cut into quarters: Stars and stripes representing the United States; bear and star of the Republic of California; lion and castle of Spain; and an eagle, serpent, and cactus of Mexico.

1854: L.A.'s first Protestant and first Jewish religious services were held.

1860: Los Angeles population = 4,385. A severe drought in 1862-1864 ended the Rancho period. Citrus agriculture later attained prominence as irrigation technology was developed and water was brought to the dry plains from distant rivers and mountain streams.

1870: Los Angeles population = 5,728. Ex-Governor, Pio Pico built Pico House Hotel (designed by Ezra Kysor) in El Pueblo. However, Anglos dominated the elite, and the homes of "society" had already drifted south from the Plaza. The neighborhood around the Plaza began a long process of neglect and economic decline that continued until 1930.

1871, Chinese Massacre: Chinese workers began to settle near the Plaza on the slope of the hill leading down to the spot where Union Station stands today. A drunken Anglo mob killed twenty Chinese people near Calle de los Negros now Los Angeles Street. (See "Chapter 5 – Chinatown")

1876: The Southern Pacific Railroad, built largely with Chinese labor, reached Los Angeles from Northern California.

1880: Los Angeles population = 11,183.

1884: Firehouse #1 was built on the south side of the Plaza.

1880s, Boom of the '80s: A huge wave of Anglo immigration from the American heartland was spawned by competition and an aggressive fare war between the Santa Fe and the Southern Pacific Railroads, each trying to attract buyers for its land holdings. Although the boom collapsed in 1888, the population began to grow again following skillful marketing by real estate boosters. They told the world that Los Angeles was the land of sunshine, seashores, orange blossoms, and healthy, clean air. They were correct, and the world believed.

1890: Los Angeles population = 50,395, a 351 percent explosion of growth from a decade earlier. As railroad construction projects were finished, more Chinese workers moved to Los Angeles and many settled in Chinatown on the east side of El Pueblo.

1899: A project was started to build a huge harbor at San Pedro, twenty miles south of the Plaza. Rock-filled break-waters form the largest man-made harbor in the world. It was destined to become the leading west coast port and America's primary link to Asia–the Pacific Rim.

1900: Los Angeles population = 102,479, a 103 percent increase in ten years. Henry E. Huntington created the Pacific

Electric Railway in 1902 and rapidly enlarged it throughout the decade, mainly by buying up short municipal railways in the suburbs and connecting them together. Huntington's arrangement of the P.E. routes becomes the largest inter-urban rapid-transit rail system in the world, and later formed the template upon which the freeway system would be loosely shaped between the 1950s and 1970s.

1910: Los Angeles population = 319,198. Another decade of enormous "infracture" projects in Los Angeles. In 1913, William Mulholland completed the construction of an aqueduct 233 miles from Owens Lake. His famous speech at the ceremony marking the opening of the aqueduct: "There it is. Take it." Later extended to 338 miles, the Los Angeles Aqueduct made possible a huge expansion of agriculture and, of course, population. In 1915, California celebrated the opening of the Panama Canal which brought new business to L.A.'s new harbor.

1920: Los Angeles population = 576,673.

1928: Mrs. Christine Sterling had been working on an idea to convert the Plaza neighborhood into a Spanish-Mexican-American center. She now discovered that the oldest existing house in Los Angeles, the Avila Adobe, was badly deteriorated, condemned by the L.A. Health Department, and about to be demolished. She successfully campaigned to preserve the Avila house and clean up Olvera Street. Workers scooped out three feet of dirt and filth from the whole length of the block.

1930: Los Angeles population = 1,238,000. Olvera Street opened as a Mexican marketplace. (See a plaque honoring Christine Sterling. It is fixed to the inside of the brick border on the north side of the Plaza.)

1930s: Chinatown was demolished to make way for Union Station. Some Chinese homes and businesses were relocated three blocks north on Ord Street ("China City") and others even farther north on Broadway ("New Chinatown"). The Garnier Building, just south of Firehouse #1, which was built to house Chinese merchants, is the lone survivor of the early Chinese era. The building is being converted into the Chinese American History Museum.

1939: Union Station, the last of the great railroad terminals to be built in the United States was dedicated in a spectacular celebration and parade.

1940: (Before World War II) Los Angeles population = 1,504,000.

1950: (After World War II) Los Angeles population = 1,970,000.

1953: Forty-four acres around the Plaza was designated a State Historic Park.

1970: Los Angeles population = 2,816,000.

1980: Los Angeles population = 2,967,000.

1981: Los Angeles celebrated its Bicentennial.

1990: Los Angeles City population = 3,485,000. Of these, forty percent were Latino, thirty-seven percent were Anglo, fourteen percent were African-American, and ten percent were Asian. Los Angeles has come full circle and is once again ethnically diverse with more Latinos than Anglos.

PROSPECTS

At the time of publication, workers are refurbishing some of the older structures of the El Pueblo Historic Monument, including seismic strengthening and installing better handicapped access. (Artifacts from before and after the arrival of Mexican and Spanish settlers, were found under the buildings lining Olvera Street when elevator shafts were dug in 1995.)

The El Pueblo Historic Monument: A visible symbol and narrative of the city's past, and many important sites are identified and commemorated. The Garnier Building, after waiting more than forty years, is being converted into a Chinese historical museum. The beautiful Pico House and its neighbors, the Masonic Hall and the Merced Theater, are also returned to life.

This park also needs to be reconnected to other Downtown districts. The Community Redevelopment Agency (C.R.A.), in its Downtown Strategic Plan (D.S.P.) envisions better pedestrian walkways between the Plaza area and the neighborhoods nearby. It also hopes to build 12,000 dwelling units and try to make El Pueblo, once again, a residential neighborhood as well as a tourist attraction.

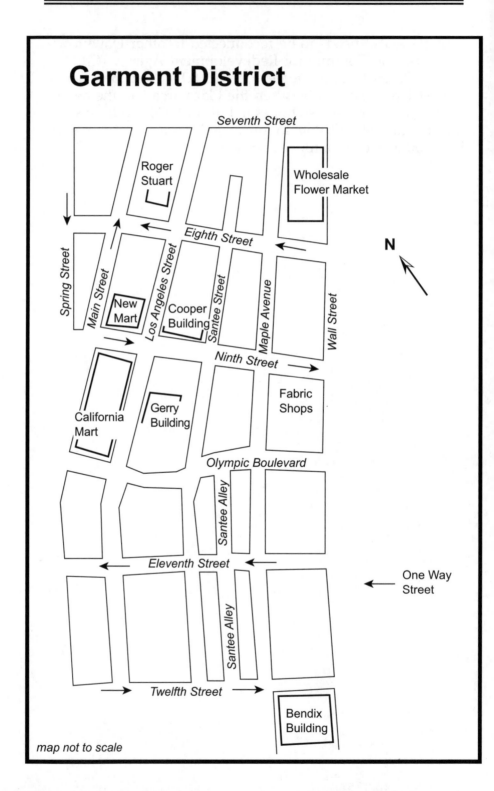

Garment District

Seventh Street

Roger Stuart

Wholesale Flower Market

Eighth Street

Spring Street

Main Street

Los Angeles Street

New Mart

Cooper Building

Santee Street

Maple Avenue

Wall Street

N

Ninth Street

Fabric Shops

California Mart

Gerry Building

Olympic Boulevard

Santee Alley

Eleventh Street

One Way Street

Santee Alley

Twelfth Street

Bendix Building

map not to scale

8. GARMENT DISTRICT
ALSO KNOWN AS THE FASHION DISTRICT

The Garment District is one of the liveliest showplaces in Southern California. It can't be beat for color, energy, variety, delicious food smells, and terrific people watching.

The street scenes are surrealistic fantasies. Over here are ranks of mannequins staring introspectively into the near distance and garbed in variations of whatever suits, dresses, or uniforms the sellers are pushing. The shop next door sells fabrics, and the sidewalk is half-filled with rows of yard goods draped over tall cardboard tubes. The place next to that specializes in jeans–blue jeans, green jeans, red, yellow, white, purple, and black jeans. Over there are shoes, and purses, and watches all massed together. Dresses and gowns of every variety hang on wall hooks or on wheeled racks. A lineup of disconnected plaster legs display hosiery in a rainbow of colors. On the ground, where the little kids can get at them, are seductive battery-driven plastic toys, incessantly gyrating and squawking. Around the corner, a boom box blasts away. Over here, next to a tie rack, a rotating light beacon shoots out dazzling red, white, blue, and green flashes. Hawkers shout. Customers laugh. Self-conscious teenagers prance or slouch by. Harried mothers try to distract their kids from the costume jewelry and grotesque cosmetics.

It's a carnival, a comedy of manners set on a richly decorated stage. It is one of L.A.'s most amazing public spaces. If you haven't seen the Garment District recently, give it a try! Weekends are more crowded and playful than weekdays. Go there any time! You've been missing a grand show!

LOCATION

The Garment District sprawls over fifty square blocks (Think of it!) between Broadway and Wall Streets, and Seventh Street and Pico Boulevard.

The Garment District has Six Sections

• **California Market Center (formerly CaliforniaMart or CalMart) and nearby wholesale only shops-** The entrance to "CalMart" is on Ninth Street between Los Angeles and Main Streets. You can't shop in "CalMart" unless you have a resellers license, but you can eat lunch there. "CalMart" opens its main floor to the public on occasional Saturdays. Across Ninth Street from "CalMart" is the New Mart, a major designer building, at 127 East Ninth Street. Look around the stores in this building and ask when they're having their next "sample sale."

• **Cooper Building-** at Ninth and Los Angeles Streets, contains six floors of outlet shops in what was formerly a factory loft.

• **Santee Alley-** lies just east of Santee Street between Olympic and Twelfth. The Alley and its neighbors–tiny shops and stalls tightly packed together in an open street-market–make up the best amusement park around. And it is free!

• **Small retail shops-** Between Los Angeles and Wall Streets and between Ninth and Pico Boulevard Several streets of small shops carrying discounted apparel, fabric, costume jewelry, and other accessories.

• **Menswear stores-** Los Angeles Street north of the Cooper Building, between Seventh and Ninth Streets. The best known of these is Roger Stuart Clothes, 729 South Los Angeles Street.

• **Southern California Flower Market-** (wholesale only) Takes up the entire block between Seventh and Eighth and Maple and Wall Streets. This is where Southern California florists pick up the stock for their stores. You can stroll inside (but keep out of the way!), breathe the lovely aroma, and watch the action.

GETTING THERE FROM UNION STATION

DASH bus, Route D: On weekdays, you'll find the DASH bus at the Patsaouras Transit Plaza. Every five minutes; free to Metrolink riders, otherwise $.25. From the Metrolink train platform, go down the ramp to the pedestrian tunnel and turn right–away from Union Station itself. Walk past the Red Line Subway entrance, and head for the bus plaza. The bus takes you straight to the Garment District in about twenty minutes. Pull the "Stop Requested" cord above the bus windows when you pass Ninth Street. You will get off on Main Street between Ninth and Olympic across from the CaliforniaMart.

Red Line Subway: The Red Line Subway does not go near the Garment District.

DRIVING AND PARKING

From the north: Take the Pasadena Freeway (I-110) south to the Ninth Street exit. Follow curve left to Ninth Street and go east for about nine blocks. Park in the Main Street or Spring Street lots ($4.00 or $5.00 all day) or drive four more blocks to the Ninth and Wall Street lot ($3.00 all day) for the eastern part of the Garment District.

From the east: Take the 101 Freeway west, then the transition to the Harbor Freeway South (I-110). Drive to the Ninth Street exit. Follow the curve left to Ninth Street and go east for about nine blocks. Park in the Main or Spring Street lots ($4.00 or $5.00 all day) or drive four more blocks to Ninth and Wall Street lot ($3.00 all day) for the eastern part of the Garment District. If you prefer traveling west on the I-10 Freeway, take the Maple Street exit, turn right, and drive six blocks into the district from the south.

From the south: Drive north on the Harbor Freeway (I-110) to the Ninth Street exit. Turn right onto Ninth Street. Parking lots are on Ninth or Eighth at Spring Street.

From the west: Take the Santa Monica Freeway (I-10) past the 110 Freeway, and take the Maple Street exit. Turn left onto Maple and drive to lots near Pico and Maple Streets or seven blocks to lots on the north part of the Garment District ($3.00 all day).

From the northwest, Hollywood, and the San Fernando Valley: Take the Hollywood Freeway East. Go through the transition to the Harbor Freeway South (110). Drive to the Ninth Street exit. Follow the curve left to Ninth Street and go east for about nine blocks. Park on Main Street or Spring Street lots ($4.00 or $5.00 all day) or drive four more blocks to the Ninth and Wall Street lot ($3.00 all day) for the eastern part of the Garment District.

WHO'S THERE?

Near the *California Market Center*, you'll see wholesalers, manufacturer's representatives, salespeople, and buyers for retail stores, many in trendy dress, all going about the serious business of merchandising. Shoppers are drawn from the full cross-section of society making the Garment District the most diverse section of the City.

Behind the showplace facade of the Garment District is another world. The five-story and twelve-story buildings in the area are factories–sweatshops, crowded with sewing machines and their operators, mostly immigrant women from Mexico, El Salvador, Guatemala, the Philippines, and other Asian lands. The factories of this district constitute the center of a huge manufacturing industry–L.A.'s largest! It extends out into the industrial suburbs of Los Angeles and into Orange County.

WHAT'S THERE FOR THE VISITOR?

The Garment District is a marketplace with bargains, variety, quantity, and discount shopping. This brings the crowds and the near-circus atmosphere.

California Market Center, formerly CalMart- For an introduction to the magnitude of the wholesale segment of this district, you can step into the biggest single apparel market in the world. The CalMart is composed of four connected buildings containing two thousand showrooms. Eight thousand people work in this place and generate six billion dollars in sales of apparel and accessories each year. Six billion!

Step into the front entrance on Ninth Street, and stroll around the lobby. Television screens show slinking models parading the latest gowns. You might consider coming back to the CalMart for lunch, but remember it's closed on weekends.

New Mart- 127 East Ninth Street, across the street from CalMart. Another wholesale building, this is a "major designer" place with up-scale labels like Leon Max, David Dart, Emil Rutenberg, T.J. & The Boys, Margaret O'Leary, and Pamela Carone. Several firms have occasional "sample sales." Just ask.

Cooper Building- Now head for the retail outlets. This might be a good time to check out the Cooper Building on Ninth and Los Angeles Streets, catty-corner from the CalMart. Pick up a pamphlet at the entrance to get a general idea of the locations of stores and what they carry. Take the stairs or the elevator. Be sure to notice the signs: "No Returns" and "No Refunds". (Before you leave the Cooper Building, consider using one of the rest rooms located on each floor. You may have trouble finding one later down among the shops and alleys.)

Next stop, Santee Alley!

Santee Alley- This is the most colorful, and most crowded section of the Garment District. It is one-fourth mile long, sandwiched between Santee and Maple Streets and between Olympic and Twelfth Streets. It is jammed with 150 shops and stalls. This is the place to buy inexpensive clothing, shoes, watches–if you examine the items carefully!

Just look at all the stuff! You, and throngs of others, will find dresses for women and girls, pants of all types, every kind of outerwear and underwear, swimwear, partywear, menswear, shoes of all qualities, toys, ties, socks, party favors, watches (including $35.00 "Rolex" watches made in China. Aren't they all?), pins, buttons, visors, costume jewelry, belts, and sunglasses–whatever the heart desires, all in a gloriously chaotic jumble.

You can bargain, sometimes. Tell them you saw that blouse for $5.00 less up the block. Many people haggle loudly in Spanish, or English, or whatever language works.

Best of all, the people and their antics are as varied and colorful as the merchandise. There's every ethnic group and language, every age, and all imaginable styles of dress. The Alley is an extraordinary place for people watching.

The din! Vendors clap their hands to get your attention, then call out in Spanish or English, urging you to look at their wares. Powerfully amplified, a rapper sings about discount prices in his shoe store. Boom boxes and car stereos compete with the rapper. The smells of sizzling onions and sausages smack the senses. Fresh sliced mangos beckon on every corner.

Why is this neighborhood the place for possible buys? The garment business is labor-intensive, rapidly changing, and high-volume. The resulting overcuts, mistakes in design, and other manufactured oddities are "dumped" into the shops and stalls of the Garment District. Many shops also sell seconds (flawed goods) and other products that haven't sold elsewhere. You'll see labels on items from department stores whose clearance sales and bargain basements failed to move them.

In the Cooper Building and the street shops, you get the general impression of masses of overcuts and styles from previous seasons. Sometimes, in-season overcuts are also sold here with new labels substituted for brand names, to prevent complaints from people who paid full price elsewhere. Some shops specialize in the products of single countries or narrow lines, say, women's vests from India.

No returns. No refunds. And, sometimes, no identifiable shop to return to. Fitting-rooms are few and far between. In these streets, trades people come and go frequently and unpredictably.

Security

Garment District merchants are aware of shoppers' concerns about safety. They employ sporty looking, bicycle riding security people to zip around the area in pairs.

Remember: Downtown is the safest area in Los Angeles. And the Garment District is one of the safest areas of Downtown.

If you're interested in shopping for fabric, try *Michael Levine*, a huge fabric and notion store on Ninth and Maple Streets (920 South Maple).

For tourists and suburban visitors, the Garment District offers quick access by train and DASH Bus. You would enjoy an unharried trip here to see the sights, eat a cheerful lunch, and watch people and activity you can't see in your conventional suburban malls. It's an urban adventure–entertaining, stimulating, and easy as pie to get to.

Southern California Flower Market

700 block of Maple and Wall Streets. Flowers from around California and Hawaii are funneled into two buildings on both sides of Wall Street. Flower cultivation in Los Angeles began in 1892 when Japanese-American farmers planted fields just south of the growing city and near Santa Monica. This Flower Market was started in 1913, a few blocks north and west of here, and moved to this location in 1923. Japanese names are still much in evidence: Nakashima, Tayama, Kimura, Endo, and Miwa. Anglo names pre-dominate on the east side of Wall Street.

Monday, Wednesday, and Friday are market days, and the place opens early. Tuesday, Thursday and Saturday are slower, but still worth a look and a sniff. The hours of the Flower Market Coffee Shop (on Wall Street): Monday, Wednesday, Friday 3:00 a.m. to 2:00 p.m.; Tuesday, Thursday 5:30 a.m. to 2:00 p.m., Saturday 5:30 a.m. to 12:00 p.m. Breakfasts until 10:00 a.m. This is a good place to see and hear shop talk.

SHOPPING

But what about the *shopper's* point of view? Can you find first-class bargains? Can you locate hard-to-find clothing, shoes, glitz, beads, or trimmings? Is this a place you would revisit occasionally to do some serious hunting and gathering? Maybe.

Visitors will think the *Garment District* has suffered from the growth of factory outlet malls on the fringe of the city. *Garment District* shops and stalls are tiny, chaotic, and oddly specialized. You'll need to maneuver around piles of shlocky stuff to find items worth a closer look, but many customers delight in the excitement and challenge of shopping here. If you're accustomed to upscale, quieter stores that run frequent sales, or if you like the well-organized and consistent discount stores down the road from your home–T.J. Maxx, Ross Dress for Less, Marshall's, Nordstrom Rack–you probably won't enjoy the relative rough and tumble of the Garment District.

The Cooper Building might appear more orderly than the alleys and streets. However, inside its shops you find labels mixed up in little confusing sub-areas–a few Anne Kleins here, a bunch of Liz Claibornes there, something else over here in the corner. There are variations in quality that require a fine eye and a sure memory for prices. Some shoppers will be confused, others stimulated.

If you are looking only for bargains, you may be happier if you take the sinful alternative and drive your car to an outlet mall.

BUILDINGS

California Market Center- Ninth Street between Main and Los Angeles Streets. Four blank-faced, modern buildings covering two square blocks. This is the world's largest single apparel market. Eight thousand people work here, handling more than $6,000,000,000.00 worth of merchandise annually. In the plaza entrance on Ninth Street, a tall sculpture in black steel, a silhouette of *Hammering Man* makes his perplexing commentary in slow motion.

Bendix Building- (Lee, W. Douglas) 1206 Maple at Twelfth Street. Eleven-story factory loft with large windows and fancy gothic detailing. The building is handsome enough on its own, but its huge BENDIX sign rising on a steel frame-work gives it a special cachet. In an earlier life, this was used as an office building and a place for light manufacturing. During the World War II, the federal government censored mail here.

Printing Center Building- next to Bendix Building on Maple Street, south of Twelfth Street. Another factory loft with large windows and delicate decoration. The name shows this area was formerly occupied by other industries as well as garment manufacture.

1200 Santee Building- Twelve-story loft with more gothic details.

Gerry Building- (Fleischman, Maurice 1947) 910 Los Angeles Street, across from CalMart. Eight-story factory loft. On the front, a continuous line of windows on each floor project as bays, rounded off at the ends. A fine example of streamline Art Deco factory architecture.

PUBLIC ART

Hammering Man- (Borofsky, Jonathan, 1988) Sculpture, painted corten steel. Twenty-two foot tall man slowly striking hammer blows (motorized). Front court of CaliforniaMart, Ninth Street between Main and Los Angeles Streets.

Arrogant Man, and **Surprised Woman-** (Frey, Viola, 1986) Sculptures. Glazed ceramics, ten feet high. CaliforniaMart, Ninth Street luncheon court on Los Angeles Street side.

CONVENIENCES AND NECESSITIES

Public Rest Rooms

In California Market Center- Ninth between Main and Los Angeles Streets. Escalator to second floor, then walk two lefts; on left hand side of hallway.

In Cooper Building- Ninth and Los Angeles Streets, each floor.

In the food court area of the Fashion Building- Small entrances on 934 Los Angeles Street or 900 block of Santee Street.

Public Telephones

Many phones throughout **California Market Center, Ninth** and **Los Angeles Streets**.

Mid-block of almost all streets in the **Garment District**.

ATMs

There are several ATMs around the perimeter and in the front court of **California Market Center, Ninth** and **Los Angeles Streets**.

Many other ATMs are scattered around the **Garment District**. The businesses of the area know you may need cash.

Places to Sit

California Market Center- Ninth Street between Main and Los Angeles Streets. Inside and outside in the front courtyard.

Food court in the Fashion Building- small entrances on 934 Los Angeles Street or 900 block of Santee Street.

Some of the larger shops and stores have benches or couches just inside the entrances for weary shoppers or their companions.

Bus Information

MTA Customer Service, CaliforniaMart- 1016 South Main Street. Tuesday-Saturday 10:00 a.m. to 6:00 p.m.

RESTAURANTS

Price Guide to average lunch entrees:

$ = $3.00 - $8.00	$$$ = $13.00 - $17.00
$$ = $9.00 - $12.00	$$$$ = $18.00+

Angelique Cafe- 840 South Spring Street. Triangular corner where Main and Spring Streets join; just north of California Market Center. Simple French food. Sidewalk seating. Lunches only. Monday through Saturday they are open from 7:00 a.m. to 4:00 p.m. (213) 623-8698. (**$$**)

Lucas L.A. European Cafe- Northwest corner of Ninth and Main Streets. Bright and cheerful with fine views of this active corner across from the California Market Center. ($$)

El Pollo Loco- Corner of Ninth and Santee Streets. ($)

New Moon- 102 West Ninth Street–that's West Ninth–across Main Street from the California Market Center. Chinese food. The New Moon is an industry favorite. *Everyone*, they say, from the fashion industry eats here. They swear the New Moon has the best Chinese chicken salad ($7.95) in the world! (213) 624-0186. ($$)

Lilit Deli Restaurant- 109 East Ninth Street. More than a dozen pasta dishes ready for fast service. Also soup and sandwiches. Small, cheerful place. Hours: lunches Monday through Friday. (213) 622-0321. ($)

Afshan Glatt Kosher Restaurant- 306 East Ninth Street. Poultry, white fish, and beef dishes, stews, kabobs, and sandwiches. Popular and lively; promises to last longer than the Italian restaurant that recently occupied this space. Monday through Friday 11:00 a.m. to 5:00 p.m. (213) 622-1010. ($$)

Food court in the Fashion Building- small entrances at 935-B Los Angeles Street or 934 Santee Street. Good range of ethnic food possibilities. Not quite enough tables and chairs during noon lunch hour, but it's much calmer than the crush of humanity out on the sidewalks of the Garment District. ($)

Setha's- 978 South San Pedro Street. Monday through Friday from 7:00 a.m. to 4:00 p.m., and Saturday from 7:30 a.m. to 2:00 p.m. Closed Sundays. (213) 624-9865. ($)

In the California Market Center - Ninth and Los Angeles Streets:

Thai Dishes- Pleasant, modern restaurant convenient to California Market Center workers; up-scale from the fast food outlets in front of the California Market Center. Closed on weekends. ($$)

Moda Café- 110 East Ninth Street, the southwest corner of the main building. Breakfast and lunch. Italian style. M-F.

The Mixed Green- In front entrance court of California Market Center. Salad and potato bar. ($)

HISTORY

The Garment District was first developed as a manufacturing and wholesale center, not as a retail shopping district. The plethora of small specialty shops and stalls is a recent creation. Santee Alley, for example, is the product of a marketing philosophy developed by Middle Eastern entrepreneurs.

In the mid-1970s, an Israeli immigrant found that the quality of his imported dresses was inferior to standard American merchandise and not marketable, so he unloaded his inventory in a "swap meet"–an ad hoc street fair. He quickly saw that he could sell overcuts and seconds directly into the streets surrounding the clothing factories. Soon manufacturers were aiming some of their merchandise at two tiers of buyers–ordinary retail stores and the continuing street fair.

However, the business of manufacturing garments first came to Los Angeles from New York fifty years earlier–in the 1920s–as runaways from East Coast labor unions. Workers aplenty could be found in Los Angeles, and they were accustomed to "open shops" (nonunion factories). Mostly Mexican women, they were later joined by other minorities.

By the 1930s, designers here were taking advantage of the growth of Hollywood and its success in displaying the latest fashions to the world. Among the first Los Angeles labels to win national prominence were women's swimwear companies, Cole of California and Catalina. After World War II, Los Angeles came into its own as a fashion center, second only to New York. Over the years, the old labels have lost sales to Guess?, Cherokee Group, Bugle Boy Industries, Paul Davrill, Carole Little, Cal-Togs/Breton Industries, Jonathan Martin, E-Z Sportswear, and Chorus Line. Sadly, Cole and Catalina fell into bankruptcy in 1993.

Southern California has never befriended labor unions. Latina workers trying to organize one in the 1930s, had to fight racial and gender prejudices as well as the fierce opposition of managers. The International Ladies Garment Workers Union managed to stage a major strike in 1933. Organizational meetings were held in the Trinity Auditorium, now the Embassy Auditorium, on Ninth and Grand Avenue, just a few blocks west of the Garment District. Latina workers struck some apparel factories even in 1943, a wartime year. Still, only one percent of today's sweatshop workers belong to the I.L.G.W.U.

One of the obstacles faced by unions is the fragmentation of the industry. Nowadays, apparel manufacturing is splintered into hundreds of small pieces. For example, Guess?, the largest clothing firm in L.A., designs its garments, acquires and cuts the fabric, and then employs 100 sewing contractors to assemble the goods. The contractors, in turn, employ, "as needed," up to 7,000 workers to assemble goods sold under the company's label. These contract workers are hired and dismissed at a moment's notice and paid no benefits.

Los Angeles County alone has nearly ten percent of America's apparel jobs and twenty-two percent of all women's wear jobs. There are 100,000 "on-the-books" textile workers in this area and an estimated 25,000 "off-the-books" workers, mostly undocumented immigrants. Sewing machine operators are paid on a piecework basis, but factories are also required to have time clocks to prevent pay from falling below minimum wage for slower workers.

The dispersion of the work force in the garment business makes it prone to abuses. In the 1990s, however, the Federal Labor Department can and has taken legal action against designing firms pretending ignorance of working conditions and accepting only indirect responsibility for labor environments.

Then in mid-1995, a revelation of horrific worker abuse hit news media around the world: seventy-two Thai sewing machine operators were discovered inside a virtual prison in the nearby town of El Monte. For as long as seven years, they had been terrorized by nine slave masters from their own country, completely isolated from outsiders, forced to work long hours (from 7:00 a.m. to 12:00 a.m., six days a week), paid only $2.00 an hour, and threatened with machetes. All retailers who had sold goods sewn in the El Monte prison/factory denied any knowledge of the matter, and all state and federal agencies affected ignorance, in spite of complaints and warnings over several years.

Of course, few garment workers are slaves. Their jobs are merely arduous. However, industry people point out that sewing machine employment is open to newcomers from Mexico, Central America, Vietnam, and Korea. And in the stalls and shops that line the streets of the Garment District, many other Latin American and Asian salespeople are also at their starting points in the American economy.

The Garment District is profoundly linked to the world economy, especially that of the Third World. The apparel business is now the largest manufacturing industry in L.A.–one-third of all the non-durable manufacturing jobs–even though most clothing worn by Americans is made in other countries.

PROSPECTS

L.A.'s clothing manufacturers are carefully watching the effects of NAFTA, the North American Free Trade Agreement, passed in 1993.

If Mexican factories can create popular designs, sew them up quickly while maintaining convincing quality controls, they will be tough competitors in a changing business. They will also be able to maintain their cost advantage in goods, like tee shirts or socks, that do not change rapidly.

California has a special advantage in this new economic environment. The fact that L.A.'s designers compete aggressively near each other in a dynamic business arena means that they also react quickly to the rapidly changing fashions created here in Los Angeles. The fastest way to get a new style off the sketch pads and onto store racks is to produce the clothing immediately, right here.

Although U.S. labor costs are much higher than in Mexico, U.S. firms are promoting the quality and prestige of the home-grown product. This is the reason many of L.A.'s up-scale designers (e.g. Brazcan Tricot, David Dart, J.R. Morrissey, and Leon Max) now insist their labels say: "Made in the U.S.A."

Recently, fashion industry employers were surprised by a growing shortage of sewing machine operators in California. NAFTA's lower tariffs on imported goods created more jobs for stay-at-home Mexicans, and new immigration restrictions have reduced supplies of low-wage apparel workers. This may herald a shift from piecework pay to hourly wages and innovative teamwork systems. It's becoming a worker's market.

The California Market Center briefly encountered new competition from a crosstown rival, the Pacific Design Center in West Hollywood. The P.D.C.'s traditional wholesale business is in office furnishings, but with the pace of new office construction, slowed by the economy, a large portion of its showrooms were designated for the fashion industry in an effort to draw upscale labels away from the Garment District. In response, the CalMart undertook a renovation and redecoration job, and the Garment District now prefers to call itself the "Fashion District." The struggle was won by CalMart in 1996. CalMart now calls itself California Market Center.

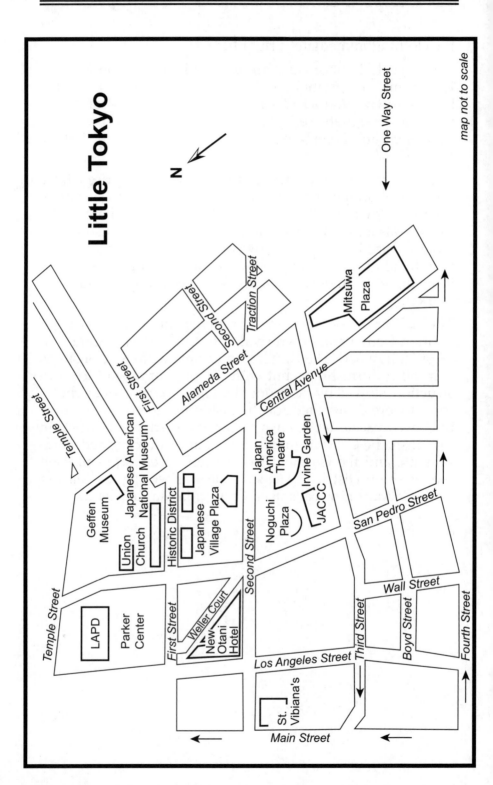

map not to scale

Little Tokyo

N

One Way Street

Temple Street

First Street

Second Street

Traction Street

Alameda Street

Central Avenue

Mitsuwa Plaza

Japanese American National Museum

Geffen Museum

Union Church

Historic District

Japanese Village Plaza

Japan America Theatre

Noguchi Plaza

Irvine Garden

JACCC

San Pedro Street

Temple Street

LAPD

Parker Center

First Street

Weller Court

New Otani Hotel

Second Street

Los Angeles Street

Third Street

Wall Street

Boyd Street

Fourth Street

St. Vibiana's

Main Street

9. LITTLE TOKYO

People of Japanese ancestry have lived in Los Angeles for 110 years–except for three grim years during the Second World War.

Although most of the Japanese and Japanese-Americans in Los Angeles now make their homes in the suburbs (with concentrations in Gardena, Sawtelle, and Crenshaw), some still live Downtown in Little Tokyo. The 1990 Census showed that six hundred eighty-five Japanese, eighty Korean, and twenty-eight Chinese people reside here. Nevertheless, today Little Tokyo is less a residential community than a destination for tourists and a business center. The main attractions for visitors are the several clusters of shops, two fine museums, several restaurant complexes, and the fact that Little Tokyo continues to be the symbolic and cultural center of Japanese and Japanese-Americans in Los Angeles.

It is the site of the *Japanese American Museum*, the elegant *New Otani Hotel and Garden*, the *Noguchi Plaza*, the *Japanese American Cultural and Community Center*, and the *Japan America Theater*. The *Nisei Week Parade and Festival* are celebrated here every August.

Visit Little Tokyo for a fascinating mixture of old and new, Western and Eastern, kitschy and classy. All attractions lie in a safe, compact, and walkable area.

LOCATION

Little Tokyo is only a half-mile south of Union Station. The district's historic buildings are on East First Street between San Pedro Street and Central Avenue. Newer sections were built in the 1970s and 1980s between First and Third Streets and Los Angeles and Alameda Streets. The southern border of Little Tokyo is Third Street.

GETTING THERE FROM UNION STATION

Walking: From the front of Union Station, walk across Alameda Street and up the slope to Los Angeles Street which borders El Pueblo Historic Plaza; hike south (left) for three blocks. At First Street you will be in front of the *New Otani Hotel*, which marks the northwest corner of Little Tokyo.

DASH Bus, Route D: The best ride to Little Tokyo from Union Station is DASH bus, route D, boarded at *Nick Patsaouras Transit Plaza*; free to Metrolink Riders. (When you detrain, go down the ramp to the tunnel and turn *right*–away from Union Station.) On the DASH bus, pull the "Stop Requested" cord over the window when you get to Los Angeles Street on Temple. You will be on the south side of the Federal Building, one block north of Little Tokyo's *New Otani Hotel*. Hike south on Los Angeles Street, in front of the *Parker Center*, headquarters of the Los Angeles Police Department. On weekends, catch DASH across Alameda Street from Union Station. It goes directly to Little Tokyo.

Red Line Subway: The subway's *Civic Center* station on First and Hill Streets is four short blocks away from Little Tokyo. This hike is fine on weekdays when other people are around, but on weekends the Civic Center and First Street itself, west of Los Angeles Street, is nearly empty and may make you feel uneasy.

DRIVING AND PARKING

From the north: Drive toward Downtown on the Pasadena Freeway (I-110) and take the transition ramp to the I-101 Freeway going east. Take the exit marked Los Angeles Street and turn right. Drive down to Second Street. Parking lots are on the right between Second and Third. For *Yaohan Plaza*, turn left on Second, drive to Alameda, and turn right to Yaohan Plaza a block ahead.

From the east: Take the I-101 Freeway going east. Exit at Alameda, turn left, and drive to First Street. Turn right on First, then left on Central for parking at the Japanese Village Plaza or in nearby lots. For *Mitsuwa Plaza*, continue on Alameda to Third Street.

From the south and west: Drive north on the Harbor Freeway (I-110). Take the transition ramp to the I-101 Freeway going east. Take the exit marked Los Angeles Street and turn right. Drive down to Second Street. Parking lots are on the right between Second and Third. For *Mitsuwa Plaza*, turn left on Second, drive to Alameda, and turn right to the Plaza a block ahead.

From the northwest (Hollywood and the San Fernando Valley): Take the Hollywood Freeway (I-101 East) to the exit marked Los Angeles Street and turn right. Drive down to Second Street. Parking lots are on the right between Second and Third. For *Mitsuwa Plaza*, turn left on Second, drive to Alameda, and turn right to the Plaza a block ahead.

Note: Most parking lots are no more than $4.00 all day and even cheaper after 4:00 p.m.

WHO'S THERE?

Japanese settlers, the *Issei*, first arrived here in the 1880s at a time when most other people in Los Angeles were living several blocks north and west, near the dusty El Pueblo Plaza. The first Issei were mostly men, but eventually Japanese women were permitted to come to California, joining husbands and communities that were already stable and well organized. For decades, farming provided a secure economic base, encouraging the more densely concentrated enclave of Little Tokyo to grow into a social and commercial center and a residential neighborhood.

Today, Little Tokyo is home to several generations of Japanese and Japanese-Americans. The children of the Issei (*Nisei*), and their grandchildren (*Sanse*) are joined by more recent migrants and large numbers of Japanese visitors: students, tourists, and business people.

WHAT'S THERE FOR THE VISITOR?

Most of Little Tokyo is new. Many old hotels, stores, restaurants, and apartments that served the community from the early 1900s have been demolished to make way for the structures we see today. The only intact historical block is the row of thirteen shops and apartments on the north side of First Street between San Pedro Street and Central Avenue. The U.S. Department of the Interior proclaimed this entire block to be a National Historic Landmark, a distinction it richly deserves.

Japanese American National Museum- Located in two buildings, one the former *Nishi Hongwanji Buddhist Temple* (Edgar Cline, 1925, remodeled 1992). 369 East First Street, corner of First Street and Central Avenue. The second, and larger, building, directly across Central Avenue is the new *Pavilion* (Hellmuth Obata and Kassabaum, 1999). Not only do both buildings contain exhibits about Japanese-American people and their role in American history, but both are architecturally strong structures in themselves. Hours: Tuesday through Sunday 10:00 a.m. to 5:00 p.m., Thursday 11:00 a.m. to 8:00 p.m. Closed Mondays. (213) 625-0414.

In 1942, Little Tokyo's citizens were rounded up and loaded onto buses on this corner, beginning their three-year internment in distant camps away from the Pacific Coast. Members of the temple used the building as storehouse for their household belongings during their imprisonment.

The museum sponsors a lecture and concert series and issues a quarterly calendar of its events. The museum's fine bookstore carries many works about Japanese life in America. It also sells a delightful range of gift items.

Noguchi Plaza/Japanese American Cultural Community Center (J.A.C.C.C.)- 244 South San Pedro Street. The circular red-brick plaza was designed by Isamu Noguchi who also created the sculptured stones, *To the Issei*, in 1984. Noguchi was born in Boyle Heights, next to East L.A., in 1904, of an Irish-American mother and a Japanese (*Issei*) father. One of America's most productive sculptors of stone and wood abstractions, here he positions huge carved rocks on a brick platform.

The J.A.C.C.C. was designed to combine the groups and activities that were formerly scattered among church and school rooms around the city. It contains a library, exhibition spaces, offices of social service agencies, and classrooms for teaching traditional Japanese arts–from flower arranging to dance. It is the location of Japanese festival celebrations such as *Hanamatsuri* (Buddha's birthday), Girls' Day and Boys' Day.

The *Japan America Theater* in the Cultural Center stages performances of traditional Japanese music and dance, contemporary plays about the Japanese-American experience, classical western music, and even karaoke. For information about the J.A.C.C.C., call (213) 628-2725. For the theater, call (213) 680-3700.

James Irvine Memorial Garden- Located next to the *Japanese American Cultural Community Center/Noguchi Plaza*. 244 South San Pedro Street, 1979. Japanese-American farmers in Orange County used to rent land from the Irvine Co. This exquisite garden was partially funded to commemorate that relationship. Native California and rare plants grow in a sunken garden alongside a three-part stream. The top of the stream is turbulent, suggesting the difficult times endured by the Issei. It then divides, symbolizing the divided loyalties of the Nisei during World War II. Hopes for the future are expressed in the stream's calm finish. You can look down on the garden from the plaza above. Better still, take the elevator inside the *Japanese American Cultural Community Center*. Go to the basement level, down a hallway, to a display explaining the garden and its iconography. You can then go directly into the garden for a stroll.

Japanese Village Plaza (a.k.a. Little Tokyo Plaza)- First Street between Central and San Pedro Streets. A shopping and restaurant complex designed to resemble a small Japanese village. Tile pictures and signs on either side of the fire watchtower frame an entranceway and tell the story of Little Tokyo's history.

Mitsuwa Plaza- Corner of Third and Alameda Streets. Three-story enclosed shopping mall containing restaurants, food markets, and retail and service shops. An animated clock tower stands near the second floor escalator entry; balls roll and click their way down two-rail channels. Hard to tell time by it, but it is mesmerizing. Little kids will enjoy the colorful play areas.

New Otani Hotel and Garden- (1977). First and Los Angeles Streets. This 448-room luxury hotel attracts a clientele of Japanese nationals, as do several stores next to the hotel and along Weller Court (Second and San Pedro Streets). Take an elevator from the Lobby to the fourth floor Garden Level, and walk out onto the lovely garden with a quiet stream, waterfall, and ponds. From the south edge of the garden, you can see a spectacular view of high rise office towers in Downtown's financial district. St. Vibiana's Cathedral is in the immediate foreground, just a block away.

The *New Otani* and its adjacent stores are branches of businesses whose headquarters are in Japan. The many banks here indicate Little Tokyo's importance as an offshoot of Japanese commerce as well as a community center for Japanese-American citizens.

Geffen Contemporary Museum of Art (formerly the Temporary Contemporary Museum of Art)- (1983). A branch of Museum of Contemporary Art (M.O.C.A.). The Geffen resides at 152 North Central Avenue, across the street from the Japanese American National Museum. An admission ticket also gets you into M.O.C.A. located eight blocks west on Bunker Hill. The building began life as a large warehouse, unrelated to the existence of Little Tokyo, but three years before M.O.C.A. was constructed on Bunker Hill, collectors and other members of L.A.'s modern art community converted it into a "temporary" art museum. Architect Frank Gehry designed the front entrance and interior partitions, ramps, and railings to frame exhibitions of modern art. The *Geffen* is especially suited for very large sculptures and installations that cannot fit into more conventional spaces such as those in M.O.C.A. When M.O.C.A. finally opened in 1986, the directors realized they would need the older museum to continue indefinitely. David Geffen is an entertainment mogul and art collector.

Fugetsu Do- A confectionery shop, 315 First Street. The oldest store in continuous operation in Little Tokyo. It was founded in 1903 by Seiichi Kito. His grandson, Brian Kito runs it today. The shop, originally on Weller Street, later was moved to the block where the Parker Center (L.A.P.D. headquarters) was built. It was moved again to this spot on First Street in the 1960s. The fortune cookie was created by

Seiichi Kito in this store (it is not a Chinese invention, but a Japanese-American one). Old photographs and cooking equipment used in the early days are displayed inside the front window. Traditional Japanese confections are unlike American pastries. The Japanese use *mochi* (pounded rice), bean paste, and other ingredients more subtly sweet than the refined sugar of American confections. Try a few!

Fugetsu Do is just one of the small, old shops on the north side of First Street between San Pedro Street and Central Avenue, an entire block designated a National Historic Landmark. Look into Anzen Hardware, 353 First Street, or Far East Cafe, 347 First Street. You can't find many turn-of-the-century blocks like this in Southern California. Redevelopment work strengthened and upgraded these evocative old structures.

Brunswig Square- (1936, remodeled by Reeves and Associates, 1986), 360 East Second Street. The Brunswig Drug Company was founded in 1887 and manufactured and distributed drugs from buildings still standing in the *El Pueblo Park,* just west of the *Pico House.* Later, the company built this structure, originally a warehouse, a few blocks from the older ones. Now beautifully refurbished in Art Deco style, this imposing building houses retail spaces, medical offices, and government facilities.

Higashi Hongwanji Buddhist Temple- 505 East Third Street (Kajima International, 1976). Elegant, imposing traditional design, but constructed in concrete rather than wood. If you take the *L.A. Conservancy* tour, you will see the gorgeous interior containing an altar, shrines of Buddha and the founder of the sect, and many ceremonial objects.

Jodosha Buddhist Temple- 442 East Third Street. Including L.A. extension of Bukkyo University.

Union Center for the Arts (formerly Union Church, 1922)- 120 North Judge John Aiso Street (extension of San Pedro Street). The building served originally both as a Japanese Protestant church for three congregations and as a community center. It is now remodeled as a theater, the home of the East West Players.

SHOPPING

If you're looking for Japanese kitchen appliances, dishes, decorative dolls, fans, lacquerware, or other household items, try:

Little Tokyo Arts & Gifts- 317 First Street. A real mom and pop store. Look around–you'll find lots of hidden treasures in this cluttered, homey little place.

Plaza Gift Center- 111 Japanese Village Plaza. This shop looks deceptively small from the outside, but it's bursting with stuff inside. It advertises the best deal on rice cookers in Little Tokyo. Invest in a bamboo back scratcher for only $1.39.

Rafu Bassan Inc.- 326 Second Street. A big, beautiful store with lots of lovely things to look at. Pretty porcelain, lacquerware, and glassware. All the cooking accessories you'll ever need, from bento boxes to spam sushi molds. Clocks with Japanese numerals, photo albums, and cookbooks. Buy a traffic safety amulet for the car you left at home.

Ryumondo- Located in the *Mitsuwa Plaza*, corner of Alameda and Third Streets, third floor. Gorgeous wood and lacquer ware. It's expensive, but good quality.

Bookstores

Little Tokyo bookstores carry both Japanese and English titles. You'll find cookbooks, children's books, guidebooks, history books, literature, teach-yourself-Japanese books, magazines, and, of course, *manga*, the comic books that are a Japanese obsession.

Nippon Book Company- in Japanese Village Plaza. First Street. A friendly family store with good variety. It also carries origami paper and Japanese stationery.

Asahiya- in Mitsuwa Plaza (corner of Alameda and Third Streets), first floor. Large selection. They carry some lovely photo books of Japan to admire at your leisure. Small CD section of current Japanese pop music.

Kinokuniya- Weller Court next to the *New Otani Hotel*. Huge store with comprehensive selection of books on Japan, origami and rice papers, stationery, CDs, language software, and videos. Will also special order books from Japan for you.

Souvenirs

There are many tourist shops with overpriced items catering largely to out-of-town and Japanese tourists. They have some very nice things, but better bargains could probably be found elsewhere. However, if you'd like to visit these shops, stroll down Onizuka Street and Japanese Village Plaza. It's fun to see what people are selling to foreign tourists these days. The more entertaining souvenir stops are:

Western Gift- 402 Honda Plaza. Wins the prize for largest Indian chief head for sale in Little Tokyo.

Olympic Shop- Onizuka Street. Take your picture with Bill Clinton and an Indian chief.

Supermarkets

Little Tokyo has two: The largest is inside *Mitsuwa Plaza* shopping mall at Third and Alameda Streets. Try also Enbun Market, in the middle of Japanese Village Plaza (#124), open daily.

Miscellaneous Stores

Marukyo- 448 Honda Plaza. Traditional Japanese clothing, including yukata (cotton kimonos), obi (sash), tabe (split-toe socks), and zori (slippers). Also, large and fluffy futons.

Michi- Second floor of Mitsuwa Plaza, Third and Alameda. Stickers, book bags, sweatshirts, albums, and school supplies decorated with the cuddly Japanese cartoon characters of Hello Kitty, KeroKeroKeroppi, Ahiru no Pekkle, and Pochacco. Cute for kids.

L.A. Sing-Along- First floor of Mitsuwa Plaza. Karaoke CDs and laser discs. For living room lizards. Sorry monolinguals– Japanese only.

Note: The Los Angeles Conservancy offers informative guided walking tours of Little Tokyo one Saturday each month. Call (213) 623-CITY for information.

SIGHTS

Symbols and Signs

Manekineko- Beckoning cat. In shop windows or just inside doorways, you'll often see stylized pottery figures of a cat with one front paw held up against its ear as though greeting the passerby. The other arm usually holds a gold coin or two. This icon is a traditional mascot bringing good luck and inviting guests to come inside and spend some money. Variety stores in Little Tokyo sell these charms in various sizes. Take one home and see if it works for you.

Fire Watchtower (hinomi-yagura)- (David Hyun and Associates, 1979). First Street entrance to *Japanese Village Plaza*. Watchtowers of this design were used in Japanese villages by fire-fighting companies to alert everyone to fires in their areas. Watchmen would ring a huge bell once for distant fires or repeatedly for closer ones. Because such towers marked villages, why not use this traditional structure to identify the northern portal of this shopping and restaurant complex suggesting a small Japanese village? Tile pictures and signs on the walls on either side of the watchtower tell the story of Little Tokyo's history.

PUBLIC ART

To the Issei- (Noguchi, Isamu, 1984) Sculpture, stone. Located in the Plaza designed by Noguchi himself. Huge stones on a brick platform near the east side of the plaza.

Ellison Onizuka- (Hernandez, Joseph E., 1990) Bas relief. Onizuka Street runs diagonally north from the corner of Second and San Pedro Streets. The work honors the first Japanese-American astronaut, who was killed with other crew members in the tragic accident of the *Challenger* space shuttle in 1986. His cheerful smile seems to reassure viewers of this image of a national hero.

Friendship Knot- (Tajiri, Shinkichi, 1981) Sculpture, fiberglass. Stands at entrance to Astronaut Ellison Onizuki Street at corner Second and San Pedro Streets. Clever version of a recognizable symbol of affiliation.

Sontuko (Kanjiro) Ninomiya- (Hannya, Junichiro, 1983) Bronze sculpture of a legendary peasant/scholar (1787-1856) carrying a bundle of sticks while reading a book. A marker indicates that the sculpture is dedicated to the Issei pioneers and that it "symbolizes the treasured values of perseverance, integrity and social consciousness."

North entrance of *Japanese Village Plaza* ceramic mural (Matsukuma, J., 1980). Photographs on tiles. A statement on the wall reads, "America is a continuing story of breaking from the past. The late nineteenth century boats bringing Japanese immigrants to the United States carried a cargo of ambition, industry, and energy."

Toyo Miyatake's Camera- (Nagasawa, Nobuho, 1993) On sidewalk, corner of First Street and Central, in front of Japanese American National Museum. Sculpture of the camera used by studio photographer Miyatake when he was interned in the wartime camp at Manzanar. He built a box to hold a lens that he had smuggled into the camp. After dark, this sculpture/camera becomes a projector showing his photographs on a screen in the Museum window. Miyatake's prewar studio was located across First Street from Fugetsu Do, but it is now gone, replaced by a small parking lot.

CONVENIENCES AND NECESSITIES

Public Rest Rooms

New Otani Hotel- First and Los Angeles Streets. First floor near lobby.

Mitsuwa Plaza Shopping Mall- Third and Alameda Streets. Second floor near front escalators.

Public Telephones

Sumitomo Bank- Corner of San Pedro and First Streets.

Japanese Village Plaza- Between First and Second Streets.

Mitsuwa Plaza- At Third and Alameda Streets.

Bank of California- 231 East Second Street, near the Japanese Village Plaza.

ATMs

Pacific Heritage Bank- 324 East First Street.

Sumitomo Bank- Corner of San Pedro and First Streets.

Japanese Village Plaza- Between First and Second Streets.

Mitsuwa Plaza- Third and Alameda Streets.

Bank of California- 321 East Second Street.

Places to Sit

Noguchi Plaza in front of the **Japanese American Cultural Community Center-** Hard benches. 244 South San Pedro Street.

Sumitomo Bank- Stone benches. Corner of San Pedro Street and First Street.

Onizuka Street- Concrete benches.

Japanese Village Plaza- Wood deck of band shell in center. Between First and Second Streets.

Mitsuwa Plaza- Third and Alameda Streets, many wooden benches.

Pharmacy

Kyodo Pharmacy- 420 East Third Street. Open Monday through Friday from 9:30 a.m. to 5:30 p.m.; on Saturday from 9:30 a.m. to 3:30 p.m.; and is closed Sunday.

RESTAURANTS

Price Guide to average lunch entrees:

$ = $3.00 - $8.00 $$$ = $13.00 - $17.00
$$ = $9.00 - $12.00 $$$$ = $18.00+

First Street

Aoi Restaurant- 331 First Street. Small place for lunches on week days, dinners every night except Tuesday. ($)

Koraku- Los Angeles Street between First and Second Streets. Ramen, croquettes, teriyaki, and typical Tokyo cheap, fast food. Brightly lighted, wood tables with orange plastic tops, and orange plastic bar; booths in back; cheerful. Ramen prepared behind the counter, Japanese style. Pleasant bilingual waiters. ($)

Nirvana- 314 First Street. New restaurant with art deco decor. American and Japanese menu. Open daily except Sunday.

Tokyo Kaikan- 225 South San Pedro Street. A well-known restaurant in Little Tokyo. Separate sushi and shabu-shabu rooms, as well as a general dining area and a bar. Areas are separated by bamboo walls. Extensive menu includes shabu-shabu, sushi, sashimi, teriyaki, tempura, udon, sukiyaki, nabe, and ton-katsu, as well as some tempting appetizers. The staff is cordial. A special occasion possibility. Monday through Friday lunches, Monday through Saturday dinners until 10:00 p.m., closed Sunday.($$$)

Mr. Ramen- 341 First Street. A good possibility for a quick meal. Offers ramen, curry rice, tempura, teriyaki, gyooza, and includes a vegetarian menu. Busy at weekday lunch times. Open 11:30 a.m. to 11:30 p.m. Closed Monday. ($)

Suehiro Restaurant- 337 First Street. Many patrons come from L.A. Police Department and City Hall. Sashimi, deep-fried tempura dishes, Chinese style stir-fried beef and vegetables, noodles. Try katsu don-pork or chicken cutlets cooked in a bowl with eggs and onion. Sunday through Thursday from 11:00 a.m. to 1:00 a.m. and Friday and Saturday from 11:00 a.m. to 3:00 a.m. (213) 626-9132 ($)

Sushi Amai- Small sushi place in the Japanese American National Museum building, 359 First Street. Boiled fish, tempura, and teriyaki chicken. Tuesday through Saturday lunches and dinners to 10:00 p.m. Sunday dinner only. ($)

Usui- 343 First Street. Popular weekdays at noon. Serves nabe, sashimi, sukiyaki, tempura, and teriyaki. Booths and a sushi bar. Daily except Sunday. ($$)

Far East Cafe- (closed) First Street between San Pedro Street and Central Avenue. Big neon sign in front says "Chop Suey." Chinese food adapted to Japanese tastes. An old building, it has been used as a setting for movies. Just after World War II, this was the only place in Little Tokyo that served rice; locals can remember relying for a time on a cheap dish of rice and minced pork called homyu. The building was damaged in the January 1994 earthquake and remains closed at the time of this writing.

Mitsuru Sushi Bar & Grill- 316 First Street. Specializes in sushi. Also serves western breakfasts, sandwiches, and noodles at lunch; and teriyaki, tempura, beef, and noodles at dinner. Young, sporty atmosphere, and a hangout for local citizens–a good sign. Open for all meals, daily. (213) 626-4046 ($- $$)

Señor Fish- 422 East First Street. Across from Pavilion. Tacos and fish dishes. Popular lunch place. ($$)

Japanese Village Plaza (Fire Tower Mall) – Entrances on First and Second Streets between San Pedro Street and Central Avenue

Rascals- #103. Just under the fire watch tower. Fast food. Mostly outdoor tables. (213) 687-4811. Daily ($)

Tokyo Gardens- #333. On Second Street corner. Sandwiches, udon, sukiyaki, sashimi, teriyaki, tempura, vegetable dishes, beer. Brown plastic tables and chairs. Like a coffee shop, but with Japanese food. A local hangout. Daily except Sunday. 8:00 a.m. to 10:00 p.m. ($)

Al Mercato- #137. Japanese and Italian! Pastas, meat, and seafood. Lunch and dinner. Closed Sunday (213) 626-6967.

Shabu-Shabu House- #127. Serves shabu-shabu, a fun dish to eat. Very popular with both young and old crowd. Round bar with high stools. Boiling broth shared by every other person. Brightly lit, cheerful. Closed Monday. ($)

Frying Fish- #120. Emphasizes sushi, but they also have tempura. Buy two sushi on a plate for $1.30 to $1.80, or in pre-arranged boxes called bento. Sushi plates rotate on a conveyer belt, and you pick off the plates you want. You might expect to eat five to seven plates. Popular with young people. Round bar and high stool arrangement typical of Japan's sushi and ramen places. Daily 11:00 a.m. to 10:00 p.m. ($) to ($$)

Mikawaya- #123. This sweet shop serves up traditional Japanese confections made of mochi (pounded rice), as well as ice cream, sodas, and iced tea and coffee. A place to relax and take a rest from trotting about the mall. Sunday through Friday 9:30 a.m. to 7:00 p.m., Saturday 9:30 a.m. to 8:00 p.m. ($)

Mitsuru Cafe- #117. The main attraction here is the imagawayaki, made fresh in their front window while you watch. Imagawayaki are made of a pancake-like dough with a sweet bean filling. These are delicious when piping hot, fresh from the griddle. You can also get a snack of yakitori, shumai, tempura, or egg rolls. Daily, lunch and dinner to 9:00 p.m. ($)

Oiwake- east side, up stairs of parking structure. Upon entering Oiwake, the first thing you see is a tranquil fountain playing over a bed of rocks. The next is the giant-screen television around the corner. Oiwake offers not only reasonably priced meals, but also karaoke to go with your dinner. The menu includes noodles and combination plates of sushi, sashimi, and tempura. Daily except Monday, 11:00 a.m. to 2:00 a.m. ($)

Rokudan of Kobe- #106. Attracts a young professional crowd on weekend evenings. They offer a variety of foods: gyooza, tempura, shabu-shabu, sukiyaki, and noodles. Monday through Sunday 12:00 p.m. to 10:00 p.m. (213) 625-7444. ($$)

Oomasa- corner with First Street. Cheerful and brightly lighted with a sushi bar and booths. Caters to a diverse crowd. A good choice for families, groups of friends, and young couples. Offers noodles, tempura, sushi, sashimi, teriyaki and combination plates. 11:30 a.m. to 1:00 a.m. every day except Tuesday. ($$)

Hibachi BBQ- #135. Long, narrow restaurant, with waiters bustling back and forth between the booths. Serves Korean barbecue of pork, chicken, or beef. Open daily from 11:00 a.m. to 10:00 p.m. ($)

Cafe Focus- Little Tokyo Plaza, second floor. Just like a Tokyo western–style coffee shop. Serves coffee, sandwiches, steaks, spaghetti, ton-katsu, and desserts. Reserved atmosphere with modern furniture. Karaoke. ($$)

> **Note:** Getting sushi by the plate is fun. It can be more expensive, but you can get repeats of what you like and have more control over your selections.

Second Street –
between San Pedro Street and Central Avenue

Teishokuya- 345 Second Street. Combination plates. ($)

Sushi Komasa- 351 Second Street. They serve sushi, udon, donburi, combinations. Lunches and dinners. Daily except Monday. ($)

Kokekokko- 203 Central Boulevard (Restaurant name imitates the sound of a crowing rooster.) Serves grilled chicken pieces. Seating at counter or tables. A 1995 review by the L.A. Times suggests ordering the set course dinner. Dinners only. Open daily except Sunday. ($$$)

Mandarin Deli Restaurant- 356 Second Street. Branch of restaurant chain in Chinatown and Anaheim. "Noodles rule," as a *Times* review has it. Lunches and dinners. On Sundays the restaurant is closed. ($)

Honda Plaza –
Central Avenue between Second and Third Streets

Murasaki- A good place to go if the kids are clamoring for hamburgers. Murasaki has fast food, Japanese and American style: noodles, tempura, and other quick snacks as well as the basic burger. Order at the counter McDonald's style, and sit in plastic booths. Daily, all meals. Closes at 7:00 p.m. ($)

Sushi-Gen- Walk in and the smell of sushi smacks you. Brightly lighted and bustling with booths and a sushi bar. Full on weekday at noon with business people and families. ($$)

Mitsuwa Plaza –
Corner of Third and Alameda Streets

Mifune- First floor. Specializes in soba and udon. Pleasant atmosphere, low-lit, and wood tables. Right next to the Yaohan supermarket. Daily 11:00 a.m. to 9:00 p.m. ($)

Hanaichi Monme- Third floor. Serves up ramen and its tasty accompaniment, gyooza. Popular with young shoppers in the mall. They also have treats such as shaved ice with sweet beans. Daily 11:30 a.m. to 8:30 p.m. ($)

Issen Joki- Third floor. Serves udon, ton-katsu, yaki-tori, and soba, in a more subdued atmosphere than its next door neighbor, Hanaichi Monme. Daily except Monday, lunches and dinners until 9:00 p.m. ($)

Coaster- Third floor. A nice family place to go if someone does not want to eat Japanese food. Serves teriyaki, fried shrimp, hamburgers, and sandwiches in a brightly lit, blond wood table atmosphere. Weekday breakfasts; daily (except Thursday) lunches until 4:00 p.m.; Saturday 9:00 a.m. to 7:00 p.m., Sunday 9:00 a.m. to 6:00 p.m. ($)

Lauren- Third floor. Spaghetti, combinations, and children's dishes. Daily except Thurs. 11:30 a.m. to 9:00 p.m. ($)

Yodo-ya- Third floor. The largest range of food among the restaurants in the mall. Offers soba, udon, teriyaki, sashimi, and tempura. Quiet and pleasant atmosphere. Daily lunches and dinners until 9:00 p.m. ($$)

Shibucho- Third floor. Quiet, removed from the bustle of the mall. Specializes in sushi. Daily lunches and dinners. ($)

New Otani Hotel –
Corner of First and Los Angeles Streets

Azalea- American and European style, sandwiches, salads, fish, and pasta. Customers are mostly Japanese business people. Lovely cool cream decor, flowers on tables. Daily, continuous service 6:00 a.m. to 11:00 p.m. ($$)

Thousand Cranes- Richly elegant atmosphere; tables overlooking a lovely garden view, tatami rooms for privacy. Menu includes sushi, sashimi, tempura, teriyaki, hibachi, ochazuke, sukiyaki, and shabu-shabu. Separate sushi bar and tempura bar. Another special occasion possibility. Monday through Friday all meals. Dinners only Saturday and Sunday. ($$$$)

Garden Grill- Serves beef, seafood, and vegetables cooked on a grill at your table. Also overlooks the garden. Caters to business lunch crowd, as well as hotel patrons. Monday through Friday lunches; dinners every day until 9:30 p.m. ($$$$)

Akasaka Hanten- Onizuka Street, Second level in fountain court. Chinese food served the way Japanese do it in Japan: fried rice, dumplings, sweet and sour, and so forth. ($)

Curry House- Onizuka Street, Second level in New Otani Hotel fountain court. This is the place to get kare raisu, thick curries spooned over a bed of rice, a modern day Japanese staple. Also serve spaghetti and salads. Popular. Quick service. ($)

Daisuke- Onizuka Street, Second level in New Otani Hotel fountain court. Specializes in soba and udon. Informal atmosphere, brown plastic tables and chairs, and paper lanterns overhead. Attracts young people. ($)

Food Glossary

gyooza - The Japanese version of Chinese pot-stickers. Usually stuffed with meat, but on occasion they are vegetarian. Make an excellent accompaniment with ramen.

hibachi - Meat and vegetables grilled at your table. Not only tasty, but also a good show.

kaiseki - A full meal of several different dishes thoughtfully and gracefully prepared and presented. Traditionally the foods of the tea ceremony.

miso soup - A fish-base broth with cubes of tofu in it that you can chase around the bowl with your chopsticks. A delicious staple of the Japanese diet.

nabe - A steaming potful of noodles, meat and vegetables. A hearty meal, good for a cold day.

noodles - Three basic varieties, all good for a hot, quick, inexpensive and filling meal. Eat them with chopsticks and make loud slurping noises; it's not considered rude.

ramen - Thin Chinese egg noodles served in a strong broth with vegetables and slices of meat or tempura.

soba - Thin buckwheat noodles served in broth with tempura and vegetables, or in a basket with a separate dipping sauce.

sashimi - Raw fish, plain and simple, eaten dipped in soy sauce; additional wasabi optional. An acquired taste for most people, but delicious once you are accustomed to it. You can also eat the shredded white stuff they serve with the sashimi–it's shredded daikon, a mild Japanese radish. Dip the daikon in soy sauce too. Sashimi comes with rice and miso soup.

shabu-shabu - Vegetables, noodles, and thinly sliced beef served raw on platters. The diner picks up the food with chopsticks and swishes it in a pot of boiling broth to cook it, thereby making a "shabu-shabu" sound. This is a good, healthy meal, and fun to eat.

continued...

sukiyaki - A tasty, slightly sweet dish of meat and vegetables, usually served with a raw egg in the center. Comes with rice.

sushi - Raw fish, vegetables, or sweetened, cooked egg wrapped in seaweed with rice. The green paste that comes on the side and may be hiding inside your sushi is wasabi, a very hot horseradish that clears the sinuses. Stir a little into your soy sauce for extra flavor. Sushi can be eaten with fingers or chopsticks, and should be dipped in soy sauce. Sushi can be ordered in pre-arranged selections at your table or by the plate at the bar.

tempura - Shrimp and/or vegetables dipped in light batter and deep fried. Served with a dipping sauce and rice. Good option for vegetarians.

teriyaki - Fish, chicken, or meat grilled in a tasty sauce and served with rice. A good choice for finicky western tastes.

ton-katsu - A pork cutlet served with a sauce over rice.

udon - thick, white, chewy noodles, served like soba and ramen.

yakisoba - Fried noodles with vegetables and meat. A tasty, slightly salty Japanese fast food.

HISTORY

A Community of Memory: The story of Little Tokyo, as seen from its buildings and streets, is the clearest to comprehend of all the Downtown districts. It has continuity with its past, especially visible on the north side of First Street which is an Historic Landmark. Its ethnic history is unbroken, except for the experience of its Japanese and Japanese-American residents during the Second World War–three years of isolation and imprisonment in distant encampments, torn from their work and property, and denied the dignity and rights of citizenship. Still, after the war, some of the former residents returned, and here they stay.

The first Japanese immigrants to America were recruited by sugar farmers and railroad builders to work as cheap laborers in the cane fields of Hawaii or laying track in California. A few of these early immigrants filtered into Southern California, only to arrive here in the midst of an enormous surge of Anglo migrations from mid-America–the "Boom of the Eighties." In 1885, a Japanese ex-seaman called Kame started a modest restaurant on the corner of Los Angeles and First Streets. Twenty-four other Japanese *wataridori* (sojourners) soon found their way to the neighborhood, and a few Japanese businesses were opened in the 1890s: bamboo shops, tobacco shops, dry goods stores, and American-style restaurants. A diversified economy began among the growing population of *Issei* (first generation).

The migration process continued as a sequence of steady Japanese advances in the face of constant hostility and legal prohibitions imposed by the Anglo community. By 1900, more than a hundred Japanese people were bunched into the East First Street neighborhood, already anxious about the surrounding racial antagonisms. In 1903, as California's railroad expansion was concluding, more than 2,000 Japanese migrated south from San Francisco. The land surrounding Los Angeles was still rural, and Japanese farmers settled in the flatlands of Gardena, the San Gabriel Valley, and as far away as the Imperial Valley. They skillfully devised new techniques for increasing the yields of cash crops and new strategies for marketing their produce.

First Street Time Line

A delightful art project has appeared on the north side of First Street whose buildings constitute a *National Historic Landmark*. Designed by Sheila Lebrant de Bretteville (see listing for "Biddy Mason Park", in "Chapter 3 – Broadway District"), the history of Little Tokyo is represented in the sidewalk–a 1,000 foot-long strip with brass letters. It identifies the people who occupied each address on First Street over the sixty years from 1890 to World War II.

In Little Tokyo, residents developed a more urban economy. The oldest continuing business there is the *Fugetsu Do Confectionery*, now on First Street, which started in 1903. The same year saw the publication of the first issue of *Rafu Shimpo*, a Japanese and English newspaper still published today.

L.A.'s Japanese population jumped to about 10,000 in 1906 when the San Francisco Earthquake drove masses south. More than 30,000 Japanese migrated to the United States the following year. But Anglo opposition continued, and, in 1908, a "Gentlemen's Agreement" was struck with the Japanese government which curtailed further immigration, except for the wives and children of men already here. Still the Japanese came, and still they were met by virulent antagonism.

The first settlers were overwhelmingly male (3,200 men in 1905 vs. only 142 women), but soon women began arriving in large numbers. Some brides-to-be came from the villages from which the men had come, chosen by go-betweens or by other family members. Others were "picture brides," selected by their future husbands from printed advertisements.

In 1909, farmers of Japanese, Chinese, Russians, and American ancestry opened the *City Market of Los Angeles* near the railroad tracks at Ninth and San Pedro Streets, initiating a wholesale district that survives to this day. The variety of Japanese enterprises continued to grow, and soon there were forty businesses in Little Tokyo and three hundred and sixty elsewhere in Los Angeles. In time, first and second generation Japanese farmers and wholesalers were producing and marketing seventy-five percent of all the fresh produce consumed in Los Angeles.

However, their successes only increased the hostility of Anglos, who kept pushing a long series of anti-Japanese immigration laws, first by the California legislature and then by the U.S. Congress. For example, in California, the *Alien Land Act of 1913* stated that aliens ineligible to become citizens could not own land for more than three years. This unmistakably applied most directly to Asians rather than to immigrant whites or people of African descent. In 1924, the U.S.

Congress passed the *Second Exclusion Act*, aimed explicitly at Japanese people, severely limiting their further immigration and cutting it off entirely to women—even wives of American citizens.

In response to this pervasive animosity, the Japanese formed their own cooperatives, hospitals, churches, Japanese-language schools, and other organizations. Meetings and classes were held in such places as the old *Union Church*, (now *Union Center for the Arts*) 120 North San Pedro Street. The people of Little Tokyo credit this social and economic cohesion with bringing them through the Great Depression with lower unemployment rates (only five to ten percent) than were suffered elsewhere (twenty-five percent in 1932).

In 1934, Little Tokyo's merchants invented *Nisei Week*, a summer festival consisting of a parade, entertainment, fashion shows, sales, and other promotions. *Nisei Week* is still the largest single attraction of Little Tokyo.

The neighborhood also had its shady side. *The Tokyo Club* was a notorious gambling spot and a center for Bosses Yasuda and Yamatoda. It competed with similar joints in Chinatown until the late 1930s.

December 7, 1941: Soon after Pearl Harbor was attacked, FBI agents arrested Little Tokyo's merchants, newspaper editors, and other community leaders. The Army recommended that, "all alien subjects...of enemy nations" be removed to a "Zone of the Interior". President Roosevelt signed *Executive Order 9066* on February 19, 1942 which removed "all persons of Japanese ancestry" from their homes and property. The order applied to both Japanese-born and American-born Japanese people.

Thus began an exodus of six thousand people from Little Tokyo and twelve thousand from other locations in Southern California. They were first assembled on the corner of First Street and Central Avenue outside the building that is now the Japanese American National Museum. They were sent for a brief stay at the Santa Anita Racetrack, and then shipped to ten remote prison camps in the interior deserts and beyond.

Whole families had to live in sixteen-by-twenty-foot rooms in tar-papered barracks for the next three years. Of the 110,000 people of Japanese ancestry in ten camps, two-thirds were American citizens.

The war quickly brought huge masses of Anglos and African-Americans to Southern California to take jobs in defense and construction industries. Swarming through Union Station, just three blocks away, and looking frantically for housing, African-American workers from the South and Midwest discovered the recently emptied buildings and homes of Little Tokyo–and moved in. Now called *Bronzeville*, the area sprouted nightclubs and pool halls, and became a center for Big Band entertainment. As the war wound down in mid-1945, the Japanese were finally released from their internment. Many feared a hostile reception from the new residents in Bronzeville, but others confidently returned and reopened businesses. The African-Americans soon left Little Tokyo to find housing in South Central L.A.

Wartime Losses

The wartime evacuation and its aftermath left a widely dispersed Japanese-American population. Many moved to suburbs, others moved away to cities across the country. Having lost their property and businesses, most now became employees of Anglo firms. Only a tiny fraction of their wealth was ever returned. The federal government paid an average claim of only $1,388.00 in 1942 and another of $20,000.00 in 1988.

Japanese-Americans speak of a cultural trait, *shigataganai*, the ability to persevere in the face of events they cannot control. This spirit helped bring them through the years of oppression, wartime evacuation, and the struggle to succeed as American citizens.

Most of the buildings of Little Tokyo today are new, the products of a prolonged "urban renewal" crusade by City planners and the Community Redevelopment Agency (C.R.A.). Except for the row of buildings along the north side of First Street, most other old structures have been demolished.

First, a block across from the old *Union Church* on North San Pedro Street was razed to make room for Parker Center, headquarters of the L.A. Police Department. Then in the seventies and eighties, other buildings were demolished to make way for the new malls, banks, and plazas built with federal subsidies. Residents of Little Tokyo had hoped the city would try to enhance the residential community and put most of its efforts into building more housing for older people. However, the City favored projects that would earn new tax revenues–office buildings, hotels, and shopping malls.

In 1972, a group of thirty of Japan's largest banks and corporations developed plans to build a luxury hotel in Little Tokyo to be followed by other Japanese institutions. Locals worried that they would be forced out of business by large scale developments favoring corporations based in Japan.

We see today the results of a mixture of these several interests. On the one hand, the sixteen-story *Little Tokyo Towers*, offers 300 apartment units for Issei and Nisei elders (just east of the *Japanese American Cultural and Community Center*). On the other hand, the *New Otani Hotel*, the department stores on Weller Court, Yaohan Plaza, and other buildings still being planned, provide profits for Japanese corporations as well as tax revenues for the City of Los Angeles.

The 1990 Census reported that only six hundred eighty-five people of Japanese ancestry lived in the district (along with eighty Koreans and twenty-eight Chinese). It follows that the social and economic viability of Little Tokyo rests largely on Japanese-Americans who live in the suburbs but who return occasionally to buy Japanese goods and enjoy a favorite restaurant and also on tourists from Japan who prefer familiar hotel accommodations to more westernized ones.

PROSPECTS

The recession that hit Southern California in the mid-1990s slowed down a number of Little Tokyo's businesses, just as it did in other Downtown districts. However, things are happening here, and there is energy and optimism.

With the splendid *Japanese American National Museum*, and the continued successes of other cultural institutions like the *Japan America Theater*, Little Tokyo is a wonderful place to visit. It has an amazing variety of stores, restaurants, parks, and streetscapes. Little Tokyo is accessible to the growing numbers of suburban Metrolink riders.

The C.R.A. and other planners want to boost the number of residents and give more variety to the area. A proposed *First Street North* project was to have been built on Temple Street just west of the *Geffen Museum*. It would have created high-rise government offices, a new hotel, and low-income housing. However, Mayor Richard Riordan, seeing a greater need to recycle the historic buildings on Broadway, decided in early 1994 to steer funding away from Little Tokyo. So *First Street North* is on hold. However, a new C.R.A. apartment project, Casa Heiwa (architects Togawa and Smith, 1996) was built near Third and Los Angeles Streets. It houses seniors and families.

The Metropolitan Transit Authority is planning an extension of the Red Line Subway from Union Station to East Los Angeles, with a stop in Little Tokyo. But the station would be located at Third and Santa Fe Streets, five blocks east of today's center of activity. The *Downtown Strategic Plan* suggests that the Blue Line be extended north and east from Seventh and Figueroa Streets to a station to be located at Second Street and Central Avenue, thence north to Union Station.

Two other projects are being contemplated at the time of this writing: The *First Street South Plaza* would build a mix of office buildings, condos, and low-income housing on the Southeast corner of First and Alameda. And a Dutch firm wants to build a major mixed-use development on the block just east of the *Japanese American National Museum* and The *Geffen Contemporary Museum of Art*. Again, much depends on the future vigor of the economy to judge whether these projects are worth the financial risk–but they sound terrific.

A block west of Little Tokyo, on 2nd and Main Streets, developer Tom Gilmore recently acquired St. Vibiana's Cathedral just as the new Cathedral of Our Lady of the Angels was being constructed on Grand Avenue. St. Vibiana's and its outlying buildings will be converted into apartments and a performing arts complex.

Fanciful floral-based crane motifs by Hokusai

Lower Financial District

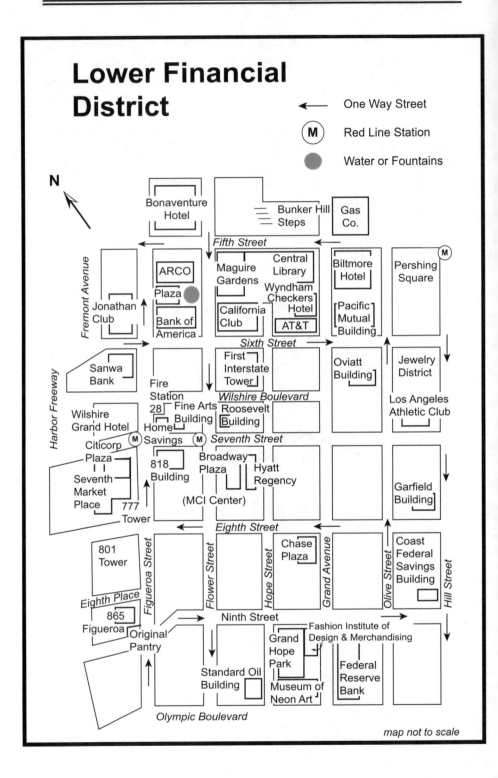

← One Way Street

(M) Red Line Station

● Water or Fountains

N

Bonaventure Hotel

Bunker Hill Steps

Gas Co.

Fifth Street

Fremont Avenue

ARCO Plaza

Maguire Gardens

Central Library

Biltmore Hotel

Pershing Square (M)

Jonathan Club

Bank of America

California Club

Wyndham Checkers Hotel

AT&T

Pacific Mutual Building

Sixth Street

Harbor Freeway

Sanwa Bank

Fire Station 28

First Interstate Tower

Oviatt Building

Jewelry District

Wilshire Boulevard

Los Angeles Athletic Club

Wilshire Grand Hotel

Fine Arts Building

Roosevelt Building

Home

Citicorp (M) Savings (M) Seventh Street

Plaza

818 Building

Broadway Plaza

Hyatt Regency

Seventh Market Place

777 Tower

(MCI Center)

Garfield Building

Eighth Street

801 Tower

Figueroa Street

Flower Street

Hope Street

Chase Plaza

Grand Avenue

Olive Street

Coast Federal Savings Building

Hill Street

Eighth Place

865 Figueroa

Original Pantry

Ninth Street

Fashion Institute of Design & Merchandising

Standard Oil Building

Grand Hope Park

Museum of Neon Art

Federal Reserve Bank

Olympic Boulevard

map not to scale

10. Lower Financial District & Grand Hope Park

This district lies south of Bunker Hill, between Olive Street and the Harbor Freeway. Along with its northern neighbor, this is the heart of the business community of Southern California. An assortment of new and old office buildings, hotels, restaurants, and department stores, it contains many reminders of the time when Downtown was a shopping destination as well as a business center. The principal attractions here today are the *Central Library*, on Fifth and Flower and the confluence of shops, restaurants, hotels, and office towers around Seventh and Figueroa.

Grand Hope Park (a.k.a. South Park)- Grand Hope Park lies on the southern edge of the Lower Financial District, south of Seventh Street. It is a smaller neighborhood with a mixture of residences, stores, offices, schools, churches, restaurants, and the cheerful new park itself–at Ninth and Hope Streets. Only a couple of blocks apart, these sub-districts are psychologically disconnected today. However, city officials plan to convert Hope Street into a pedestrian *avanida*, running south from the Central Library to Grand Hope Park and continuing to the *L.A. Convention Center*. Meanwhile, you can visit the park for which this neighborhood is named, the *Fashion Institute of Design and Merchandising*, a museum in the Federal Reserve Bank, the historic and beautiful *Embassy Theater*, and the recently expanded *Los Angeles Convention Center*.

GETTING THERE FROM UNION STATION

Red Line Subway: Take the Red Line from Union Station to Seventh Street/Metro Center Station (free with your Metrolink ticket or $1.35 without it). Ride the escalator up to the Figueroa Street exit.

DASH bus, Route B: From Union Station, walk across Alameda Street and find the DASH sign at the curb half way up the slope of El Pueblo Historic Monument (Ride free with your Metrolink ticket or $.25 without it). Exit the bus at Flower and Seventh Streets.

DRIVING AND PARKING

From the north: Take the Pasadena Freeway (I-110) south to the Ninth Street exit. Follow the curve left to Ninth Street. After four blocks, turn left onto Hope Street. Parking lots are on Ninth Street or Eighth Street near Hope Street.

From the east: Take the 101 Freeway west, then the transition to the Harbor Freeway South (I-110). Drive to the Ninth Street exit. Follow the curve left to Ninth Street. After four blocks, turn left onto Hope Street. Parking lots are on Ninth Street or Eighth Street near Hope Street.

From the south: Drive north on the Harbor Freeway (I-110) to the Ninth Street exit. Turn right onto Ninth Street. After four blocks, turn left onto Hope Street. Parking lots are on Ninth Street or Eighth Street near Hope Street.

From the west: Take the Santa Monica Freeway (I-10) to the Harbor Freeway North (I-110). Drive to the Ninth Street exit. Turn right onto Ninth Street. After four blocks, turn left onto Hope Street. Parking lots are on Ninth Street or Eighth Street near Hope Street.

From the north-west, Hollywood, and the San Fernando Valley: Take the Hollywood Freeway (I-101 East). Go through the transition to the Harbor Freeway South (I-110). Drive to the Ninth Street exit. Follow curve left to Ninth Street. After four blocks, turn left onto Hope Street. Parking lots are on Ninth Street or Eighth Street near Hope Street.

Best Parking Deal in Town

If you own a *Los Angeles Public Library library card* (not a *County* library card) and you can begin your visit after 3:00 p.m. on weekdays or any time on weekends, drive to the lot under the Maguire Gardens (524 South Flower Street). Only $1.00 flat rate!

WHO'S THERE?

This district, along with Bunker Hill, contains the largest concentration of corporate headquarters in Southern California. Sixty-one company headquarters are located Downtown, solidly ahead of Santa Monica (eighteen), Woodland Hills (eighteen), Century City (ten), Beverly Hills (eight), and Pasadena (seven). [*Los Angeles Times*, 4-25-95.]

You'll find office workers, tourists, shop clerks, delivery runners, shoppers, and even some nearby apartment dwellers. Several hotels provide a supply of visitors. Two of L.A.'s most exclusive businessmen's clubs are located a block apart in elegant older buildings–the *California Club* on Flower and Sixth Streets and the *Jonathan Club* on Figueroa and Sixth Streets. College students add to the mix. In Grand Hope Park, aspiring entrepreneurs are trained at the *Fashion Institute of Design and Merchandising*, and groups of students attending the nearby University of Southern California occupy apartments in this area.

WHAT'S THERE FOR THE VISITOR?

Shopping

Here are the remnants of Seventh Street's glory days as a shopping district. Flagship department stores were once plentiful along Seventh Street. The buildings survive, but their functions have been changed. *Robinson's* is now empty, *Bullock's* is a mass of jewelry stalls, and *Barker Brothers* is now an office building.

The only major department stores on Seventh Street now are *Macy's*, formerly *The Broadway*, inside a plaza (700 West Seventh Street), and *Robinson's/May* in the Seventh Market Place, Figueroa Street, between Seventh and Eighth Streets.

Macy's Plaza- formerly *Broadway Plaza*, is an enclosed shopping mall anchored by Macy's Department Store and the Hyatt Regency Los Angeles. Macy's Plaza also contains a fine food court and specialty shops on two levels:

Women's Apparel	Specialty Shops	
Casual Corner	Carol's Hallmark	Smoke 'N' Stuff
Express	De Sumarak Jewelers	Sunglass Hut
Lady Footlocker	Fleur de Blum	U.S. Postal Service
Lerner New York	General Nutrition Ctr.	Waldenbooks
Victoria's Secret	Jewelry Pavilion	W.H. Smith Gift Shop
Men's Apparel	Monte Carlo Boutique	
Plaza Suit & Tux Co.	Radio Shack	

Seventh Market Place- An indoor/outdoor shopping mall anchored by *Robinson's-May*. Monday through Friday 10:00 a.m. to 7:00 p.m., Saturday 10:00 a.m. to 6:00 p.m., Sunday 11:00 a.m. to 5:00 p.m. Other stores here are:

Women's Apparel	Specialty Shops
Ann Taylor	Paper Solutions
Koko	Godiva Chocolatier

ARCO Plaza- Another enclosed shopping mall. This one is buried underground at Flower Street between Fifth and Sixth Streets. (Monday through Friday 8:00 a.m. to 6:00 p.m. Mostly closed on weekends.) The only unusual store here is the *U.S. Government Printing Office Book Store* located on Level C. Otherwise, ARCO Plaza shops include:

Level B:

AM/PM Mini Market	gift shop	Radio Shack
Atkinson Photography	Hallmark	Rice Garden
Back Rub	Just Juice	Salads 2000
barber shop	Koko	Sears Shoe Repair
cleaners	Mrs. Fields Cookies	tuxedo store
dental office	optometrist	Wall St. Deli
Downstairs Florists	photo express	U.S. Post Office
General Nutrition Ctr.	PIP Printing	

Level C:

beauty shop	Printing Office
Bookstore	restaurant
Dutton's Books	stationers
Federal Express	U.S. Government
MTA Customer Service	Weight Watchers
Plaza Footcare	

Caravan Book Store- A delightful "Old and Rare" book shop, 550 Grand Avenue. It's located inside the *Pacific Mutual Building*.

Thomas Bros. Map and Guidebook Store- 521 Sixth Street, will delight anyone hunting for travel literature, globes, and maps.

Attention L.A. shoppers.
On a nice day, go inside a mall!

Nowadays, most shoppers visit stores inside malls or other enclosures–even in our mild climate. The civic delights of strolling along public sidewalks, window-shopping, and enjoying the open air were once powerful attractions to Downtown.

Only recently has L.A.'s pedestrian life started to quicken again in a trend led by restaurants that now provide tables and chairs on sidewalks and plazas. The newest Downtown buildings have been built with windows facing the sidewalks, hoping that retail stores will rent street-level spaces and invite window-shopping again.

BUILDINGS

From South to North

865 South Figueroa Building- (Martin, Albert C., 1990; adjacent waterfall sculpture by Ellen Zimmerman) Thirty-five story office tower. Notice how the setbacks of planes of the building's exterior make it possible to have up to thirty-two corner offices on each floor, offering its occupants eight times the usual number of prized quarters.

801 Tower- (Architect's Collaborative, 1992) 801 South Figueroa Street. It has a faceted granite exterior with setbacks at the corner yielding twelve corner offices on each floor. The building is capped by lighted glass towers on each corner.

801 Tower has a newfangled air conditioning system developed in France: 700,000 water-filled plastic balls are frozen during cooler off-peak hours; they absorb the heat of the building during warm hours.

Zanja Madre sculpture garden- (Leicester, Andrew, 1992) South side of 801 Tower. An award-winning space displaying "an allegorical landscape" honoring the "Mother Ditch," the irrigation conduit that brought water from the Los Angeles River into the early *Pueblo de Los Angeles*, about one mile north. Leicester, who owns the copyright to this garden, sued Warner Bros. when he saw the movie *Batman Forever* which had used his park for one of its principal sets.

777 Tower- (Pelli, Cesar, 1991) 777 South Figueroa Street. A striking white metal fifty-two story building with a built-in optical illusion: the front and back walls of the building are bowed out in the middle, but the sides are flat but appear bowed from a distance because the vertical lines of the building are thicker in the middle than near the corners. A public art gallery off the lobby holds a fine collection of Ansel Adams photographs.

Seventh Market Place- (Skidmore, Owings and Merrill, Jerde Partnership, 1986) 735 South Figueroa Street, just south of Citicorp Plaza. An intriguing three-level semi-subterranean shopping mall with fifty-four specialty shops and a food court at its base. *Macy's* and *Robinson's-May* have department stores here. You are drawn to the edge of a pit by the superstructure on Figueroa Street. Peek over the edge and then take the escalator down to join in the experience. For a surprise, try going *up* instead to a grassy park one floor above street level that contains *Poet's Walk* along with a number of art works.

Citicorp Plaza- (Skidmore, Owings & Merrill, 1985) Corner of Seventh and Figueroa Streets. Forty-one story high rise. Delicate drawings and lines of poetry are incised in the sidewalk and on the marble stumps near the corner by the entrance. Note the whimsical life-sized bronze sculpture of a businessman carrying a briefcase and heading into the building's stone wall (*Corporate Head*, by Terry Allen).

Macy's Plaza (a.k.a. MCI Center) and Hyatt Regency Hotel- (Charles Luckman Associates, 1973) 700 Seventh Street, between Hope and Flower Streets. The Macy's store anchors a thirty-one store, three-level shopping mall. MCI is the anchor tenant in the office tower. The eye-catching grand entrance from Seventh Street into this multi-use center contrasts with the other three sides of this building which are blank walls–and no windows.

818 Building- Formerly Barker Brothers furniture store (Curlett and Bellman, 1925) 818 Seventh Street. Now an office building. Go into the lovely, spacious entrance lobby to see what downtown shopping was all about in the old days. Customers would remember where they bought things and how royally they were treated. You can still see the words "Fine Furniture" and "Floor Coverings" on the window frames by the main entrance.

Fine Arts Building- (Walker and Eisen, 1925) 811 West Seventh Street. Artists and musicians worked and lived in this exquisite building, perfectly located where shoppers could stop to admire and purchase art works displayed in the elaborate lobby showcases set against walls of Batchelder tile. Outside, over the entrance, are heroic reclining figures labeled *Architecture* and *Sculpture*. This is one of the most beautiful buildings in the City, an Art Deco masterpiece, restored by architect Brenda Levin. Be sure to go inside the lobby!

Home Savings of America Tower- (Tim Vreeland of Albert C. Martin Associates, 1988) Northeast corner of Seventh and Figueroa. A twenty-four-story chateauesque structure topped by a copper mansard roof with triangular gables and turrets. Presumably inspired by its neighboring older buildings (Fire Station #28 on Figueroa Street and the Fine Arts Building next door on Seventh Street), Home Savings Tower marks the intersections of two subways, the Red Line and the Blue Line in a station called Seventh/Metro Center.

Home Savings Tower contains four delightful murals: 1) A tile mosaic by Joyce Kozloff on two panels, forty feet high, above the Seventh Street entrance. Angels and oranges (obvious Los Angeles icons) are at the rounded lunettes at the top. 2) The mural on the ceiling of the corner outdoor entrance to the Red Line Subway–*The City Above*, 1990 painted by Terry Schoonhoven. People and office towers are viewed from below ground. Best seen as you ride up the escalator. 3) The ground floor teller area in the bank displays a mural called *The Story of L.A.* by Carlos Almaraz, thirty-two-foot long. A lot to absorb! 4) Take an elevator up to the Sixth floor "Sky Lobby" to find *Latitude 34, Longitude 118, A Southern California Panorama* by Richard Haas, 1988. This spectacular room is the principal entrance to the *Home Savings Tower*. Haas's mural celebrates all the good things people in the home loan business say about urban sprawl and freeways.

Coast Federal Savings Building- (Fox, Kohn Peterson, 1987) 1000 Wilshire Boulevard, just east of the Harbor Freeway. Many freeway drivers admire this building, responding to the two-tone stone facing and the detached gateway arch. These touches provide a relief from the cool, hardness of the district. Inside the main hall, you can catch a nice lunch at the *Harbor View* coffee shop.

Sanwa Bank Plaza- (Martin, David of A.C. Martin Associates, 1991) Wilshire Boulevard and Figueroa Street. A fifty-two-story tower set at a forty-five degree angle to the street corners. It has dramatic green-house-enclosed entrances, shaded by metal lattice screens. The top three stories of the building comprise another greenhouse which lights up at night. The exterior walls are rose granite, V-grooved to enhance the sculptured effect of the building. Tenants ride in luxurious elevators lined with rose imperial marble. Though designed by a prominent Los Angeles firm, the building was the first major Los Angeles tower developed by a Japanese company, Mitsui Fudosan, a subsidiary of Mitsui Real Estate Development Co., the foremost investor in office and residential structures in that country.

Headquarters

The largest corporations once headquartered Downtown have disappeared in the wake of recent consolidations-- ARCO, Gas Company, First Interstate Bank, Home Savings of America, and even the *Los Angeles Times*.

Most spaces are rented to the full range of business firms--accountants, banks, branches of foreign corporations, lawyers, real estate agencies, stockbrokers, and others. However, advertising agencies, and entertainment businesses are located elsewhere in the city.

The Aon Building- (Charles Luckman Associates, 1973) 707 Wilshire Boulevard. Sixty-two story office building. This is a spare, untextured, dark glass-curtain style building. On May 4, 1988, a fire broke out about one-third of the way up (sprinklers were being installed but were not yet operating). The fire wiped out all offices on a couple of floors, but the structural steel was protected by insulation and survived undamaged. The building was refurbished and now has sprinklers. Aon is Gaelic for oneness.

Pacific Building, formerly Pacific Mutual Building- (John Parkinson 1908, additions by Dodd & Richards, 1921, 1926, restored in 1974) 523 West Sixth Street. An impressive Beaux Arts building with a sumptuous marble lobby. An entrance gateway is surmounted by two heraldic gods supporting a shield. It was purchased by Chinese investors from the People's Republic and Taiwan in 1996

Oviatt Building- (Walker and Eisen, 1928) 617 South Olive Street. Another of L.A.'s Art Deco masterpieces. Originally this was a fancy haberdasher, the choice of businessmen and Hollywood stars. Peek into the first floor now occupied by Cidada Restaurant (See below). Front entrance marquee and elevator doors reveal the care and imagination heaped upon this building. The top two floors (not open to the public), reached by oak elevators, contain a luxurious moderne apartment built for Mr. Oviatt himself.

Biltmore Hotel- (Schultze and Weaver, 1923, 1928; renovated by Gene Summers and Phyllis Lambert, 1973) Corner of Olive and Fifth Streets, across from Pershing Square. It was designed by the same firm that created the Waldorf Astoria in New York. Its elegant Beaux Arts style exterior masses the three-wing and three-level vertical design so common to the genre. Many of the ceilings in the ballrooms and in the main hallway were painted by Giovanni Smeraldi, in whose honor the hotel renamed one of its restaurants. The registration lobby is now a drive-in entrance on Grand Avenue, but the original Italian Renaissance main lobby facing Pershing Square, still lives as a happy hour and high tea room. And what a space!

Stroll up and down the main hallway and try the doors to the several spectacular ballrooms not in use. It's OK to peek inside. They are used for meetings, conventions, banquets, proms, and other fancy affairs. The ballrooms vary in style, but all are stunning.

If you have time for a luxurious moment in the afternoon, sit down in the old entrance lobby on Olive Street, and order cappuccinos for two ($7.50, including tip). Or, even cheaper, pick up a lunch at Smeraldi's Deli and take it into the old lobby to eat in splendor.

Checkers Hotel, formerly Mayflower Hotel- (Whittlesey, Charles F., 1927) Renovated 1989. 535 South Grand Avenue, next to new wing of *Central Library*. A small, elegant, European-style hotel in Spanish Moorish design. Sixty-five years ago you could have stayed here for between $2.50 and $7.50 a night. That was when constructing the new Central Library next door cost only $3,000,000.00.

Central Library, a.k.a. Los Angeles Public Library- (Goodhue, Bertram Grosvenor and Carleton Winslow, 1925; recent east addition–the Tom Bradley Wing–designed by Pfeiffer, Norman of Hardy Holtzman Pfeiffer, 1993; *Maguire Gardens* designed by Halprin, Lawrence 1993; older sculptures by Lawrie, Lee; inscribed literary quotations selected by Alexander, Hartley Burr) 630 West Fifth Street, between Grand Avenue and Flower Street.

Architect/author Charles Moore wrote that if Los Angeles has just one truly great building, the *Central Library* is it!

The main structure was designed by Goodhue a decade after he created, in a very different style, the Spanish Colonial Revival buildings of San Diego's Balboa Park. The theme here is an invention of Goodhue's, a mixture of Byzantine, Egyptian, modern, and even Spanish–perfectly suited to the context of eclectic Southern California.

In recent decades, officials had been pondering what to do about the rundown condition and insufficient size of the library. Then, on April 29, 1986, an arsonist (still unknown) set the building on fire. A third of the books were destroyed, but the remaining materials were temporarily relocated, pending the refurbishing of the old building and the construction of a huge addition. But where to find the money?

Maguire-Thomas Partners, builders of several neighboring high-rise office towers, purchased "air rights" from the Library, for which it had no need, to get the City's permission to erect such tall buildings. This transaction provided much of the $214,000,000.00 necessary to refurbish the Goodhue wing and build the new Bradley wing.

But how to make such an addition without dwarfing the beautiful but modest Goodhue building? The solution by architect Norman Pfeiffer was to build an eight-story wing–but mostly below ground. The Tom Bradley Wing is covered by a glass roof, creating a spectacular atrium for the escalators, and lined with glass-walled reading rooms. The librarians call it a "Grand Canyon of books."

Contributing to the brightness are huge chandeliers of painted fiberglass and aluminum designed by Therman Statom, three one-ton lanterns with depictions of nature, technology, and the ethereal realms. You can go all the way down to the History Room on the bottom level and still feel you are in bright, cheerful daylight. (Make the return trip by elevator. The elevator shaft and the car itself is papered with old index cards from the card catalog which is no longer used in this computer age.)

You enter the library through the old wing. Go up to the second floor and into the spectacular Rotunda. All the paintings and fittings survived the fire and are original. The zodiac chandelier in the main rotunda was designed by Lee Lawrie, the sculptor of most of the other icons inside and out. The upper walls are twelve murals, *California's Four Eras*, painted by Dean Cornwall from 1927-1932. Cornwall's paintings are today the same light shade they were before the fire. The two sphinxes at the north staircase were carved by Lawrie from 1926 to 1930. The sphinxes (black, unveined Belgian marble with bronze headdresses) representing the "mysteries of knowledge," guard Lawrie's *Statue of Civilization*, who holds a book of quotations in five languages. The sphinxes' open books have quotations in Greek from Plutarch's *Morals*.

One of the most delightful rooms of the Goodhue Wing is south of the rotunda, the children's library. It has beautifully painted ceilings hung with original chandeliers. Murals, painted by Albert Herter, celebrate L.A.'s Spanish history, *Finding Gold in '49, Cabrillo, Portola, de Anza, Building the Missions*, and a *Spanish Fiesta at a Mission*. Don't miss a charming, puppet and story-telling theater in the adjacent room.

Outside on the south wall, History, Letters, Philosophy, Statecraft, Arts, and Science are represented by the busts of Herotodus, Virgil, Socrates, Justinian, da Vinci, and Copernicus.

The **Maguire Gardens** are named for Robert Maguire whose firm purchased the valuable air rights. This garden has become one of Downtown's most successful public spaces. Take the time to see the several fountains in the Maguire Gardens, and study the ways language is celebrated in inscriptions on the steps. At the westernmost steps near Flower Street, look at the map of the world that serves as the basin of a small pool. It identifies great cities whose libraries have experienced terrible fires.

Library hours: Monday through Thursday from 10:00 a.m. to 8:00 p.m.; Friday and Saturday 10:00 a.m. to 6:00 p.m.; and Sunday from 1:00 p.m. to 5:00 p.m. Docent tours: Monday through Friday at 12:30 p.m., Saturday 11:00 a.m. and 2:00 p.m., Sunday 2:00 p.m.

ARCO Plaza- (Albert C. Martin & Associates, 1972) Flower Street between Fifth and Sixth Streets. Twin fifty-two-story towers straddle a plaza and a two-story Bank of America branch. The Southern California headquarters for the Bank of America are in the south tower.

ARCO has recently merged with British Petroleum AMOCO and is now controlled in London, England. The Bank of America has been been absorbed by Nation's Bank whose main headquarters are in the South.

This mega-structure replaced one of L.A.'s Art Deco gems, the **Richfield Building** which was faced in black and gold tile (Morgan, Walls, and Clements, 1929). The Richfield Building had elegance, grace, and personality; the ARCO Plaza has monumental size.

A striking fountain-sculpture designed by Herbert Bayer, *Double Ascension* (1973) adds color to an otherwise dull frontage. The owners of *ARCO Plaza* should add comfortable seats, food carts, and draw the curtains to make the plaza come alive.

Under the plaza is an underground shopping mall with bookstores, specialty shops, and restaurants. Planners today realize it would have been better to put all these stores and restaurants up on the street and in the sunlight where the pedestrians are!

Grand Hope Park Area, (South Park Area) - Ninth Street between Grand Avenue and Hope Street

You'll spot the Park itself by four striking elements: 1) A theme tower on the corner of Hope and Ninth Streets. 2) An impressive, post-modern school building, The *Fashion Institute of Design and Merchandising*. 3) The northern face of the new *Del Prado* apartment building whose tower resembles a construction elevator, and 4) The *Federal Reserve Bank*.

Otherwise, this is a neighborhood of new apartment buildings. The residents don't have to commute downtown; they're already there!

Most of the new apartment tenants are middle-class folk, the units renting from $780.00 to $1400.00/month, slightly higher than the apartments on the north side of downtown near the Music Center. About fifteen percent of the units are subsidized for people of low incomes.

Fashion Institute of Design and Merchandising (F.I.D.M.)- (Jon Jerde Partners, 1984) Jerde was the creator of the citywide decoration scheme for the Olympic Games held in L.A. in 1984 and also the architect of Horton Plaza in downtown San Diego, *Westside Pavilion* in Westwood, and *Citywalk* in Universal Studios.

In the F.I.D.M. building, you can see a catalog of the courses taught–an astonishing list of technical subjects about the design, manufacture, and sale of clothing. F.I.D.M. is just four blocks west of the huge Garment District (see "Chapter 8 – Garment District").

The Fashion Institute also contains the *F.I.D.M. Gallery* which shows creations by the school's advanced students. Open Monday through Thursday, 11:00 a.m. to 3:00 p.m. (213) 624-1201. Check out the *F.I.D.M. Bookstore* for art supplies, unusual books on fashions, furniture design, and marketing. Monday through Thursday 8:00 a.m. to 4:00 p.m. Also try the F.I.D.M. Scholarship Store on Grand Avenue for clothing bargains. Monday through Thursday, 9:00 a.m. to 6:00 p.m. and Friday, 9:00 a.m. to 4:00 p.m.

The Grand Avenue entrance to F.I.D.M. is almost blocked by a life-size sculpture by Gwynn Murrill, *Angel*, (1990, bronze). One of many attempts by artists to depict the words "Los Angeles," this one is full winged and dressed in a dreamy gown, but the angel's face is covered by a cat mask. The mask is Murrill's commentary on the ability of fashions to alter appearances and identities. Also, in *Grand Hope Park* itself, are bronze coyotes sculpted by Murrill and other fascinating works of art.

Embassy Hotel and Auditorium- North, across Ninth Street from F.I.D.M. This is now a branch of the University of Southern California. USC took over the building and students and some faculty members have resided and attended classes there. Concerts and plays have been presented in the historic theater which was also the venue for some of the garment workers' unions organizing in the 1930s and 1940s. The earthquake in January, 1994 damaged the building, which was refurbished.

Museum of Neon Art (M.O.N.A.)- Ground floor of *Renaissance Tower*, Olympic and Hope Street. Its famous collection of neon designs was previously housed east of Little Tokyo. Great view of the Downtown skyline across Grand Hope Park. Wednesday through Saturday 11:00 a.m. to 5:00 p.m. and Sunday, 12:00 p.m. to 5:00 p.m. $5.00 admission. (213) 489-9918.

Federal Reserve Bank- On Grand Avenue between Ninth and Olympic is closed to visitors, except for a permanent exhibit off the lobby called *The World of Economics*. You will get an optimistic look at how national and international economies work, and you can play computer games based on relationships between economics and public policy.

Los Angeles Convention Center- (South and West buildings, by Ki Suh Park of Gruen Associates, 1993) Figueroa at Pico Street (DASH bus A or F from Fifth near Flower Street directly to the main entrance.) The gargantuan Convention Center consists of three huge exhibit halls, theaters, food courts, and an array of business services. It's worth a visit just to gawk at the entrance halls for the South and West buildings–airy glass structures supported by cool steel framing. Shades of Orange County's *Crystal Cathedral*!

Hopes are high that increased large convention business will spur new hotel growth and enliven the whole South Park neighborhood. If the size of the buildings counts for anything, the *Convention Center* might well deliver the goods. Of course, it's the vigor of the general economy and the ability of the area to handle large numbers of convention visitors that counts most.

Staples Center- Figueroa Street, just north of the Convention Center. State-of-the-art sports arena with 20,000 seats. This arena opened in the fall of 1999 and is the home court for the L.A. Lakers and L.A. Clippers basketball teams, L.A. Kings hockey club, and L.A. Avengers arena football team. There are development plans for a new multiplex entertainment/ retail center surrounding the arena which will help draw people to the area after hours on weekdays and weekends. (See "Prospects" section later in the chapter for more details.)

Los Angeles Herald-Examiner Building- (Morgan, Julia 1912) 1111 South Broadway. A Mission Revival creation by one of California's most famous architects. Julia Morgan was the first woman from any country to study at the *Ecole des Beaux Arts* in Paris. She later designed the Hearst Castle at San Simeon. The newspaper stopped its presses in 1989, and the arches are now walled-in. This beautiful building is looking for a new life–maybe as a museum about the garment industry in California.

Mayan Theater- (Morgan, Walls, and Clements, 1927) 1040 South Hill Street. The sculptured facade carries the Mayan theme as far as it can possibly go. Colored paint was added later. Edward Doheny, the discoverer of oil in Los Angeles, financed the *Mayan Theater*. In the 1970s and 1980s, the *Mayan Theater* became a porno movie house. It was finally rescued in 1990 and is now a nightclub with two dance floors.

Garfield Building- (Beelman, Claude, 1930) 408 West Eighth Street at Hill Street An Art Deco beauty, the building is now empty and shuttered.

Standard Oil Co. Building- (Kelham, George W., 1928) 605 West Olympic Boulevard, northwest corner of Olympic and Hope Streets. Cities everywhere need to mix together new and old buildings. The Standard Oil Building's contribution here follows from its proximity to Grand Hope Park across the street and the fact that its immediate neighbors are new apartments and condos trying to display signs of becoming a community.

Variety Arts Center- Formerly *Friday Morning Club* (Allison and Allison, 1924), 940 South Figueroa Street. Beaux Arts style.

Hotel Figueroa- (Stanton, Reed, and Hibbard, 1925) 939 South Figueroa Street. This is a handsome Spanish-style hotel which, late in its life, finds itself convenient to Grand Hope Park and Convention Center. It has a charming lobby and courtyard.

Remembering Downtown Street Names
In Order, East To West

In the good old days, when families often traveled downtown for recreation and shopping, many Angelenos, especially kids, could recite this ditty:

> From Main we Spring to Broadway
> and over the Hill to Olive.
> Wouldn't it be Grand if we could Hope
> to pick a Flower that grows on Figueroa?

PUBLIC ART

Art in The Lower Financial District - North of Eighth Street

This district is especially rich with examples of works commissioned as a requirement of law–the "One Percent For Art Program" (see Glossary).

A Place for Everything and Everything in its Place- (Bunn, David, 1993) Two elevators in Bradley Wing of Central Library, Fifth and Flower Streets. What can you do with catalog index cards which are now replaced by computers?

Apotheosis of Power- (Ballin, Hugo, 1930) Mural in Edison Company Building (now One Bunker Hill). Fifth Street and Grand Avenue.

California's Four Eras- (Cornwall, Dean, 1927-32) Twelve murals in rotunda of Central Library. They seem faded, as though the color had been bleached in the clean-up after the fires, but, no, the colors are just as they were originally painted.

City Above- (Schoonhoven, Terry, 1990) Mural on ceiling of street-level entrance to the Red Line and Blue Line Subway station at Seventh and Figueroa Streets–"Seventh/Metro Center" in Home Savings Tower. Best viewed by riding the up-escalator from the subway. Delightful picture of the buildings in the neighborhood and the street scene.

Corporate Head- (Allen, Terry, 1990) Sculpture, bronze. Citicorp Plaza. Southeast corner Seventh and Figueroa Streets. Next to entrance, a businessman in a three-piece suit and carrying a briefcase is in the process of losing body and soul to his corporation. Watch tourists do double-takes. Ponder the connection between this gentleman, the headless athletic sculptures in front of the Memorial Coliseum, and the reference to "headless farmers" in Robert Mezey's poem in the park above Seventh Market Place (on other side of Citicorp Building).

Double Ascension- (Bayer, Herbert, 1973) Sculpture and fountain, painted steel steps rising out of elevated pool. ARCO Plaza, Flower Street between Fifth and Sixth Streets. Framed by dark walls of Bank of America and Atlantic Richfield buildings.

Family Baroque- (Barrett, Bill, 1992) Sculpture outside entrance of Edison Company Building, Fifth Street and Grand Avenue.

Heaven to Earth- (Gil de Montes, Roberto, 1992) Mural, ceramic tile. Red Line, Seventh/Metro Center station, Flower and Seventh Streets.

Illumination- (Preston, Ann, 1993) Four huge lamps in "Grand Canyon of Books," Bradley Wing of Central Library, Fifth and Flower Streets.

L.A. Prime Matter- (Orr, Eric, 1991) Fountain/sculpture. Corner of Wilshire Boulevard and Figueroa Street at *Sanwa Bank*. Water slowly slithers down a ribbed bronze column and then flows more rapidly down its stone base. But look! The fountain episodically catches on fire!

Latitude 34, Longitude 118, A Southern California Panorama- (Haas, Richard, 1988) Mural. *Home Savings Tower,* Seventh and Figueroa Streets in the "Sky Lobby" (take elevators to sixth floor). Cheerful interpretation of L.A.'s diversity, architecture, and suburban sprawl, painted on upper walls and ceiling of a spectacular elevator lobby.

Lithos- (1991) Interior/exterior waterfalls. 865 Figueroa Building. Walls of rocks continuing from inside the entrance lobby to both outdoor sides. Water rushes over the outdoor rocks.

Natural, Technological, Ethereal- (Statom, Therman, 1993) Three chandeliers for the *Central Library.* Flower and Fifth Streets. Sculptures, painted fiberglass and aluminum. Three one-ton lanterns illuminate the "Grand Canyon of books" inside the atrium of the new Tom Bradley wing. Depictions of nature, technology, the arts, and extraterrestrial space.

Painting with Multiple Centers for Central Library- (Petropolis, Renee, 1993) In the lower rotunda of Central Library, Fifth and Flower Streets. Ceiling mural. Three main entrance halls converge on this lobby. Multicolored swirls of lines and letters taken from the names of several Los Angeles writers and poets.

Salmon Run- (Keene, Christopher, 1982) Sculpture. *Manulife Plaza.* Fifth and Figueroa Streets. Dramatic arrangement of bears fishing.

Sculptures- (Lawrie, Lee, 1926-1930) Interior and exterior ornaments of Central Library. Fifth and Flower Streets. Be sure to admire his two sphinxes (black, unveined Belgian marble with bronze headdresses) at the north staircase. The open books they hold are quotations in Greek from Plutarch's Morals. They guard his *Statue of Civilization,* who is holding a book of quotations in five languages. See also Lawrie's zodiac chandelier in main rotunda and sculptures on south exterior: History, Letters, Philosophy, Statecraft, Arts, and Science portrayed by Herotodus, Virgil, Socrates, Justinian, da Vinci, and Copernicus.

Site, Memory, Reflection- (Albuquerque, Lita, 1993) In *550 South Hope Street Building*. Tiny meditation room commemorating the many churches that once stood Downtown, including especially the *Church of the Open Door* known to all who can remember it as the "Jesus Saves Church" which occupied this spot.

Source Figure- (Graham, Robert, 1992) Sculpture. Top of Bunker Hill Steps. Hope Street, just south of Fourth Street. An angel of the city, she is giving water to Los Angeles–or at least to the stream that gurgles down Bunker Hill to Fifth Street.

The Movies: Fantasies, and The Movies: Spectacles- (Kozloff, Joyce, 1990, 1993) Murals, ceramic tile. On walls of the platform of the Blue Line station Seventh/Metro Center. Each tile depicts a famous movie character or scene.

The Story of L.A.- (Almaraz, Carlos, 1989) Mural. Home Savings Tower, Seventh and Figueroa Streets, east wall inside the bank's teller area. Thirty-two-foot depiction of the city's history and society.

Mosaic- (Kozloff, Joyce, 1989) Above front doors of Home Savings of America Tower, Seventh and Figueroa Streets. At the top, you can just see two icons of Los Angeles–angels and oranges.

Untitled murals, friezes and ceiling decorations- (Smeraldi, Giovanni, 1920s) In the *Biltmore Hotel*. 515 South Olive Street. Main hallway and Crystal Ballroom. In a nice salute to the artist, one of the hotel's fine restaurants is named Smeraldi's.

Unity- (Komar, Vitaly and Alexander Melamid, 1993) Mural. Lobby of *Library Tower*. 633 West Fifth Street. Three Renaissance angels, a brunette and two blondes, represent figures painted in a chapel, called **Porciuncula** ("little place"), attended by St. Francis of Assisi. The original Spanish name given to the river was *El Rio de Los Angeles de Porciuncula*.

Poets' Walk- The grassy deck above Seventh Market Place, between Seventh and Eighth on Figueroa Street. A collection of poetry and scattered art objects. One provocative piece is a small sculpture by David Gilhooly depicting uncollected picnic leftovers. It is accompanied by a poem by Robert Mezey (1990): *The Public Abandons Philosophy:*

Bargains, odds and ends for sale–
Double breasted suit of mail,
Half a sandwich, slightly stale.
Unused crucifixion nail.
Hard rain to fall on U.S.A.
Shortly, headless farmers say
Man and woman
Beast and human
All too common.

On the other side of the escalators, this same artist/poet team produced another work, three pigeons poking around a fried egg, sunny side up: *Pigeons Acquire Philosophy:*

All of time's productions must
Wither soon and turn to dust.
Art appears the one exception–
Seers and scientists nonplused.

Other artist/poet concoctions: Gary Soto/Joe Fay, "The business of stray dogs..." and George Herms's art, an assemblage of "found objects" with Charles Simic's *Portals to Poetry*. Peter Alexander's illuminated glass *Puddles* (1995) on the plaza floor of 777 Tower, just south of *Seventh Market Place*, accompanies words of Ikkyu Shonin, Zen poet of fifteenth century.

Art at Grand Hope Park - South of Seventh Street

Angel- (Murrill, Gwynn, 1990) Sculpture, bronze. Entrance to *Fashion Institute of Design and Merchandising*, Ninth Street and Grand Avenue. Another take on the words "Los Angeles". The mask is Murrill's commentary on the ability of fashions to hide appearances. Is L.A. a city of angels in masquerade? See also Murrill's coyotes and a snake watched by a hawk in Grand Hope Park (see *Urban Curiosity*, below.)

Celestial Source- (Albuquerque, Lita, 1993) Fountain in *Grand Hope Park*, Olympic Boulevard and Hope Street.

Clock Tower- (Halprin, Lawrence, 1993) Northwest corner of Grand Hope Park, Ninth Street and Hope Street. All the cracked and broken crockery suggests a reference to the Watts Towers. However, Halprin deliberately broke this stuff and separated the fragments.

Ed Ruscha Monument- (Twitchell, Kent, 1978-87) Mural. North exterior wall of 1031 South Hill Street, overlooking a parking lot. Twitchell's photographically accurate portrait, six-stories tall, of his friend and fellow artist.

Homage to Cabrillo: Venetian Quadrant- (Sturman, Eugene, 1985) Sculptures. Stainless steel, bronze, and copper. 888 South Figueroa, across street from Original Pantry. This is the first of the C.R.A.'s "One Percent For Art" projects.

Lizard Bench- (Guerrero, Raul, 1993) Olympic Boulevard and Hope Street. Bench on east side of children's playground in *Grand Hope Park*.

Los Angeles Basin circa 1840- (Guerrero, Raul, 1993) "Antwall," a frieze along west wall of children's playground of *Grand Hope Park*, Olympic Boulevard and Hope Street. Follow the line of ants to the end!

Mirage Fountain- (Guerrero, Raul, 1993) Snake design worked into a fountain in Grand Hope Park, Olympic Boulevard and Hope Street.

Puddles- (Alexander, Peter, 1995) Illuminated glass in plaza floor and south side of *777 Tower*, 777 Figueroa Street. Accompanies words of Ikkyu Shonin, Zen poet of fifteenth century.

Urban Curiosity- (Murrill, Gwynn, 1993) Sculptures, bronze. Coyotes, hawk, and snake in *Grand Hope Park*, and Ninth and Hope Streets. The snake is innocently slithering on a ledge watched by the hawk perched on the pergola near Renaissance Tower, at southeast corner of the park. Murrill loves animals.

Yang-Na- (Berlant, Tony, 1990) Painted metal rotunda walls of entrance lobby, *Fashion Institute of Design and Merchandising (F.I.D.M.)*. "Yang-Na" is the name of the tribe of Native Americans who lived here before the Spanish arrived. Ninth Street and Grand Avenue.

Zanja Madre- (Leicester, Andrew, 1992) Small park next to 801 Tower. 801 Figueroa Street. Space age version of the original "Mother Ditch" which once brought water to the original Pueblo. This park also has many other suggestive icons of Los Angeles. Look for an oil drill, a drill for water, a turtle that periodically gurgles and slurps, and fence gates spooky enough to suit the makers of the third Batman movie–much to Leicester's dismay.

CONVENIENCES AND NECESSITIES

Public Rest Rooms

Macy's Plaza- Seventh Street between Hope and Flower Streets. Food court area on lower level, southwest corner.

Central Library- Fifth and Flower Streets.

ARCO Plaza- Between Fifth and Sixth Streets, on Flower Street. B-level of the underground shopping mall, near north and south escalators.

1000 Wilshire- Across hall from Harbor View Coffee Shop.

Seventh Market Place- Figueroa Street between Seventh and Eighth Streets. Food court level, near Ichiban of Japan.

Wilshire Grand Hotel (formerly Omni and Hilton)- Wilshire Boulevard, west of Figueroa Street. Downstairs, under the main entrance.

ATMs

#1 Wilshire Building- Wilshire Boulevard and Grand Avenue (CALFED)

Macy's Plaza- Seventh Street between Flower and Hope Streets, Main floor.

Bank of America- Flower and Seventh Streets.

Home Savings Tower- Seventh and Figueroa Streets.

Sanwa Bank Building- Sixth and Figueroa Streets.

Places to Sit

Macy's Plaza- Seventh Street between Flower and Hope Streets. Benches, inside on street level.

Seventh Market Place- Seventh Street and Figueroa. All levels. Also small park upstairs from the Figueroa Street entrance to plaza.

Zanja Madre Park- Next to 801 Figueroa Street.

Central Library and Maguire Gardens- Corner of Fifth and Flower Streets, park benches outside, many chairs inside.

Coast Federal Savings Building- 1000 Wilshire Boulevard; benches outside.

Grand Hope Park- Ninth and Hope Streets; park benches.

Prescription Drugs

Horton & Converse Pharmacy- On Seventh and Figueroa Streets in the Seventh Market Place.

Roosevelt Pharmacy- 729 Seventh Street.

Bus Information

MTA Customer Service- ARCO Plaza, 515 South Flower Street, Level C., Monday through Friday 7:30 a.m. to 3:30 p.m.

RESTAURANTS

Price Guide for average lunch entrees:

$ = $3.00 - $8.00	$$$ = $13.00 - $17.00
$$ = $9.00 - $12.00	$$$$ = $18.00+

Figueroa & Ninth Area

The Original Pantry- 879 South Figueroa Street. Lots of steak, eggs, butter, and fried potatoes. Open twenty-four hours every day since 1924. Owned by Richard Riordan, former mayor of L.A.. Famous and very popular; lines often extend out the door and around the corner. ($)

Ziga Trattoria- 825 West Ninth Street, just west of *The Original Pantry*. Bright, cheerful, lively place, popular with office workers from neighboring high rises. Indoor and outdoor seating. Salads, sandwiches, pizza, pasta, risotti (Italian rice). Lunches. Monday through. Dinners Tuesday, Wednesday, Thursday to 8:00 p.m. (213) 488-0400. ($$)

Figueroa Street Cafe- 939 South Figueroa Street, in picturesque, Spanish-style lobby of *Hotel Figueroa*. Salads, pastas. Old California atmosphere. Eat next to lobby or take your tray back to poolside music room. Lunches. ($)

La Bella Cucina- 949 South Figueroa Street, next to *Hotel Figueroa*. Country and Northern Italian food, with fresh pizzas and pastas. Chicken and fish. Informal, sunny, relaxed atmosphere attracts young to middle-aged professionals working nearby. Also available for take-out. Lunches are from Monday through Friday at 11:00 a.m. to 4:00 p.m., and dinner from Monday through Sunday at 6:00 p.m. to 11:30 p.m. (213) 623-0014. ($)

Pasta Firenze- 939 South Figueroa Street, in *Hotel Figueroa*. Serves a variety of pastas, from angel hair to rigatoni, with sauces as traditional as Bolognese meat sauce or as unusual as Japanese eggplant in a garlic and tomato base. Lovely tile work on the floors and doorway arches, lending a cool Southwestern feel. Cafeteria-style service. Monday through Friday, 11:30 a.m. to 2:00 p.m. and 5:00 p.m. to 10:00 p.m. Closed Saturday and Sunday. (213) 627-8971 ($)

Gill's Cuisine of India- 838 South Grand Avenue, in the *Stillwell Hotel*. An anomaly in the sea of French, Italian, and American restaurants of the Lower Financial District. Specializes in Tandoori dishes, baked in a clay oven at high temperatures. Vegetarian dishes as well. Open for lunch Monday through Friday, 11:30 a.m. to 2:30 p.m., dinner Monday through Thursday, 5:30 p.m. to 9:30 p.m., and Friday and Saturday, 6:00 p.m. to 9:30 p.m. Closed Sunday. (213) 623-1050. ($)

Window's Steaks and Martinis- 1150 South Olive Street, *Transamerica Building*, Thirty-second floor. Exquisite aerial view of Los Angeles from the south edge of Downtown. This is now a steak house, in view of its proximity to the Staples Center. Open from Monday through Friday 11:30 a.m. to 2:00 p.m.; Tuesday through Saturday from 5:00 to 10:00 p.m.; and always closed on Sunday. (213) 746-1554. ($$$$)

Fox Sports Sky Box Bar & Grill- In the Staples Center. Eleventh and Figueroa Streets. Open 11:00 a.m. to 11:00 p.m. events days. No events days, lunch from 11:00 a.m. to 5:00 p.m. (213) 742-7345. ($$)

Breadwinners Soup, Salad, Sandwiches- 801 South Grand Avenue, in *Chase Plaza*. Breakfast and lunch. 7:00 a.m. to 4:00 p.m. ($)

Seventh Street and Figueroa Area

La Salsa- Seventh and Flower Streets, above Red Line entrance. Mexican fast food. La Salsa has a printed guide to their fresh salsa bar: "Pick your picante." The hottest selection, Salsa Volcan, will burn off your eyebrows; the mildest is called Salsa Deliciosa. Tostadas, burritos, taquitos, and combination specials. Monday through Friday 7:00 a.m. to 8:00 p.m., Saturday 11:00 a.m. to 4:00 p.m. Closed Sundays. (213) 892-8227. ($)

Brasserie- In Macy's Plaza. 711 South Hope Street. Hamburgers, sandwiches, salads, and buffet. Cool subterranean enclosure. Caters to weekday business crowd and tourists. Monday through Saturday, 6:00 a.m. to 2:30 p.m. ($$)

California Pizza Kitchen- Figueroa and Seventh Streets. Next to the Seventh Market Place. Open Monday through Friday from 11:00 a.m. to 9:30 p.m., and from Saturday through Sunday from 12:00 p.m. to 9:00 p.m. (213) 228-8500. ($$-$$$)

The Grill- In Macy's Plaza/Hyatt Regency Hotel, 711 South Hope Street. Enter through bottom floor of Macy's Plaza. This is yet another conversion to a steak house following the arrival of the Staples Center to the neighborhood. Broiled, not grilled, steaks, and seafood. Dinners only. Open Sunday through Saturday from 5:00 p.m. to 10:00 p.m. (213) 683-1234. ($$$-$$$$)

Ciao Trattoria- 815 West Seventh Street, in the Fine Arts Building. Salads, soups, pasta, fish, meat, and seafood, prepared in light Italian-style with sun dried tomatoes, mushrooms, and fresh vegetables. Elegant dining space and fashionable clientele. Nice place to take a client or a date. Monday through Friday, 11:00 a.m. to 9:00 p.m., Saturday and Sunday, 5:00 p.m. to 9:00 p.m. Happy hour Monday through Friday, 4:00 p.m. to 7:00 p.m. (213) 624-2244. ($$-$$$)

Engine Co. #28- 644 South Figueroa Street. Check their luncheon specials. Hot seafood platter, cobb salad, chunky gazpacho, turkey burger, whiskey-fennel sausages, "911 fudge brownie sundae." Owned by Linda Griego, Chair of RLA (formerly called Rebuild L.A.). Beautifully restored firehouse. Monday through Friday, 11:15 a.m. to 9:00 p.m.; Saturday and Sunday 5:00 p.m. to 9:00 p.m. (213) 624-6996. ($$$)

In Wilshire Grand Hotel – Figueroa Street between Wilshire and Seventh Street

Cardini, Gorgeous interior. Also poolside tables on the outside patio. Serves tempting Italian: seafood, chicken, veal, beef, and pasta. Monday through Friday 11:30 a.m. to 2:00 p.m. ($$$)

Kyoto- Japanese food. Monday through Friday brunch, 7:00 a.m. to 10:00 a.m., lunch, 11:30 a.m. to 2:00 p.m., dinner, 5:30 p.m. to 9:30 p.m. ($$$)

City Grill- View of *Citicorp Plaza*. Plush interior, gazebos serving as buffet tables. American food, with occasional international twists such as Japanese ramen, Mexican quesadillas, and British fish and chips. Daily, 6:00 a.m. to 11:00 p.m. (213) 627-4289. ($$)

Seoul Jung- Korean cuisine. Lunches and dinners. Daily. (213) 688-7880.

Pacific Grille- (Inside) *Sanwa Bank Tower,* Northwest corner, Wilshire Boulevard and Figueroa Street. A portion of the building's atrium is framed by steel and wood ribs (designed by *Morphosis* architect Michael Rotondi) to enclose the intriguing and popular restaurant. Monday through Friday 11:00 a.m. to 2:00 p.m. (213) 485-0927. ($$)

The Kiosk- (Outdoors) Figueroa & Wilshire Boulevard. Plaza next to *Sanwa Bank Building.* Sandwiches, salads, snacks. Try grilled eggplant on cubatta bread with asiago, oucou, and arugula or roast chicken with walnuts on onion bread with watercress and tomato. Great place on the many days of good weather in L.A. ($)

Harbor View Coffee Shop- Main hallway in 1000 Wilshire Building (Coast Federal Bank Building). The name is a joke; L.A.'s harbor is twenty miles south, but the Harbor Freeway roars by on the other side of the windows. Still, the atmosphere is relaxing. Monday through Friday, 7:30 a.m. to 2:30 p.m. ($)

Food court in **Seventh Market Place-** Figueroa Street between Seventh and Eighth Streets, on lowest level (third level). Sit inside or out in the circular courtyard:

  California Crisp- Sandwiches, pasta and salads. ($)
  Euro Coffee- Gourmet coffee shop. ($)
  Noodle House ($)
  Panda Express- Chinese. ($)
  Sbarro- Pizza, pasta, and salads. ($)
  Stan's Donuts ($)
  Tacomole Healthy Mexican ($)
  Tokyo Kitchen ($)

Food court in **Macy's Plaza-** 700 West Seventh Street. Excellent possibilities in a civilized atmosphere:

  Carl's Jr.- American fast food. ($)
  Checker Cab Pizza- Pizza and pasta. ($)
  Cravings Dreyer's Ice Cream ($)
  Fresh and Tasty- Sandwiches (including hand carved turkey on a California roll), soups, salads, gourmet coffee. ($)
  Gourmet Fruit Bowl- Fruit (fresh & dried), drinks. ($)
  The Lovin' Oven ($)
  Plaza Deli- Breakfast, hot and cold sandwiches. ($)
  Plum Tree Express- Chinese fast food. ($)
  Sushi Wakana- Sushi. ($)

Coffee Bean & Tea Leaf- 801 West Seventh Street, corner of Flower Street ($)

It's A Wrap!- 818 West Seventh Street. ($)

Pershing Square Area

Cicada- In Oviatt Building, 617 South Olive Street. Originally, Oviatt's was the premier haberdasher serving Hollywood stars in the 1920s and 1930s. It's now the site of excellent, lavishly-presented Italian food. Plush, Art Deco interior with high ceilings and low lighting and ornate decorations. Large comfortable chairs. Bar in luxuriously appointed mezzanine. Lunch Monday through Friday 11:30 a.m. to 2:30 p.m. Dinner Monday through Saturday, 5:30 p.m. to 9:30 p.m. (213) 488-9488. (\$\$\$)

In Biltmore Hotel – Olive and Fifth Streets

Bernard's- Excellent continental cuisine. Seafood, chicken and duck, beef and even venison in tasty combination with lots of vegetables. Daily specials. Low-lighted, dark wood walls, and ornate pillars. The kind of place you'd want to go before attending the opera. Lunches are Monday through Friday until 2:00 p.m., Dinners are Monday through Thursday, 5:30 p.m. to 10:00 p.m., Friday and Saturday 6:00 p.m. to 10:30 p.m. For reservations (213) 612-1580. (\$\$\$\$)

Smeraldi's- (Named for the artist who painted the Biltmore's lobby and ballroom ceilings). Italian food, including lobster or Peking Duck pizza; pasta with chicken, fresh vegetables, and cheese; green salads; and Italian-American sandwiches like Philly cheese steak. Airy, modern decor. Attracts young professionals. Sunday and Monday from 6:30 p.m. to 10:00 p.m. (213) 612-1562. (\$\$)

Smeraldi's Deli and Bakery- Pizzas, sandwiches, salads, coffees, and bakery items. You could buy a lunch box and carry it into the Biltmore's original entrance lobby, the Rendezvous Court, or eat at the Deli's counter, or take your lunch across the street to Pershing Square to eat outside. (\$)

Sai Sai- Japanese food served in a spacious dining room, complete with lacquer serving trays and decorative sake bottles. Sushi, sashimi, Japanese-style steak, tempura, kaiseki, and more. Daily sushi lunch special for $9.50. Try some green tea or red bean ice cream for dessert. Frequented by business people. Monday through Friday, 11:30 a.m. to 2:00 p.m. and 5:30 p.m. to 9:30 p.m. Happy hour from 5:30 p.m. to 6:30 p.m. (213) 624-1011 ext. 1288. ($$$)

Grand Avenue Bar- 520 South Grand Avenue, in back of hotel. Sports lounge with several TV screens. Luncheon buffet on weekends. Open Monday through Friday, 3:30 p.m. to 12:00 a.m.; Saturday and Sunday 11:00 a.m. to 12:00 a.m. (213) 612-1532. ($$)

Rendezvous Court- The Los Angeles version of New York's Tea at the Plaza Hotel. Seating on luxurious chairs in the Biltmore's original entrance lobby, a lovely marble room with a soaring ceiling. They serve individual cups of tea in several tempting varieties, as well as "traditional tea," with canapés and tarts–and cocktails. Daily, 11:00 a.m. to 11:00 p.m. ($) You can also bring lunches and bakery goodies in from Smeraldi's Deli and Bakery in the next room. ($)

Checkers- in Checkers Hotel, 535 South Grand Avenue. Highly rated French-American food. Menu changes frequently according to what can be bought fresh. Also special vegetarian entrees. Breakfast, brunch, lunch, afternoon tea, and dinner. Elegant and comfortable continental atmosphere. Sunday through Saturday, 7:00 a.m. to 10:30 a.m. for breakfast and 5:30 p.m. to 9:00 p.m. for dinner. (213) 624-0000. ($$$)

Water Grill- 544 South Grand Avenue. A chic, acclaimed seafood restaurant. Extensive menu divided into the fish's waters of origin. Seafood prepared in Californian French and Italian-influenced style. Seafood pastas, sandwiches, meat and poultry also on the menu. Highly polished wood and glass lend it a classy, private feel. Known as a place for client dinners. Sunday through Saturday, 11:30 a.m. to 3:00 p.m. for lunch and 4:00 p.m. to 9:00 p.m. for dinner. (213) 891-0900. ($$$)

New York Pizza- 518 West Sixth Street. Serves up New York-style pizza in a Big Apple atmosphere complete with signs from the New York City Subway system. Thin crust and Sicilian. Can be ordered by the slice or by the pie; to stay or to go. Monday through Friday, 10:00 a.m. to 5:30 p.m.; Saturday, 11:00 a.m. to 5:00 p.m. ($)

Yorkshire Grill- 610 West Sixth Street. Fifties-era green naugahyde booths and stools, and dark formica tables under fluorescent lighting. Caters to business crowds. Sandwiches, entrees (pastrami, salami, baked frankfurters, brisket, etc.). Monday through Friday, 6:00 a.m. to 4:00 p.m. and Saturday 6:00 a.m. to 2:00 p.m. (213) 629-3020. ($)

Aloha Teriyaki- 609 South Grand Avenue. Japanese-Hawaiian charbroiled fast food. Monday through Friday, 8:00 a.m. to 6:00 p.m.; Saturday, 10:00 a.m. to 4:00 p.m. (213) 622-1895. ($)

Casey's Bar and Grill- 613 South Grand Avenue. Popular with business folk for lunches, dinners, and happy hour. Burgers, sandwiches, pasta, and deli specialties. Kitchen hours are Monday through Friday 11:00 a.m. to 8:30 p.m.; bar Monday through Friday 11:00 a.m. to 10:00 p.m. (213) 629-2353. ($$)

Flower and Fifth Street Area

McCormick and Schmick's- At top of Bunker Hill Steps in Library Tower. 633 West Fifth Street. Famous for its huge selection of fresh seafood. Menu changes according to season. There is $12.95 lobster every Friday. Sporty atmosphere. Also has an extensive wine list, bar, and a "$1.95 Menu" happy hour Monday through Friday, 3:00 a.m. to 7:00 p.m. Open Monday through Friday 11:00 a.m. to 10:00 p.m., Saturday and Sunday 4:00 p.m. to 10:00 p.m. The bar stays open Monday through Friday until 12:00 a.m. (213) 629-1929. ($$)

Cuidad- 445 South Figueroa in the Union Bank Plaza. Food of "the Latin world" offered by media personalities Mary Sue Milliken and Susan Feniger. Cuidad is their latest addition to their *Border Grill* in Santa Monica and Las Vegas. Open Monday through Friday from 11:30 a.m. to 11:00 p.m.; Saturday from 4:30 p.m. to 11:00 p.m.; and Sunday from 4:30 p.m. to 10:00 p.m. ($$-$$$)

Bookends Cafe- In Central Library, Fifth and Flower Streets. Food court in southwest corner of main floor—seating indoors or out (overlooking Maguire Gardens. *Panda Express, T.C.B.Y.* (yogurt), and *Creative Croissants.* Open Monday 10:00 a.m. to

6:00 p.m., Tuesday and Wednesday 11:00 a.m. to 7:00 p.m., Thursday to Saturday 10:00 a.m. to 6:00 p.m., Sunday 11:00 a.m. to 5:00 p.m. The Central Library receives eight percent of the gross sales. ($)

Cafe Pinot- In *Maguire Gardens* of Central Library. Fifth and Flower Streets. When the Central Library was reconstructed in 1993, this glass-sided restaurant structure was built into the Maguire Gardens. Success! On weekdays lunch hours, this French bistro is filled with office workers from the surrounding district. Casual indoor and outdoor dining featuring rotisserie chicken. The restaurant is an offspring of Joachim Splichal's Westside *Patina/Pinot* (Melrose Avenue). TV personality Huell Houser calls this his favorite location in L.A. Monday through Friday, breakfast and lunch is served, Monday through Saturday, dinner is from 5:30 p.m. to 9:30 p.m. (213) 239-6500. ($$$)

In Westin Bonaventure Hotel –
Fifth Street between Figueroa & Flower Streets

Sidewalk Cafe- Ground floor. A classy coffee shop in atrium lobby near one of several fountain/pools. Salads, sandwiches, and entrees served American-style with occasional Asian and Mexican accents. Salad bar. Frequented by business people, hotel guests, and shoppers. Open Sunday through Thursday, 6:00 a.m. to 11:00 p.m.; Friday and Saturday 6:00 a.m. to midnight. Sunday brunch is 11:00 a.m. to 3:00 p.m. ($$)

Top of Five- Thirty-fifth floor. Terrific view of the city. Rotating bar just down the stairs from the restaurant. Serves "California steak and seafood" (read French-American food) at booths and tables arranged so you can see the city while you eat. Prime rib, filet mignon, charred lamb loin, mixed grill, and seafood. Monday through Friday, lunch; Sunday through Thursday, dinner 5:30 p.m. to 10:00 p.m.; Friday and Saturday 5:30 to 10:30 p.m. (213) 624-1000. ($$$)

Mandarin West- Sixth floor. Mandarin and Szechwan cuisine in sleek modern decor. Specializes in seafood. Open Monday through Friday from 11:00 a.m. to 3:00 p.m. for lunch. Dinner is from 4:30 p.m. to 9:00 p.m. Saturdays 4:30 p.m. to 9:00 p.m. (213) 683-8866. ($$-$$$)

Market on Fourth -
Fourth Level, Food Court on the Balcony

The Health Winner- Salads, sandwiches, baked potatoes. ($)
Bonaventure Brewing Co.- ($$)
Cap'n Lee's Seafood- Fried and grilled seafood. ($)
Jyokamochi ($)
Uncle Mustache Falafel- Middle Eastern fast food. ($)
Korean BBQ Plus- Korean BBQ combination platters. ($)

In ARCO Plaza –
Flower Street between Fifth and Sixth Streets

FLOOR 50- Bank of America Tower. 555 South Flower Street. Daily changing selection of European, American, and Asian-influenced entrees. Menu headings include "Bankers' Favorites," such as New York Steak or Chicken Stir Fry with Spicy Soy Sauce, and "Healthier Choices," including Fresh Fruit Platter or Greek Salad. Terrific view from each of the six dining rooms. "Your clients will appreciate the prestige" says their advertising. Monday through Friday, lunches only, 11:30 a.m. to 2:00 p.m. Business attire. Reservations suggested, call (213) 228-5050. ($$$$)

Salads 2000- Level B ($)

HISTORY

The Seventh Street Story: A huge population explosion hit Los Angeles in the late 1880s. Thousands of new settlers came by train from the midwest, pouring into Southern California and settling in the neighborhoods near the old Plaza. Most of the resulting expansion would have to flow out onto the flatlands jammed between Bunker Hill and the Los Angeles River. With no other direction available, the movement would be to the south.

The first buildings south of the Plaza were late-Victorian single family homes and shops. In time, the residential neighborhood evolved into a mixed collection of small apartment buildings, hotels, business offices, stores, warehouses, small factories, and repair shops–diverse, lively, dusty, and full of promise.

By 1900, the midpoint of commercial activity had moved down Broadway and was approaching Second Street. Yet, businesses, hotels, and shops were already becoming widely dispersed. Two railway stations were located several blocks east, near the river. Speculators were buying rural property well to the south and west. Smokestack industries were forming along the railroad tracks to the north on both sides of the river. L.A.'s fabled urban sprawl had already been born.

The southern expansion of commerce accelerated, once it moved past Fifth Street at the foot of Bunker Hill, and swung west. By 1910, Seventh Street had become the major avenue to the west and was lined with buildings all the way out to Westlake Park (now *MacArthur Park*).

Twenty years later, at the beginning of the Great Depression, Downtown's center of gravity had arrived at Seventh and Hill Streets. Seventh Street (east-west) and Broadway (north-south) had become the two main axes of L.A.'s shopping and entertainment districts. Broadway's department stores included *The Broadway*, at Fourth Street; *Fifth Street Store* at Fifth; May Co., at Eighth; and *Eastern Columbia* at Ninth Street. Spectacular movie palaces on Broadway had joined its shops and department stores: the largest theaters were located south of Sixth Street.

Bullock's Department Store, (two big buildings whose upper floors bridged an alley), stood at the northwest corner of Seventh Street and Broadway. Farther west on Seventh were two other flagship stores, *Robinson's*, between Grand and Hope, and *Barker Brothers*, on Figueroa. In 1930, the *Los Angeles Times* described Seventh Street as "Los Angeles' counterpart of New York's Fifth Avenue". From Spring Street, west Seventh is lined with beautiful shops and some of the newest and finest buildings in the city."

Banks, insurance companies, and other financial institutions were concentrated on Spring Street, sometimes called the "Wall Street of the West." (You can still find the handsome Classical and Beaux Arts bank buildings on Spring Street, but many are now empty and looking for new purposes.)

After the First World War, the Downtown center continued its western shift. Among the important office buildings and hotels headed in that direction in the 1920s were: The Pacific Mutual Building on Sixth Street between Olive and Grand Avenue, the Roosevelt Building on Seventh between Flower and Hope Streets, the *Mayflower Hotel* (now *Checkers Hotel*) on Grand and Fifth Streets, and the splendid *Biltmore Hotel* on Olive and Fifth Street, across from Pershing Square. The Central Library and two elite businessmen's clubs (the *California Club* on Sixth and Flower and the *Jonathan Club* on Sixth and Figueroa) were completed in this district. The beautiful black and gold Richfield Oil Building rose across Flower Street from the Central Library. All these buildings still exist–except the Richfield Building which was demolished to make way for the massive dark towers of the *ARCO Plaza*.

Cars and Urban Sprawl: The reign of the automobile began in earnest in the 1920s, greatly accelerating the pace of decentralization. By 1927, *Bullock's* had spun off a store and sent it one and one-half miles west on Wilshire Boulevard. Hollywood Boulevard was building elaborate movie palaces to rival, and take business from, the older theaters on Broadway. In 1939, another department store, *May Co.,* placed a large branch store out on Wilshire and Fairfax–five and a half miles away. In the same year, 1939, the twelve-mile long Arroyo Seco Parkway–a new monument to the automobile's prowess–created a high-speed connection from Downtown to Pasadena.

Then came the Second World War. The huge new factories of the burgeoning defense industry were situated dozens of miles away, on the distant periphery of the metropolis, continuing the outward spread of population and their places of work. Eager highway planners waited for the war's end so that the model offered by the Arroyo Seco Route could be replicated many times over.

In the 1960s and 1970s, most of L.A.'s great freeways were cut through already urbanized neighborhoods, citrus orchards, small towns, and fragile canyons–and extended across the length and breadth of Southern California. Shopping malls erupted in the distant suburbs and began to draw energy, money, and attention away from the original Downtown stores and shops.

Other changes also damaged Downtown's attractiveness as a shopping destination: The last of the electric inter-urban trains of the *Pacific Electric Railway* made its final run to Long Beach in 1961. No longer could people hop aboard a train for a quick shopping trip to the city's center. Downtown parking was increasingly expensive and irksome, even though parking lots were replacing entire blocks of older buildings. With the encouragement of the federal government, Bunker Hill was scraped clean of absolutely all of its old Victorian houses, hotels, and apartment buildings, which effectively removed the last traces of a resident population of Downtown shoppers.

Then in the 1960s and 1970s, many handsome new office towers were built in a way that displayed contempt for the sidewalk and the pedestrians who might want to walk on it. The buildings had no retail spaces at street level. No more windows or doors, and certainly no window-shopping. What little shopping remained was devoted to just one category per district–the Jewelry District, or Japanese merchandise in Little Tokyo, or inexpensive dry-goods in the Broadway District.

The diversity–the *mixture* of things to see and do–so essential to a lively urban street, was being replaced by single-purpose neighborhoods. Adding further insults to street life, *ARCO Plaza*, *Macy's Plaza*, the *Bonaventure Hotel's* shops, and *Seventh Market Place* were built with their shops and services hidden underground or inside windowless mega-structures.

Shoppers, tourists, and other visitors were utterly abandoned by developers who were reshaping downtown streets to become little more than race courses connecting freeways to parking lots.

In time, all the major downtown department stores deserted their original sites. *The Broadway's* flagship store is a state office building; the beautiful *Eastern Columbia* is an office building; so is *Barker Brothers*. *Robinson's* Seventh Street department store closed in 1993. The firm had been sold to a holding company headquartered in New York, which promptly closed many of its stores. Ironically, they ignored the fact that L.A.'s new Red Line Subway had just opened its major station one block from *Robinson's* front door so that a new population of shoppers was suddenly poised to spend time and money there.

Today, a quick glance down the streets that intersect Seventh Street–especially Olive, Grand, Hope, and Flower Streets–will reveal the devastation of the last few decades. Whole neighborhoods of buildings were demolished to produce a sea of parking lots–which may be full of cars on weekdays, but are always empty of human life.

Figueroa Street, on the other hand, has enjoyed a renaissance in recent decades. The office towers now lining it from Wilshire Boulevard to Ninth Street are striking, modern, first-rate structures–"Class A," as they say in the trade. They were built in the optimistic glow of the 1980s but stood half-empty when the recession hit in the early 1990s. By 1995, however, many insurance companies and other businesses occupying expensive quarters along the westside Wilshire corridor and in Century City discovered that Downtown building owners were asking lower rents and offering the conveniences of central location near related businesses, banks, and law firms–and also the advantages of proximity to rapid transit systems. Life among the skyscrapers is picking up!

Until very recently, city planners have continued to divide the city into isolated, single-purpose segments. In the 1970s and 1980s, the historic core was walled off from the new financial towers by a row of apartments on Hill Street acting as a barrier. Important buildings, like *Philharmonic Hall* on Fifth and Olive Streets, were demolished and their places taken by still more parking lots–in the very blocks where continuity was most needed. This process has driven away L.A.'s pedestrians from the financial district.

However, change is afoot.

PROSPECTS

On June, 11, 1993, Mayor Tom Bradley dedicated the hopeful little Grand Hope Park (Ninth Street, between Grand Avenue and Hope Street) which had been in the works for several years. The distinguished San Francisco landscape architect Lawrence Halprin was the principal designer of the park, signaling its importance in the eyes of city officials. He was joined by artists who created a friendly and appealing urban greenspace, a destination not just for visitors from other areas, but for residents of this very district. Especially notable and unlike other Downtown projects in recent times, this park has a playground for kids!

Something for children? The design for this park was a signal of new ways of thinking by city planners and the *Community Redevelopment Agency (C.R.A.)*.

The new program- This district–at least that part of the Lower Financial District lying south of Seventh Street–is now intended to have mixed uses. Planners have finally realized that single function zones are death to the city. A civil society needs people on the streets and in public spaces–all kinds of people doing all kinds of activities at all hours of the day and night. Downtown districts need to have many more people actually living in them–including families with children. And the districts need to have things for residents to do. A children's playground is a beginning.

There are other signs of a change. The city is trying, at last, to re-connect the separate fragments of Downtown:

- **Angels Flight-** Now connects Bunker Hill with the Broadway historic core. Another funicular is planned for Second Street.

- **Pershing Square-** Now more colorful than ever, is intended to bridge the Bunker Hill business culture with Broadway's Latino culture.

- **Central Library-** Is back in action and draws people of all ages from all parts of Los Angeles.

- **Bunker Hill Steps-** Like Angels Flight, is both a pedestrian route between two districts and a destination for visitors.

In Grand Hope Park, the City wants to lure people out of their cars, into apartments in the neighborhood, and get them actually to walk to work! They're trying to attract people to Downtown residences and then give them the pleasures and comforts of community life.

For that to succeed, three ingredients are needed: attractive apartment buildings; places for shopping, entertainment, recreation, and education–and, of course, supermarkets.

So far, apartment buildings are springing up, but the other essentials are scarce or entirely missing. For example, at this writing, there are no supermarkets here or anywhere else downtown except in Little Tokyo and Chinatown.

But there is hope. Maybe even Grand Hope!

The L.A. Sports and Entertainment District- This proposed development will be built on 1,700,000 square feet of land adjacent to the Staples Center. The district will include a 1,200-room headquarters hotel, entertainment, retail spaces, restaurants, office space, parking, theater for award shows and plays, and an outdoor plaza for hosting events, celebrations, and festivals. The Master Plan will be built in two phases, to be completed in eight to ten years. The project is considered to be a catalyst for the tourism industry to Los Angeles by attracting more overnight stays, while enhancing the environment to provide local residents and the business community an after hours and weekend entertainment destination.

Turning office buildings into residences- Many office buildings south of Sixth Street built in the 1950s and 60s have stood empty and unused for years having lost their businesses to other parts of town. Then, during the dot-com boom of the 90s, Internet firms filled some structures with fiber-optic cables and electronic switching gear, but that did little for the social life of the neighborhood. Today, developers are hurrying into the vacuum, converting offices into hotels, apartments, and condominiums. A supermarket chain is planning a store near the Staples Center. The district anticipates a rapidly expanding residential population.

11. MacArthur Park

Once called *Westlake Park*, this seven square-block lawn is now the centerpiece of the *Pico Union District*, an enormous Latino enclave. Migrants from Mexico and refugees from the civil wars and grim economies of El Salvador, Guatemala, and Nicaragua have flocked to the apartment houses of *Pico Union*, making it the most crowded and among the poorest sections of the city.

In the daytime you can safely visit the Park and its once-fashionable neighborhood. The park is well policed. The rule is: Where there are many people about, you will be secure. At night, this area becomes infested with drug dealers and buyers. Stay aware of the hour and the number of people in sight.

LOCATION

MacArthur Park straddles Wilshire Boulevard at Alvarado Street, one and a half miles west of Pershing Square. It is almost exactly in the geographic center of the City. You can look east and see the Downtown office towers shining just a few blocks away. From Alvarado and Seventh, look west to see the city's most wonderful Art Deco masterpiece, *Bullock's Wilshire*. From Alvarado and Sixth, look west at the gothic tower of the *First Congregational Church*.

GETTING THERE FROM UNION STATION

Red Line Subway: Take the subway to the Westlake/ MacArthur Park Station, the fourth stop, and only seven minutes from Union Station.

WHO'S THERE?

The residents of Pico Union invariably live in apartment houses, hence the population density is the highest in Los Angeles. According to the 1990 U.S. Census, Latinos made up about eighty-two percent of the one hundred and twenty thousand people living between Sixth Street, and the Santa Monica Freeway and between Hoover and the Harbor Freeway. Mexicans and Mexican-Americans were forty-one percent of the population, Salvadorans twenty-two percent, and Guatemalans ten percent.

The apartments of Pico Union are jammed full. In 1990 there were two people per room in this district, compared to .65 per room for the city as a whole. The people here are poor; the average annual income of a resident of the neighborhood between Downtown and MacArthur Park was approximately $4,800.00 (in 1990) compared to $16,149.00 for the City. About forty-seven percent of the people were below the poverty line in Pico Union, compared to eighteen and nine-tenths percent for the City as a whole.

The area attracts visitors, especially Downtown office workers, coming by the Red Line to the famous New York-style delicatessen, *Langer's.*

WHAT'S THERE FOR THE VISITOR?

MacArthur Park and Westlake- The park and lake were recently refurbished. In 1991, all the water and astonishing accumulations of muck and trash were sucked out of the lake. The tunnels of the Red Line Subway were cut beneath the park directly under the old lake bed, and a new concrete one was built. The subway's roof is now the lake's bottom!

A fountain blasts water a hundred feet high from the center of the lake providing a powerful exclamation mark for the Park and also serves as an aeration mechanism for the lake. The fountain requires a 100-horsepower pump to do the job.

General Douglas MacArthur- In 1942, Westlake Park was renamed for the flamboyant, haughty commander of World War II's "Pacific Theater" and, later, the first part of the Korean War. He is remembered today for his statement, at the beginning of World War II when he barely escaped Japan's invasion of the Philippines, "I shall return." And he did–eventually receiving surrender documents signed by Japanese commanders.

In 1951, during the Korean War, General MacArthur was relieved of his command by President Harry Truman after they openly quarreled about the conduct of the war. Many people today can remember his farewell speech to Congress, in which he dramatically quoted a song: "Old soldiers never die, they just fade away." But the kinds of statements that got him into trouble with Truman are represented by the quotation printed on the wall behind his statue in this Park: "Battles are not won by arms alone. There must exist above all else a spiritual impulse–a will to victory. In war there can be no substitute for victory."

Another military commander associated with this park is General George Patton whose father owned much of the land in the district. As a child, Patton played in and around the park.

Westlake Theatre- (Bates, Richard D., 1926) 636 1/2 South Alvarado Street, just north of Wilshire. Now a swap meet, its most noteworthy feature is the huge sign atop the building facing the Park. Inside, behind all the clutter of toys, children's clothes, and trinkets, notice the remains of the original movie house. There is an old fire curtain hanging half-way down at the front of the stage. Clearly labeled Asbestos, it will remind us of a time when we were blissfully unaware of environmental hazards. Balconies and side-boxes, gilt painted elaborate sconces and other ornaments bespeak a glorious past when the neighborhood was occupied by upper-middle class people who lived in beautiful apartment buildings around the Park.

Parkview Hotel (formerly Elk's Club)- (Curlett and Beelman, 1925). Another Art Deco masterpiece marking the northwest corner of the Park. A vaulted entrance is set into a magnificent front facade with splendid *herms* surmounting the pilasters that give the building a strong verticality. Take the time to go into the lobby for a sense of the elegance that once marked this district.

La Fonda Restaurant Building- (Morgan, Walls and Clements, 1926) 2501 Wilshire Boulevard, just west of the park. Spanish Colonial Revival with typical ornamental frame separating main entrance from otherwise plain walls.

Mexican Consulate- Sixth Street, across from *Parkview Hotel*. In 1994, this institution moved to Pico Union from the historic *Biscailuz Building* in El Pueblo Park.

PUBLIC ART

Pyramids- (Simonian, Judy) North side. Two tile-covered, stepped pyramids or ziggurats, thirty yards apart, connected by an underground speaking tube. Try it!

Clock Tower: A Monument to the Unknown- (Herms, George) Corner of Wilshire Boulevard and Park View. A pile of rusty "found objects" (junk), dedicated to the old men who used to play chess in this section of the park. The sculpture of discarded and forgotten objects expresses Herms' thoughts about the neglect of this corner.

El Sol and La Luna- (Francisco, Letelier, 1992) Murals, ceramic tile. Beautiful faces of the people who live in this district. Both ends of Red Line Subway station at MacArthur Park. Alvarado Street and Wilshire Boulevard.

Otis Art Institute of Parsons School of Design

2401 Wilshire Boulevard, on west side of the Park. Founded in 1918, the school was the oldest art college in Los Angeles. Now a division of the *New School for Social Research* in New York, it shares its parent's concern for urban people and conditions. Otis/Parsons' artists have contributed most of the sculptures and murals found in the MacArthur Park, its front yard, especially those installed after 1984 under the direction of Adolfo Nodal. His artists worked shoulder-to-shoulder with young people from the district to design and execute a number of the pieces in the Park. This building is now an elementary school.

Hungarian Freedom Fighters- Monument (1969) Sixth Street and Park View.

Into the Light- (Statom, Therman, 1992) Sculpture, glass and metal, inside the skylight of Red Line station at MacArthur Park. Alvarado Street.

Why We Immigrate- (Dago, 1993) Monument and time capsule. Park View, north of Wilshire Boulevard. Capsule "contains our memories as immigrants."

Promethus- (Samundsson, Nina, 1935) Concrete. Southwest corner of Wilshire Boulevard and Alvarado Street. Harshly vandalized.

General Harrison Gray Otis, 1837-1917 and Newspaper- (Troubetzkoy, Paul, 1920) Corner of Wilshire and Park View. Delightful statue of the pugnacious founder of the *Los Angeles Times* and the Otis Art Institute across the street.

General Douglas MacArthur- (Burnham, Roger Noble, 1955) Southeast corner of the Park. Ramrod straight statue of the commander after whom the park was named. His statue overlooks a dried-up pond in which are represented the islands and nations of the Pacific Theater of War in World War II.

RESTAURANTS

Langer's- 407 South Alvarado Street, half-block south of subway station. Famous pastrami sandwiches. Office workers take the short Red Line trip from the financial districts just to get Langer's thick deli sandwiches. A true L.A. institution, it's got all the clamor and activity of a real urban deli. Not cheap, but big portions. Serves breakfast, lunch and dinner daily, 6:30 a.m. to 9:00 p.m. ($$)

La Fonda- 2501 Wilshire Boulevard, just west MacArthur Park and Otis Art Institute. Inexpensive Mexican food served in a cool Spanish-style interior. Patronized by local office workers during the day. At night this is the "Home of the World's Greatest Mariachi, *Los Camperos.*" You can get a full meal for about $4.00! Pleasant staff and a full bar, too. Monday through Friday 11:00 a.m. to 2:30 p.m., Sunday through Thursday 5:00 p.m. to 12:00 p.m., Friday and Saturday 5:00 p.m. to 1:30 a.m. ($)

HISTORY

The lagoon in the middle of the park was originally a fetid swamp in a low spot among alkali hills. In 1885, Mayor Henry Workman, under pressure from people who had bought land nearby, gathered private donations and city funds, bought the site, and converted it from an eyesore into a civic amenity. The city cleaned up the swamp and surrounded the lake with lush plantings of an elaborate Victorian garden, and named it Westlake Park.

By 1892, property owners in the neighborhood had subsidized the construction of an electric street railway connecting downtown with Westlake Park. In that year, Edward Doheny discovered oil near Glendale Boulevard and Second Street, half-way between downtown and Westlake Park, providing an additional economic boost. Soon Westlake District land owners constructed a neighborhood of single-family houses, apartment buildings, and residential hotels–the housing stock we still see today.

In the 1920s, Wilshire and the streets across from northern Westlake Park were dotted with handsome, Art Deco hotels and apartment buildings. The more luxurious buildings were proudly surmounted by their names in neon signs, some of which remain to this day. This was an affluent and fashionable district, and it attracted imposing institutions: *The Elk's Club Lodge, Bullock's Wilshire Department Store, the First Congregational Church*, and *Westlake Theatre*. Most of the other apartment buildings near the park were plainer–brown brick, with relatively small rooms intended for single individuals or couples. A few blocks south of the park was a large neighborhood of imposing Craftsman and Victorian homes, the northern reaches of the upscale West Adams District.

In 1935, Orange Street, which connected Westlake Park to Downtown, was renamed Wilshire Boulevard and built across the lake itself on a dramatic, sweeping causeway. Wilshire Boulevard eventually pushed farther west–all the way to Santa Monica.

By the 1930s, Wilshire Boulevard had become one of America's grandest urban esplanades, the "Main Street of Southern California." Wilshire was the principal route–certainly the most scenic one–for the fifteen-mile drive from downtown to Santa Monica Bay.

After the Second World War: came the freeways and rapid suburbanization–and everything changed!

1) Decentralization: Los Angeles planners and builders created the land development process that generated the sprawl for which the city became famous–rapidly building huge subdivisions of single-family houses in remote suburbs. Industries, offices, and jobs, moved from close-in industrial districts to distant flatlands and valleys.

The postwar decades also saw the rapid expansion of large retirement communities which were usually built in remote towns. The old people were now enticed to move out of the Westlake apartments and away from the center of the city.

2) Isolation: At the same time, the formerly efficient streetcar system that once served Pico Union's apartment dwellers was abandoned and destroyed. Residents of the inner city found themselves increasingly separated from jobs, shopping centers, and theaters. Crowded apartment districts were sliced into fragments or completely obliterated by freeways and parking lots. Automobiles ruled, not people.

3) Speculation and Neglect: Between Westlake Park and Downtown, whole blocks of apartments were bought up by speculators anticipating a lucrative commercial expansion of the downtown commercial blocks which would be spurred by government subsidies. Land owners stopped maintaining their properties, hoping the buildings would soon be demolished and be replaced by high rent business structures. A few blocks east, the Bunker Hill District served as a visible example of this demolition-and-reconstruction process. Everyone expected it to continue and to spread west along Wilshire Boulevard.

But other, farther-out commercial developments were booming even faster. New concentrations of office towers popped up in Century City on the old lot of the Twentieth

Century Fox studios. Next to UCLA, Westwood Village blossomed with huge new office buildings and apartment structures. "Edge cities" were springing up with energy and purpose in Orange County and the West Valley.

4) Overcrowding: The Westlake neighborhood became a typical example of the slumlord modus operandi: Let the property run down, but try to keep the rents up by crowding ever more people into the same spaces. Apartments along Wilshire and around the Park that had once been congenial to single older people were now converted to crammed apartments for young, large, poor families.

People of advanced years, who at an earlier time might have moved into the district, were put off by its obvious deterioration, the growing absence of shops, stores, and other amenities, and the rapid demographic shifts that openly proclaimed poverty and instability.

Latinos: The 1960s saw the first of the influx of great numbers of Latinos into the near westside apartments. At first, they were recent immigrants from Mexico, young people with large and growing families. By 1970, it was clear that Mexicans and Mexican-Americans had become the dominant populations in the area. (The area was now called Pico Union, named for two of its streets. Westlake Park had been renamed MacArthur Park in 1942. Today the Red Line has brought back the older name, calling the subway station Westlake/MacArthur Park.)

Refugees: In the 1970s and 1980s a new population arrived in Los Angeles, especially in Pico Union–waves of immigrants fleeing civil wars and murderous dictatorships in El Salvador, Guatemala, Nicaragua, and Honduras. Pico Union became the entrance gateway for Central American refugees hoping for sanctuary and economic stability.

On arrival, they found overcrowded neighborhoods, a fragmented city, and a nation governed by inconsistent and muddled immigration policies. For example, Congress first granted temporary asylum to Salvadorans in 1990, extending those protections in 1992 with an expiration date set for 1994.

Then, 190,000 work permits were further extended to September, 1995. To qualify for longer stays in this country, a Salvadoran had to demonstrate a "well-founded fear of persecution" or "extreme hardship" if returned to El Salvador–both vague and uncertain tasks.

The commercial life of Pico Union had also been transformed. Across from MacArthur Park, the Alvarado Street shopping district was no longer a bustling neighborhood of stores serving a white middle class. It had become a street of economically marginal shops pressed into gutted movie theaters, swap meets, and old storefronts.

Along with crowding and poverty, the Pico Union District has acquired a city-wide reputation as a center of gangs and drugs. In occasional efforts to assert more control, the police have tried several strategies, from mass arrests of drug dealers to blocking cars from some residential side streets. Politicians, the media, and others, lacking perspective and sympathy, have too often described the district in negative stereotypes.

PROSPECTS

The Los Angeles *Community Redevelopment Agency (C.R.A.)* has refurbished some of the old houses in the Pico Union District, but most of the population still lives in older, run-down units. MacArthur Park itself was rebuilt after the Red Line Subway plowed through. The park lawn is beautiful, with an open and airy quality about it. And it is heavily used by residents of the neighborhood.

The construction of the Red Line Subway on Alvarado Street has not had the impact that many observers expected. Some feared that opportunistic developers would buy up property, erect expensive residential and commercial structures, drive up rents, and drive out the low-income population. These ills of gentrification apparently have not happened and do not at the moment seem likely.

On the other hand, the hope that the Red Line station would bring new economic vitality to the streets around it has not been fulfilled either. The Metropolitan Transit Authority's (MTA) soulless design for the Red Line station's street-level plaza is one of the obstacles. The MTA bought and demolished the old buildings surrounding the subway entrance and cleared a wide, empty space in the very center of what should be a cluster of retail stores. The subway entrance plaza is now a vacuum and an economic and visual drag on the neighborhood.

Still, there is reason for optimism. The prospects for Pico Union residents are more likely to be driven by the people themselves than the underfunded efforts of city planners and developers.

The people of Pico Union are a select group. They had to make courageous decisions to flee the oppression in their homelands. Many had been singled out there because they stood out in some way—as individualists, entrepreneurs, dissidents, or opinion leaders. Although they were often penniless when they arrived in Los Angeles, they possessed valuable skills, family-centered convictions, and determination. Their future in the United States promises to be brighter than the current physical condition of the district suggests.

12. Museums, Public Gardens, Visitors' Center & Tours

Avila Adobe- (1818) L.A.'s oldest residence. East side of Olvera Street. Free admission.
EL PUEBLO HISTORIC PARK DISTRICT

Central Library, a.k.a. Los Angeles Public Library and **Maguire Gardens-** 630 West Fifth Street, between Grand Avenue and Flower Street. Library hours: Monday 10:00 a.m. to 5:30 p.m.; Tuesday & Wednesday 12:00 p.m. to 8:00 p.m.; Thursday through Saturday, 10:00 a.m. to 5:30 p.m., Sunday 1:00 p.m. to 5:00 p.m.   LOWER FINANCIAL DISTRICT

El Pueblo Historic Monument Visitors' Center- First floor of the *Sepulveda House* (entrance is half-way down Olvera Street on the west side). Gift shop and free movie about L.A.'s early history. Open Monday through Saturday 10:00 a.m. to 3:00 p.m. Movie shown 11:00 a.m. & 2:00 p.m.
EL PUEBLO HISTORIC PARK DISTRICT

Fashion Institute of Design and Merchandising- Contains the *F.I.D.M. Gallery* which shows creations by the school's advanced students. Open Monday through Thursday, 11:00 a.m. to 3:00 p.m. (213 624-1201). See also the *F.I.D.M. Bookstore* for art supplies, unusual books on fashions, furniture design, and marketing. Monday through Thursday 8:00 a.m. to 4:00 p.m.   LOWER FINANCIAL DISTRICT

Federal Reserve Bank- On Grand Avenue between Ninth and Olympic. This small museum called *The World of Economics* gives an optimistic look at how national and international economies work, and you can play computer games showing some relationships between economics and public policy.   LOWER FINANCIAL DISTRICT

Geffen Contemporary Museum of Art- (1983). A branch of Museum of Contemporary Art (M.O.C.A.). 152 North Central Avenue, across the street from the Japanese American National Museum. An admission ticket also gets you into M.O.C.A. located eight blocks west on Bunker Hill.
LITTLE TOKYO DISTRICT

James Irvine Memorial Garden- Next to the **Japanese American Cultural Community Center/Noguchi Plaza-** 244 South San Pedro Street. See the garden from the plaza above or take the elevator inside the Japanese American Cultural Community Center.   LITTLE TOKYO DISTRICT

Japanese American National Museum- Formerly *Nishi Hongwanji Buddhist Temple* (Edgar Cline, 1925, remodeled 1992). 369 East First Street, corner of First Street and Central Avenue. Open Tuesday through Sunday from 10:00 a.m. to 5:00 p.m.; Thursday 10:00 a.m. to 8:00 p.m. Closed Mondays. (213) 625-0414.   LITTLE TOKYO DISTRICT

Los Angeles Conservancy TOURS- (727 West Seventh Street, Suite 955) offers entertaining and informative guided walking tours. Free to members of the *L.A.Conservancy*; $8.00 to the general public. For reservations, call (213) 623-CITY. Most tours begin at 10:00 a.m.:

> *Angeleno Heights-* First Saturday each month. One hour. $10.00.
> *Art Deco-* Every Saturday. Two hours.
> *Biltmore Hotel-* Second Saturday each month. One hour.
> *Broadway Theaters-* Every Saturday. Three hours.
> *Little Tokyo-* First Saturday each month. Two hours.
> *Marble Masterpieces-* Second Saturday each month. Two hours.
> *Mecca for Merchants-* Fourth Saturday each month. Two hours.
> *Palaces of Finance-* Third Saturday each month. Two hours.
> *Pershing Square-* Every Saturday. Two and a half hours.
> *Terra Cotta-* First Saturday each month. Two hours.
> *Union Station-* Third Saturday each month. Two hours. Fourth Saturday. One hour.

Los Angeles Department of Water and Power- 135 North Hope Street. The "Historical Gallery" in the main lobby displays a collection of photographs and artifacts. This is a promotional exhibit celebrating the achievements of the engineers and workers of this department.
                    BUNKER HILL DISTRICT

Los Angeles Times Building a.k.a. Times Mirror Square- Southwest corner of First and Spring Streets. Visit the museum inside the entrance for a promotional history of the *Times*. Tours can also be arranged to visit the newspaper's editorial operations. (213) 237-5757.

CIVIC CENTER DISTRICT

Museum of Contemporary Art (M.O.C.A.)- 250 South Grand Avenue. The building itself (Arata Isozaki, 1986) is a work of modern art. M.O.C.A.'s bookstore is especially fine. Twenty-four hour information (213) 626-6222. Open Tuesday through Sunday 11:00 a.m. to 5:00 p.m., Thursday 11:00 a.m to 8:00 p.m., closed Monday and some holidays. M.O.C.A. has an older sibling, **The Geffen Contemporary**, on Central Avenue in Little Tokyo. One admission ticket, gives you both museums.

BUNKER HILL DISTRICT

Museum of Neon Art (M.O.N.A.)- Ground floor of *Renaissance Tower*, Olympic and Hope Street. Its famous collection of neon designs was previously housed east of Little Tokyo. Great view of the Downtown skyline across Grand Hope Park. Wednesday through Saturday 11:00 a.m. to 5:00 p.m. and Sunday, 12:00 p.m. to 5:00 p.m. $5.00 admission. (213) 489-9918.

LOWER FINANCIAL DISTRICT

Wells Fargo History Museum- in *Wells Fargo Center*, formerly *Crocker Center*. 333 South Grand Avenue. Open every banking day.

BUNKER HILL DISTRICT

Angels Walk L.A.

"Millennium markers" suddenly appeared on Downtown streets late 1999. Each has pictures, maps, and stories (written by *Los Angeles Times* columnists Patt Morrison and Cecilia Rasmussen) describing the identity and history of the location. The first fifteen stanchions (more are coming) are:

Corner of Third and Spring Streets
Bradbury Building- Corner of Third and Broadway
Million Dollar Theater & Grand Central Market
Angels Flight
California Plaza/Watercourt- near Omni Los Angeles
   Hotel
Grand Avenue- At Wells Fargo Center
Bunker Hill- South end of Wells Fargo Center
Bunker Hill "Spanish" Steps- Top end
Central Library- 630 West Fifth Street
One Bunker Hill- 601 West Fifth Street
Biltmore Hotel- 506 South Olive Street
Pershing Square- 550 South Hill Street in front of the
   Jewelry Center
Oviatt Building- 617 South Olive Street
Pacific Mutual Building- 523 West Sixth Street
Fine Arts Building- 811 West Seventh Street

13. Public Art:
Sculptures, Murals, And Other Constructions

Los Angeles has an enormous inventory of public art, works placed on street corners, parks, and plazas, or attached to walls of buildings and freeways. Some works have private sponsors, but more typically, artists are paid from a fund required by law, the "One Percent For Arts Program".

One percent of the development cost of a new building or other project financed by public money must be used to create works of art, either on-site or nearby.

The resulting variety is amazing–abstract, representational, colorful, colorless, metallic, plastic, small, medium, large, extra-large, funny, sad, heroic, or frivolous. Some works comment on the city, its people, or its spirit. Others are completely detached from their contexts and seem only to address the artists themselves. Some artists take their tasks seriously, others take only their fees seriously.

All this leaves the job of interpreting up to you, and you'll get little help from plaques and markers. We want only to encourage readers to look.

(Please see appropriate district chapters for expanded descriptions.)

Albuquerque, Lita, Entrance fountain, *Cathedral of Our Lady of the Angels*, 2002. Hill and Temple Streets. Civic Center. *I shall give you living water* in many languages spoken in Southern California.

Albuquerque, Lita, *Site, Memory, Reflection*, 1993. 550 South Hope Street Building. Room commemorating churches that once stood Downtown. Lower Financial District.

Albuquerque, Lita, *Celestial Source*, 1993. Fountain in Grand Hope Park, Olympic and Hope Streets, Lower Financial District.

Alexander, Peter, *Puddles*, 1995. Illuminated glass in plaza floor and south side of 777 Tower. Accompanies words of Ikkyu Shonin, Zen poet of fifteenth century. 777 Figueroa Street. Lower Financial District.

Allen, Terry, *Corporate Head*. 1990. Sculpture, bronze; verse by Philip Levine. Citicorp Plaza, southeast corner Seventh & Figueroa Streets. Three-piece-suit business man with briefcase in process of loosing body and soul to his corporation. Lower Financial District.

Almaraz, Carlos, *The Story of L.A.*, 1989. Mural. Home Savings Tower, Seventh and Figueroa Streets, east wall inside the teller area. Lower Financial District.

Antonakos, Stephen, *Neons for Pershing Square Station*, 1992. Sculpture, Hill Street at Fourth or Fifth Streets. Twelve neon abstractions suspended over tracks of Red Line Pershing Square station. Broadway/Pershing Square District.

Avilla, Glenna Boltuch, *L.A. Freeway Kids*, 1984. 225-foot mural on south wall of Hollywood Freeway (I-101) between Los Angeles and Main Streets. Children running and playing just under the L.A. Children's Museum. Seen from El Pueblo Park.

Baca Judith, *Hitting the Wall*. 1984. Mural on east side of Harbor Freeway. (I-110) at Fourth Street exit. Commissioned by L.A. Olympics Organizing Committee. West side of Bunker Hill.

Ballin, Hugo, *Apotheosis of Power*, 1930. Mural in Edison Company Building (now One Bunker Hill). Fifth and Grand Avenue. Lower Financial District.

Ballin, Hugo, *Treaty of Cahuenga*, 1931. Mural in lobby of Title Guarantee Building, Fifth and Hill Streets. Broadway/ Pershing Square District.

Barrett, Bill, *L.A. Family Baroque*, 1992. Sculpture outside entrance of Edison Company Building, Fifth and Grand Avenue. Lower Financial District.

Bayer, Herbert, *Double Ascension*, 1973. Sculpture and fountain, painted steel rising out of elevated pool. ARCO Plaza, Flower Street between Fifth and Sixth Streets. Lower Financial District.

Bell, Bill, *Atrain*, 1996. Wall of moving light patterns. Gateway Center at Union Station.

Bengston, Billy Al, Sedan 98, 1990. Mural and painted columns/cross bars. Ronald Reagan State Building, 300 South Spring Street. Broadway/Pershing Square District.

Berlant, Tony, *Yang-Na*, 1990. Painted metal rotunda walls of entrance lobby, Fashion Institute of Design and Merchandising (FIDM), Ninth and Grand Avenue. Lower Financial District.

Borofsky, Jonathan, *Hammering Man*, 1988. Sculpture, (motorized), painted corten steel. Front court of CaliforniaMart, Ninth Street between Main and Los Angeles Streets. Garment District.

Borofsky, Jonathan, *Molecule Man*, 1991. Sculpture, brushed steel. Four men grappling with each other. Edwin R. Roybal Federal Building and U.S. Courthouse, 255 East Temple Street. Civic Center.

Borofsky, Jonathan, *I Dreamed I Could Fly*, 1992. Sculpture, six fiberglass men suspended in air above Red Line Subway track in Civic Center station. Civic Center.

Bunn, David, *A Place for Everything and Everything in its Place*, 1993. Central Library, Fifth and Flower Streets. Two elevator cabs and shafts lined with old catalog index cards. Lower Financial District.

Burnham, Roger Noble, *General Douglas MacArthur*, 1955. Sculpture overlooking a map of the "Pacific Theater of War" for which MacArthur had responsibility in the early 1940s.

Calder, Alexander, *Four Arches*, 1974. Sculpture, painted steel, sixty-three feet high. Security Pacific Plaza, 333 South Hope Street. Bunker Hill.

Carlson, Cynthia, *City of Angels*, 1992. Mural, Union Station entrance to Red Line Subway. Eleven wings, one each for the eleven founding families of Los Angeles. Union Station.

Chomenko, Mary, *California Grizzly*, 1990. Sculpture, bronze. Ronald Reagan State Building, 300 South Spring Street. Broadway/Pershing Square District.

Cornwall, Dean, *California's Four Eras*, 1927-32. Twelve murals in rotunda of Central Library. Lower Financial District.

De Bretteville, Sheila, et. al., *Biddy Mason*, 1990. Timeline wall. 331 South Spring Street. Broadway District.

DiSuvero, Mark, *PreNatal Memories*, 1976-80. Corten steel. In front of Omni Los Angeles Hotel on California Plaza. Bunker Hill.

DiSuvero, Mark, *Shoshone*, 1981. Painted steel I-beams on third level of 444 Building overlooking Flower Street, across from Bonaventure Hotel. Bunker Hill.

Doolin, Jim, *Los Angeles, 1870, 1910, 1960, after 2000*, 1995-1996. Four murals inside main lobby of MTA Building. Gateway Center at Union Station.

Dubuffet, Jean, *Le Dandy*, 1973-1982. Sculpture, painted fiberglass. Ten feet high. West side of Wells Fargo Court, 333 South Grand Avenue, Bunker Hill.

Eatherton, Thomas, *Unity*, 1991. Eighty-two fiber optic light paintings on tunnel walls of Blue Line, south of Seventh Street. Lower Financial District.

Eino, *Fountains in Biddy Mason Park*. 331 South Spring Street. Broadway District.

Flores, Elsa and Carlos Almaraz, *California Dreamscape*, 1990. Mural, acrylic on canvas. Above the pool in the Ronald Reagan State Building, 300 South Spring Street. Broadway/ Pershing Square District.

Frey, Viola, *Arrogant Man, and Surprised Woman*, 1986. Sculptures, Glazed ceramics, ten feet high. CaliforniaMart, Ninth and Los Angeles Streets, luncheon courtyard on east side. Garment District.

Gage, Merrill, *Abraham Lincoln*, 1960. Sculpture, bronze. Corner of First Street and Grand Avenue. Bunker Hill.

Gil de Montes, Roberto, *Heaven to Earth*, 1992. Mural, ceramic tile. Red Line Seventh/Metro Center station. Lower Financial District.

Gilhooly, David, Bary Soto, George Herms, *Poet's Walk*, sculptures and plaques, 1990. Seventh Market Place, Seventh and Figueroa Streets. Lower Financial District.

Gold, Betty, *Redwood Moonrise*, 1990. Sculpture/fountain, stainless steel, bronze. Atrium of Ronald Reagan State Building, 300 South Spring Street in the Broadway/Pershing Square District.

Graham, Robert, *Crocker Fountain Figures-Numbers 1, 2, & 3*, 1984. Sculptures, bronze. Stepps atrium in Wells Fargo Court, 333 South Grand. Bunker Hill.

Graham, Robert, *Source Figure*, 1992. Sculpture, bronze. Top of Bunker Hill Steps, Hope Street near Fourth Street. Bunker Hill.

Graham, Robert, *Our Lady of the Angels*, Sculpture over entrance of the Cathedral of Our Lady of the Angels. Temple Street. Civic Center.

Graves, Nancy, *Sequi*, 1985. Sculpture, bronze with polychrome finish, Grand Avenue side of Wells Fargo Plaza, 333 South Grand Avenue. Bunker Hill.

Guerrero, Raul, *Mirage Fountain*, 1993, Snake fountain in Grand Hope Park, Olympic and Hope Streets. Lower Financial District.

Guerrero, Raul, *Los Angeles Basin circa 1840*, "Antwall," a frieze along west wall of children's playground of Grand Hope Park, Olympic and Hope Streets. Lower Financial District.

Guerrero, Raul, *Lizard Bench*, 1993. Bench on east side of children's playground of Grand Hope Park, Olympic and Hope Streets. Lower Financial District.

Haas, Richard, *Latitude 34, Longitude 118, A Southern California Panorama*, 1988. Mural. Home Savings Tower, Seventh and Figueroa Streets, Sky Lobby (take elevators to Sixth floor). Lower Financial District.

Halprin, Lawrence, *Clock Tower*, 1993. Northwest corner of Grand Hope Park, Ninth and Hope Streets. Lower Financial District.

Hamrol, Lloyd, *Uptown Rocker*, 1986. Sculpture, painted steel. Huge cutouts of six cars on a rocker base. Fourth street, below and west of Grand Avenue. Bunker Hill.

Hannya, Junichiro, *Sontuko (Kinjiro) Ninomiya*, 1983. Sculpture, bronze, four feet high. Southeast corner San Pedro and Second Streets. Little Tokyo.

Hawkinson, Tim, *Inverted Clocktower*, 1994. Interior of "historic" clock tower. Southeast corner of Third and Hill Streets in Grand Central Square. Broadway District.

Heizer, Michael, *North, East, South, West*, 1967-81. Sculptures, brushed stainless steel, eight feet high. Ground level of 444 Building, northeast corner of Fifth and Flower Streets. Bunker Hill.

Herms, George, *Clock Tower: A Monument to the Unknown*, Wilshire Boulevard and Park View Street. MacArthur Park.

Hernandez, Joseph E., *Ellison Onizuka*, 1990. Bas relief. Onizuka Street. Little Tokyo.

Hibald, Milton, *Handstand*, 1986. Sculpture, bronze. East end of foot-bridge over Flower Street connecting the Y.M.C.A. to the Bonaventure Hotel. Bunker Hill.

Hooper, Melvinita, *California*, 1990. Mural. Dining area of Ronald Reagan State Building, 300 South Spring Street. Broadway/Pershing Square District.

Keene, Christopher, *Salmon Run*, 1982. Sculpture. Manulife Plaza. Fifth and Figueroa Streets. Bears fishing. Lower Financial District.

Komar, Vitaly and Alexander Melamid, *Unity*, 1993, Mural. Lobby of Library Tower. 633 West Fifth Street. Three angels. Bunker Hill.

Kozloff, Joyce, *Mosaic*, 1988. Over front doors of Home Savings Of America Tower, Seventh and Figueroa Streets. Lower Financial District.

Kozloff, Joyce, *The Movies: Fantasies*, and *The Movies: Spectacles*, 1990, 1993. Murals, ceramic tile. Approach platform to Blue Line and Red line station, Seventh/ Metro Center. Seventh and Figueroa Streets. Lower Financial District.

Lawrie, Lee, *Untitled sculptures,* (1924-1930). On interior and exterior faces of Central Library. Fifth and Flower Streets. Lower Financial District.

Leicester, Andrew, *Zanja Madre,* 1992. Pocket park next to 801 Figueroa Tower. Lower Financial District.

Letelier, Francisco, *El Sol* and *La Luna,* 1992. Murals, ceramic tile. Red Line Subway station at MacArthur Park. Alvarado and Wilshire. MacArthur Park.

Liberman, Alexander, *Ulysses,* 1988. Painted steel. Southeast corner, Hope and Fourth Streets. Bunker Hill.

Lipchitz, Jacques, *Peace on Earth,* 1969. Sculpture, bronze. Plaza of the Music Center. Civic Center.

Matsukuma, J., Tile mural, 1980. Photographs from the past. North entrance of Japanese Village Plaza. First Street and Central Avenue. Little Tokyo.

McCarren, Barbara, *Pershing Square Art Program,* 1994. Constellations of stars, three telescopes, old postcard scenes, quotation from Carey McWilliams, and an earthquake fault. Sixth and Hill Streets. Broadway/Pershing Square District.

Miro, Joan, *La Caresse d'un Oiseau,* 1967. Painted bronze. South side of Wells Fargo Court. 300 block Grand Avenue. Bunker Hill.

Mullin, Christina Miguel, Mural, 1995. Cesar Chavez Avenue and Broadway. Chinatown.

Murrill, Gwynn, *Angel,* 1990. Sculpture, bronze. Entrance to Fashion Institute Design and Merchandising, Ninth and Grand Avenue. Lower Financial District.

Murrill, Gwynn, *Urban Curiosity,* 1993. Sculptures, bronze. Coyotes, hawk, and snake in Grand Hope Park, Ninth and Hope Streets. Near Renaissance Tower, at southeast corner of the park. Lower Financial District.

Murrill, Gwynn, *California Cougars,* 1990. Sculptures, bronze. In atrium of Ronald Reagan State Building, 300 South Spring Street. Broadway/Pershing Square District.

Nagasawa, Nobuho, *Toyo Miyataki's Camera,* 1993. Sculpture. On sidewalk, corner of First Street and Central Avenue, in front of Japanese American National Museum. Little Tokyo.

Nagatani, Patrick, *Epoch*, 1996. Mural (collage). MTA Building, third level. Gateway Center at Union Station.

Nielsen, Margaret, *L.A. Dialogs*, 1996. Mural. MTA Building, third level. Gateway Center at Union Station.

Nevelson, Louise, *Night Sail*, 1985. Sculpture, painted aluminum and steel. Wells Fargo Plaza. 333 South Grand Avenue. Bunker Hill.

Noguchi, Isamu, *To the Issei*, 1984. Stone sculpture. On plaza in front of Japanese American Cultural Community Center, 244 South San Pedro Street. Little Tokyo.

Orr, Eric, L.A. *Prime Matter*, 1991. Fountain/sculpture. Corner of Wilshire Boulevard and Figueroa Street, at Sanwa Bank. Lower Financial District.

Otterness, Tom, *The New World*, 1982-91. Sculpture, fountain, and frieze on a curved arcade. Bronze and caste stone. Plaza behind Federal Building, 300 North Los Angeles Street. Civic Center.

Petropolis, Renee, ceiling mural in the lower rotunda of Central Library, Fifth and Flower Streets. Lower Financial District.

Poethig, Johanna, *Calle de la Eternidad (Street of Eternity)*, 1992. Mural on wall of 351 South Broadway. Broadway District.

Politi, Leo, *Blessing of the Animals,* 1974-1978. Mural on wall of Eugene Biscailuz Building on north side of Plaza in El Pueblo Historic Park, Los Angeles Street and Olvera Street. El Pueblo/Olvera Street.

Preston, Ann, *Illumination*, 1993. Four huge lamps in "Grand Canyon of Books" of Central Library, Fifth and Flower Streets. Lower Financial District.

Saar, Bettye, *Biddy Mason's House of the Open Hand*, 1990. Photographs in elevator entrance of parking structure. 350 Spring Street. Broadway District.

Schoonhoven, Terry, *City Above*, 1990. Mural on ceiling of street-level entrance to Red Line Subway station at Seventh and Figueroa Streets ("Seventh/Metro Center") in Home Savings Tower. Lower Financial District.

Schoonhoven, Terry, *Traveler,* 1992. Mural, ceramic tile. Red Line Subway station east entrance. Union Station.

Sheets, Millard, *Untitled.* 1971. Murals in mosaic tile. City Hall East, 200 North Main Street. Civic Center.

Sheets, Tony, Friezes incised in walls of parking structures of *Los Angeles Times* and Reagan State Building, Third and Spring Streets. Broadway/Pershing Square District.

Sheets, Tony, *Stele.* Bronze. Tokyo Villa Apartments. Japanese immigrants arriving on a ship. 222 Central Avenue. Little Tokyo.

Simonian, Judy, *Pyramids.* Tile pyramids near center of the park, north of Wilshire Boulevard. MacArthur Park.

Siqueiros, David Alfaro, *America Tropical,* 1932. Mural, sixteen by eighty feet, obliterated by whitewash. On south wall of Italian Hall, Olvera Street. Covered by a shed while being restored. El Pueblo/Olvera Street

Smeraldi, Giovanni, *Untitled.* Murals, friezes, ceiling decorations. In Biltmore Hotel. 515 South Olive Street. Lower Financial District.

Sproat, Christopher, *Union Chairs,* 1992. Sculpture, granite benches, Red Line platform under Union Station. Union Station.

Statom, Therman, *Into the Light,* 1992. Sculpture, glass and metal, inside the skylight of Red Line station at MacArthur Park. Alvarado Street. MacArthur Park.

Statom, Therman, *Natural, Technological, Ethereal,* 1993. Three chandeliers for the Central Library. Flower and Fifth Streets. Sculptures, painted fiberglass and aluminum. Lower Financial District.

Stella, Frank, *Long Beach,* 1982. Sculpture/painting, painted aluminum. Twenty-two feet wide. Ground level of 444 Building, corner of Fifth and Flower Streets. Bunker Hill.

Stella, Frank, *Dusk,* (a part of Stella's Moby Dick Series), 1991. Enormous abstract mural, on south wall of Pacific Bell/AT&T Building on Grand Avenue, looking down on corner of Fifth and Olive Streets. Bunker Hill.

Sturman, Eugene, *Homage to Cabrillo: Venetian Quadrant*, 1985. Sculptures, stainless steel, bronze and copper. 888 South Figueroa Street, across from Original Pantry. Lower Financial District.

Sun, May, *River Bench*, 1995. Chinese crockery, bottles, and other artifacts rescued from excavations around Union Station. Gateway Center at Union Station.

Tajiri, Shinkigi, *Friendship Knot*, 1981. Sculpture, fiberglass., 123 South Weller Court at entrance Onizuki Street. Little Tokyo.

Torrez, Eloy, *The Pope of Broadway*, 1985. Mural. Movie actor Anthony Quinn dancing on south wall of Victor Clothing Company, Broadway & Third Streets. Broadway/Pershing Square District.

Troubetzkoy, Paul, *General Harrison Gray Otis*, 1920. Sculpture of the rambunctious founder of the *Los Angeles Times*. Southeast corner of Wilshire Boulevard and Park View Street. MacArthur Park.

Twitchell, Kent, *Bride & Groom*, 1972-1976. Mural. North exterior wall of Victor Clothing Company. 242 South Broadway. Broadway/Pershing Square District.

Twitchell, Kent, *Ed Ruscha Monument*, 1978-1987. Mural. North exterior wall of 1031 South Hill Street overlooking parking lot between Eleventh Street and Olympic. Lower Financial District.

Wyatt, Richard, *City of Dreams/River of History*. 1996. Mural of the diverse populations that make up Los Angeles. Over tunnel portal. Gateway Center at Union Station.

Yashuda, Kim, Noel Korten, Torgen Johnson, Matthew Vander Borgh, *ReUnion*, 1995. Six pavilions (bus platform). Gateway Center at Union Station.

Young, Joseph L., *Triforium*, 1972-1975. Sculpture, reinforced, concrete, glass, steel, colored lights, loudspeakers. Los Angeles Mall, 300 North Main Street Civic Center.

14. Restaurants

Listed By Type
(Please see Chapters on the Districts for details)

District

AMERICAN

Angels Flight in *Omni Los Angeles Hotel*	Bunker Hill
Back Porch *Marriott Hotel*	Bunker Hill
Brasserie in *Macy's Plaza*	Lower Financial
Casey's Bar and Grill	Lower Financial
Coaster Yaohan Plaza	Little Tokyo
Engine Co. #28	Lower Financial
Epicentre Restaurant in the *Kawada Hotel*	Civic Center
FLOOR 50 in *ARCO Plaza Bank of America Tower*	
	Lower Financial
Fountain Court in *Wells Fargo Plaza*	Bunker Hill
Grand Avenue Bar	Lower Financial
Grand Cafe in *Omni Los Angeles Hotel*	Bunker Hill
Harbor View Coffee Shop	Lower Financial
Langer's	MacArthur Park
McCormick and Schmick's in *Library Tower*	Bunker Hill
Moody's Bar and Grille in *Marriott Hotel*	Bunker Hill
Nick & Steff's Steakhouse in *Wells Fargo Court*	Bunker Hill
Original Pantry	Lower Financial
Philippe, The Original French-Dipped Sandwiches	
	Chinatown
Redwood 2nd Street Saloon	Civic Center
Sidewalk Cafe in *Westin Bonaventure Hotel*	Bunker Hill
Traxx Restaurant	Union Station
Water Grill	Lower Financial
Yorkshire Grill	Lower Financial

CHINESE

ABC Seafood	Chinatown
Dragon Inn	Chinatown

Eden Restaurant in *Chinatown Plaza*	Chinatown
Empress Pavilion in *Bamboo Plaza*	Chinatown
Fu Ling Restaurant	Chinatown
Golden Dragon	Chinatown
Hop Louie	Chinatown
Hop Woo BBQ	Chinatown
Hong Kong Harbor	Chinatown
Kim Chuy	Chinatown
Lucky Deli	Chinatown
Mandarin West in *Westin Bonaventure Hotel*	Bunker Hill
Mandarin Deli Restaurant in *Far East Plaza*	Chinatown
Mandarin Shanghai Restaurant in *Mandarin Plaza*	
	Chinatown
Mon Kee's Seafood	Chinatown
New Lucky Restaurant	Chinatown
New Moon	Garment District
Panda Express	Bunker Hill & Lower Financial
Regent Seafood	Chinatown
Ocean Seafood	Chinatown
Sam Woo Chinese BBQ	Chinatown
Taipan in *Wells Fargo Court*	Bunker Hill
Yang Chow	Bunker Hill
Yin Yang	Bunker Hill

FRENCH

Angelique	Garment District
Bernard's in *Biltmore Hotel*	Lower Financial
Cafe Pinot in *Maguire Gardens Central Library*	
	Lower Financial
Checkers in *Checkers Hotel*	Lower Financial
Top of Five in *Westin Bonaventure Hotel*	Lower Financial
Windows Steaks in *Transamerica Building*	Lower Financial

INDIAN

Gill's Cuisine of India in *Stillwell Hotel*	Lower Financial
Pacific Indian Cuisine	Garment District

ITALIAN

California Pizza Kitchen in *Wells Fargo Court*	Bunker Hill
and *Seventh* and *Figueroa Street*	Lower Financial
Cardini in *Wilshire Grand Hotel*	Lower Financial
Ciao Trattoria in *Fine Arts Building*	Lower Financial
Cicada in *Oviatt Building*	Lower Financial
Impresario Ristorante e Bar in *Dorothy Chandler Pavilion,*	
Music Center, Bunker Hill & Civic Center	
La Bella Cucina	Lower Financial
New York Pizza	Lower Financial
Pacific Grille in *Sanwa Bank Tower*	Lower Financial
Pasta Firenze in *Hotel Figueroa*	Lower Financial
Smeraldi's in *Biltmore Hotel*	Lower Financial
Tesoro Trattoria	Bunker Hill
Three Thirty Three *Marriott Hotel*	Bunker Hill
Ziga Trattoria	Lower Financial

JAPANESE

Al Mercato	Little Tokyo
Aloha Teriyaki	Lower Financial
Aoi	Little Tokyo
Akasaka Hanten	Little Tokyo
Azalea in *New Otani Hotel*	Little Tokyo
Cafe Focus in *Little Tokyo Plaza*	Little Tokyo
Curry House	Little Tokyo
Daisuke	Little Tokyo
Frying Fish in *Japanese Village Plaza*	Little Tokyo
Garden Grill *New Otani Hotel*	Little Tokyo
Hanaichi Monme *Yaohan Plaza*	Little Tokyo
Hibachi BBQ in *Japanese Village Plaza*	Little Tokyo
Issen Joki *Yaohan Plaza*	Little Tokyo
Kokekokko	Little Tokyo
Kouraku	Little Tokyo
Kyoto	Little Tokyo
Mifune *Yaohan Plaza*	Little Tokyo
Mikawaya in *Japanese Village Plaza*	Little Tokyo
Mitsuru Cafe in *Japanese Village Plaza*	Little Tokyo
Mitsuru Sushi Bar & Grill	Little Tokyo

Mr. Ramen	Little Tokyo
Murasaki *Honda Plaza*	Little Tokyo
Nirvana	Little Tokyo
Oiwake in *Japanese Village Plaza*	Little Tokyo
Oomasa in *Japanese Village Plaza*	Little Tokyo
Rokuden of Kobe in *Japanese Village Plaza*	Little Tokyo
Sai Sai in *Biltmore Hotel*	Lower Financial
Sarashina	Little Tokyo
Serina *Japanese Village Plaza*	Little Tokyo
Shabu-Shabu House in *Japanese Village Plaza*	Little Tokyo
Shibucho *Yaohan Plaza*	Little Tokyo
Suehiro	Little Tokyo
Sushi Amai	Little Tokyo
Sushi-Gen *Honda Plaza*	Little Tokyo
Sushi Komasa	Little Tokyo
Teishokuya	Little Tokyo
Thousand Cranes *New Otani Hotel*	Little Tokyo
Tokyo Gardens in *Japanese Village Plaza*	Little Tokyo
Tokyo Kaikan	Little Tokyo
Usui	Little Tokyo
Yagura Ichiban *Japanese Village Plaza*	Little Tokyo
Yodo-ya *Yaohan Plaza*	Little Tokyo
Yuwa-sei *Honda Plaza*	Little Tokyo

KOREAN

Hibachi BBQ in *Japanese Village Plaza*	Little Tokyo
Seoul Jung in *Wilshire Grand Hotel*	Lower Financial

KOSHER

Afshan Glatt Kosher Restaurant	Garment District

MEXICAN

La Casa Golondrina	El Pueblo
El Pollo Loco in *Grand Central Market*	Broadway
La Fonda	MacArthur Park
La Luz del Dia	El Pueblo
La Salsa	Lower Financial
Pan Mexico	Broadway
Señor Fish	Little Tokyo

MIDDLE EASTERN

Farid Middle East Cuisine in *St. Vincent's Alley*	Broadway
Garo's Deli in *St. Vincent's Alley*	Broadway
St. Vincent Deli in *St. Vincent's Alley*	Broadway
The Sultan	Broadway

SOUTHWESTERN

Cuidad	Lower Financial
Kachina Grill in *Wells Fargo Court*	Bunker Hill

VIETNAMESE

Eden Restaurant in *Chinatown Plaza*	Chinatown
Pho' 79 in *Far East Plaza*	Chinatown
Thanh Vi	Chinatown

LIGHT LUNCHES & FOOD COURTS

Bookends Cafe in *Central Library*	Lower Financial
Breadwinners Soup Salad Sandwiches in *Chase Plaza*	
	Lower Financial
Macy's Plaza Food Court	Lower Financial
Cafe Current in *Department of Water & Power Building*	
	Bunker Hill
Cafe in *the Cathedral of Our Lady of the Angels*	Civic Center
California Crisp in *Y.M.C.A.*	Bunker Hill
Cole's P.E.	Broadway
Court Cafeteria *Wells Fargo Court*	Bunker Hill
Fashion Building Food Court	Garment District
Fiesta Grill	Broadway
Grand Central Market	Broadway
The Kiosk (Outside)	Lower Financial
Koo-Koo-Roo	Bunker Hill
Market on Fourth in *Westin Bonaventure Hotel*	
	Lower Financial
Metro Cafe in *M.T.A. Building*	
	Gateway Center,Union Station
Pasqua Lunch Outside in *El Paseo De Los Pobladores*	
	Civic Center
Pasqua Bunker Hill, Lower Financial, Civic Center	
Pastry Shop in *Biltmore Hotel*	Lower Financial
Patinette at *Museum of Contemporary Art*	Bunker Hill

Ronald Reagan State Office Building Cafeteria
                                   Broadway District
Salads Etc   Lower Financial
Seventh Market Place Food Court   Lower Financial
Smeraldi's Deli and Bakery in *Biltmore Hotel*
                                     Lower Financial
Turkey Basket   Lower Financial
Union Bagel   Union Station
Wall Street Deli   Bunker Hill

APPENDIX

DOWNTOWN STREET ADDRESSES

Simple. Buildings on north/south streets are numbered according to the cross streets from First Street south to Olympic (which is Tenth Street) and then to Pico (God forbid we should have a Thirteenth Street.). The next street named for a person is Washington Boulevard (Nineteenth Street), just south of and parallel to the Santa Monica Freeway.

Usually, **odd** numbers are on **west** and **north** sides of streets. Thus Bernard's Restaurant in the Biltmore Hotel is 515 South Olive Street; the Bradbury Building is 304 South Broadway; the Central Library is 630 West Fifth Street.

It's simpler still to find your way west from Main Street, the east/west dividing line. Broadway is 300 west, Olive Street is 500 west, and–this is too easy!–the Harbor Freeway is 1,000 west. Alvarado Street, at MacArthur Park, is 2,000 west.

Main Street, as it goes south, angles west below Seventh Street, so the numbering shifts west for streets below Seventh.

Are you aware of this handy fact about more distant reaches? Century (meaning 100) Boulevard, which zooms directly into LAX, is a hundred blocks south of First Street. And Century City is 100 blocks west of Main Street. Is this helpful or what?

ABOUT THE TRAIN SYSTEMS

Metrolink, Red Line, Blue Line, Green Line

Metrolink- Coaches are manufactured by Bombardier Corporation of Canada. In recent years, the city of Toronto has perfected these modern commuter trains consisting of double-decked coaches which have more seats than coaches made by other companies.

Some stretches of the tracks on Metrolink are brand new, and the joints between rails are welded into a continuous, smooth ribbon. No wheel clicks! Also these state-of-the-art tracks are laid on rubber-like pads ("fish plates") between the rail and the concrete ties. Trains ride more quietly and smoothly, and much of the rumbling is gone.

General Motors of Canada makes low-polluting locomotives especially for these trains. The trains are push-pull. The engineer either sits in the locomotive when it pulls or, when it pushes, in a cab at the opposite end of the train, operating the locomotive by remote control. The trains are pushed in the direction of Union Station and pulled away from it to the suburbs. Push-pull operation has been used on commuter trains in other cities for decades. These trains are safe and efficient. And fast. They can zip along straight alignments at seventy-nine miles per hour.

Union Station is not only the terminal for Metrolink trains running to Los Angeles, it is also the first station of the Red Line Subway. The Red Line platform is right under the Metrolink platform.

The Red Line Subway is the fastest way to get to the center of Downtown from Union Station. It is safe, sparkling clean, and a genuine pleasure to ride. In each station, escalators take people to the surface. The handicapped can take elevators.

Red Line trains are propelled by electricity picked up by "shoes" that slide along third rails. The cars are manufactured by the Italian firm *Breda Costruzioni Ferroviarie*, but they must be assembled in this country and are required to contain sixty percent U.S. ingredients. A car costs approximately $2,000,000.00. The Federal Transit Administration (F.T.A.) pays about half the price of the vehicles.

Red Line goes west from Downtown to Wilshire Boulevard and Western Avenue. Another branch opened in 2000 to Hollywood and Vine by way of Vermont Avenue. Eventually the system will reach the San Fernando Valley in the northwest and, still later, East Los Angeles to the east of Union Station.

Tunneling through Los Angeles is no simple matter, and the job takes about a day to go one hundred feet. The subway runs through methane gas pockets and wet areas. Precautions, such as wrapping the tunnels in plastic or rubber lining to keep gasses and water out, have been only partly effective. Water dripped into Downtown stations throughout the first year of operation, and exhaust fans are occasionally employed to freshen the air. About four hundred and fifty of Hollywood Boulevard's "Walk of Fame" terrazzo and brass stars had to be taken up and stored while the machines were grinding underground.

There were other, well-publicized problems with surface subsidence during tunneling operations in Hollywood creating a public relations nightmare for the *Metropolitan Transit Authority*. The mayor demanded the resignation of the chief administrator of the *M.T.A.* in late 1995, and revealed his recommendation that, once the tunneling under the Hollywood Hills is complete, the remainder of the planned system continue on surface tracks.

In the meanwhile, the great advantage of subway travel is, speed! You can get from Union Station to Pershing Square in four minutes, or to MacArthur Park in seven minutes.

Blue Line- Blue Line trains began running to Long Beach in July, 1990. At the station at Seventh and Figueroa called "Seventh Street/Metro Center," passengers can transfer from the Red Line to the Blue Line, a "light rail" system whose cars travel on surface tracks except for a few blocks of subway tunnels going south from Seventh Street. These trains are made by Japanese controlled Sumitomo Corp. of America.

Green Line- About eight miles south of Downtown, the Blue Line crosses the Green Line (which opened in 1995). The Green Line occupies the median of the new Century Freeway (I-105) and goes west almost to Los Angeles International Airport (LAX). A shuttle bus takes people from the Green Line the short distance to the airport. The Green Line also goes east from the Blue Line to the City of Norwalk. Green Line trains are made by Sumitomo Corp. of America.

PEOPLE WATCHING

All the world's a stage, and the number one activity when people are out in public is–watching other people!

Faces and shapes are not the only entertainment. Consider, for example, how people perform their public roles when they are on stage? What scripts do they follow?

Comportment

On downtown streets and public spaces, where everyone is a stranger, the paramount, unwritten rule seems to be: Try to appear detached and impassive. Privatize your personal space!

This requirement leads to some odd rituals of which most people are unaware. It's worth the price of admission to watch. Of course, when *you* do them, they're only natural and not at all comical.

The very act of entering a space, say a subway train, lobby, or reading room, places a person momentarily in the spotlight. The new arrival takes a quick reading, and scans the area to see who might be looking. If someone stares back and holds the gaze, one quickly looks away–maybe by focusing on some inanimate object (seats, tables, posts), staring into the middle distance, or fussing with something being held. One can try to affect the concentrated look of an Important Person.

Minimize body contact! No bumping or brushing. Look before sitting. Keep apart. Take a seat that splits the distance evenly between other sitters. (This results in an even placement along a row, with no clumping. Notice how people sitting at a lunch counter or on the long benches on Pershing Square are spread along precisely equal intervals.) Don't look directly at a person seated opposite. If possible, take a seat or table off-axis. Try to appear cool and indifferent, unless you're with someone.

Groups of people offer cover. Notice how they often give off "tie signs" indicating their relationships to each other. Teenagers often travel in packs. For that matter, so do older people.

Notice how some people camouflage their identities–or try to. A man sleeping on a plaza bench or in a library is less likely to be disturbed by officials if he holds something, say a briefcase or umbrella. Police or security guards give tacit approval to some individuals while pressuring others to move along. People reading, or pretending to read, newspapers can stay longer in a given resting place than "loiterers."

Notice how people are more relaxed when "backstage." Postures are less erect when co-workers or friends talk together than when they are with people like customers, clients, patients, or visitors, who are formal audiences for one another.

And so it goes. It's the human comedy. As Colonel Stoopnagle used to say, "People are funnier than anybody."

GLOSSARY

Art Deco Style (art, architecture): The term was coined in 1968 to refer to styles popular in the 1920s and 1930s. The name comes from a 1925 world's fair in Paris that had been held to celebrate the **Arts Deco***ratifs et Industriels Modernes.* Architects of the time used new materials (plastics, glass brick, various metals, terra cotta) in their buildings to expressed the optimism and exuberance of the machine age. Artists and builders ornamented their work with repeated geometric figures, lively colors, and stylized depictions of industrial power and streamline transportation. Downtown Los Angeles provides dozens of excellent examples: the *Eastern Columbia Building* is the most colorful one still left, but *Bullock's Wilshire* is often cited as the best example. *Union Station,* built a decade after Bullock's, represents a mixture of Art Deco and Spanish styles.

Beaux Arts Style (architecture): Named for the famous school of architecture in Paris, *Ecole Nationale Superieure Des Beaux-Arts.* The term applies to the style of large civic buildings and avenues that dominated European architecture in the nineteenth century and inspired the designs of many of America's grandest structures. *Biltmore Hotel* is an especially visible example.

Blue Line (transportation): Electric train route between downtown's Seventh/Metro Center station on the Red Line Subway and downtown Long Beach. The twenty-mile journey takes about one hour from end to end. $1.35 one way.

Bunker Hill (district): The area between Hill Street and the I-110 Freeway, and the Music Center and Fifth Street. Once nearly covered with Victorian mansions, the neighborhood declined in the 1920s and 1930s. All its old buildings were bulldozed in the 1950s and 1960s, and Bunker Hill is now home to office towers, M.O.C.A., and the Music Center.

California Market Center (or "CalMart"): Huge wholesale fashion center in the Garment District. It also has several restaurants open to the public, but the showrooms usually are not. Closed weekends.

Cooper Building: In the Garment District, Ninth and Los Angeles Streets. Six floors of "outlet store" merchandise in what was once a factory loft.

Community Redevelopment Agency (C.R.A.), (government): Branch of city government responsible for planning and encouraging new buildings to replace rundown neighborhoods termed "project areas." Attempts to encourage businesses to erect smart, new, money-earning, tax-paying, buildings such as the high-rise offices of Bunker Hill.

DASH Bus (transportation): Small buses with frequent service on four routes through downtown L.A. The fare is $.25 or free to Metrolink riders. DASH is a way to extend your reach.

film noir (media): The sarcastic, tough guy detective movies of the 1940s, were filmed in black-and-white. Color film was unavailable through the war years but movie makers also wanted to create a dark mood. The term *noir* applies more widely to a genre of grim, biting novels, short stories, and dramas which were literary reactions to the Great Depression, World War II, and the widespread corruption in L.A.'s city government. The best exemplars are the novels of Raymond Chandler: *The Big Sleep, Farewell My Lovely, The High Window, Lady in the Lake*, and others.

funicular (transportation): A short railway slanting steeply up the side of a hill. A cable is attached to the upper ends of two counterbalanced cars on adjacent tracks; the machinery at top raises one car while lowering the other. Los Angeles once had two funiculars between Hill Street and the top of Bunker Hill– *Angels Flight* at Third Street and another at Second Street. Refurbished, after twenty-seven years in storage, Angels Flight was returned to a grateful city in February of 1996

Gold line (transportation): Electric train route between Union Station and Pasadena. Station stops include Chinatown, Southwest Museum, South Pasadena, Memorial Park (Old Pasadena), and stations along the 210 freeway to Sierra Madre Villa.

Issei (Japanese): pronounced EE-say. Japanese natives who immigrated to the U.S.-the first generation. They are the parents of the *Nisei* generation.

Metrolink (transportation): The commuter rail system operated by the Southern California Regional Rail Authority connecting Union Station in downtown Los Angeles to cities in the San Fernando Valley, San Gabriel Valley, Riverside County and Orange County. Cities as far away as San Bernardino, Riverside, and Moorpark are served.

Mixed use development (city planning): Cluster of buildings having a variety of functions-commercial, residential, entertainment, industrial. Such planning attempts to reduce the need for cars to go from one place to another and to increase diversity within each district, making it a "twenty-four-hour neighborhood." Live, work, and play in the same district.

M.O.C.A. and Geffen Contemporary (art museum): Museum of Contemporary Art. One ticket gains entrance to both buildings. Specializing in recent art including paintings, sculpture, performance art. M.O.C.A. was designed in 1986 by the Japanese architect, Arata Isozaki. The interior of the *Geffen*, formerly a county warehouse, was remodeled by famous L.A. architect Frank Gehry.

Modernism (architecture): Buildings of plain, stripped-down styles popular since the First World War. Supported by a steel framework, surface materials (curtain walls) can be composed of glass, thin slabs of stone, metal sheets or ribs, usually in simple rectangular elevations. Mies van der Rohe, Walter Gropius, and Richard Neutra led the movement which dominated architecture for several decades. In untalented hands, Modernism yielded flat-walled, feature-less buildings, like the L.A. County Courthouse, the County Hall of Administration, *ARCO Plaza*, 1 Wilshire, and the Grand Wilshire Hotel.

Nisei (Japanese-Americans): pronounced NEE-say. The second generation in the U.S.–the children of I*ssei* parents.

noir: See *film noir*.

Percent for Art Program (art): Starting in 1985, the C.R.A. has required that all developers receiving its assistance must dedicate one percent of the cost of development to public art. Sixty percent of the money is allocated to on-site works; the rest goes into a trust fund for art on public sites downtown. Memorable sculptures, carvings, murals, and other constructions have resulted.

plazas (architecture): (1) In downtown areas of cities, the public spaces created by setback requirements for large building construction. The builder gives space to the front sidewalk for additional floors he wants to go up. (2) Any large, outdoor space built as a stage for a building or for other urban purposes.

post-modern style (architecture): Over-general term for structures made of modern materials (steel, concrete, glass), but whose flamboyant shape or decoration attracts most of the attention. A building that could be merely a box or container might add imaginative flourishes, maybe a decoration from an older tradition, or an outlandish bracket, sculpture, or surprising combination of colors. For example, *Home Savings Tower* on Seventh and Figueroa Streets. An entire building might be an audacious sculpture (M.O.C.A. by Arata Isozaki or Frank Gehry's plan for the *Walt Disney Concert Hall of Music).*

Red Line (transportation): L.A.'s name for the subway connecting Union Station, Civic Center, Pershing Square, Seventh Street/Metro Center, and MacArthur Park–and later, points west and north. The first four miles began operating January, 1993.

Spanish Colonial Revival Style (architecture): Developed in 1915 by the architect Bertram Grosvner Goodhue for the buildings of San Diego's Balboa Park (for a world fair, the Panama-California Exhibition). It appeared perfectly suited to a warm climate and to the longings of sentimental, romantic Californians trying to create a regional identity. The style swept the state. Modified version of this style continue to appear to this day in commercial, academic, and home construction in other parts of the country.

terra cotta (architecture, art): Clay carved or pressed into various shapes and then fired. Surfaces often colored and glazed. Many L.A. buildings are faced or ornamented with terra cotta tile. Spectacular examples: *Eastern Columbia Building* in blue, turquoise, and gold; *Embassy Hotel/Theater* in white; and the *Palace Theater*.

Watercourt: California Plaza's name for its outdoor stage with a spectacular fountain built into it. The water can be turned off and drained from the fountain basin, creating a stage for public performances. Angels Flight's topmost station is the upper level of the Watercourt.

Zanja madre: (ZAHN-hah mah-dray). Literally, mother ditch. The long trench carved into the ground supplying water from the Porciuncula (Los Angeles) River to the original Pueblo. This is also the name of a $2,000,000.00 small park designed by Andrew Leicester on south side of 801 Figueroa Tower.

THE AUTHORS

Robert D. Herman is a professor emeritus of sociology at Pomona College in Claremont. Tracey Reim lives in New York.

ACKNOWLEDGMENTS

Los Angeles Downtown News is by all odds the most valuable reference for keeping up-to-date. It is a free weekly newspaper distributed each Saturday all around Downtown. Consistently the best source about the ever-changing districts covered in this book, it also contains informative features about food, politics, commercial real estate, and Downtown culture–all showing a refreshing commitment to Downtown and its denizens.

Other essential publications include *Los Angeles Times*, *Los Angeles Business Journal*, and the booklets and pamphlets of the *Los Angeles Conservancy*.

Knowledgeable people have supplied information and advice, including Brian Kito, Donna Yoshida, Jan Levitt, Donald Loze, Mickey Gustin, Michael Several, Tamara Thomas, and Jennifer Wong. Thanks also goes to patient librarians of the Los Angeles Public (Central) Library and the Honnold Library of the Claremont Colleges.

Christian Curtis drew the maps and Robert Thomas updated them for this edition. Rochelle and Jay Winderman, and Richard D. Burns and Mark Dodge provided editorial and production services.

Finally, many thanks to Janet Francisco of Gem Guides Book Co. for production help on the fourth edition.

INDEX

NOTES

NOTES